IT RAINS MURDER SOMETIMES IN JUNEAU

IT RAINS
MURDER
SOMETIMES
IN JUNEAU

by
Roy J. Varni

TO MRS. WONDERFUL

ACKNOWLEDGMENT

While this book is a work of fiction, still, I and my wife and son did experience this adventure in the mountains above the town of Juneau, Alaska, during the early 1970's. For our family it was a thrill of a lifetime – a far cry from our previous life in the crowded suburbs of California.

Almost all of the sites and many of the people and events are real. Thankfully, the murders are not. Most of the names have been changed "to protect the innocent."

I have, perhaps, gone to excessive lengths to describe our workplace at Upper Salmon, and I may have underplayed my description of Juneau. It is truly a most unique and beautiful place. I could have written pages and pages of things to see and places to go in and around our 'little' town, but then I would be creating a travelogue instead of a psychological thriller.

I am most grateful to Billie Wilson who has given me permission to include her beautiful poem in this book. It was the title of her work that sprouted the idea for the story and the name of my effort.

A special thank you and all my love goes to my daughter, Sharon Perkins, whose editing skills prove to me, at least, that she paid close attention to her English teachers both in high school and in college.

The distinctive cover for this book was designed by my grandson, Todd Perkins. More of his expertise can be seen on his company website: www.newestwave.com

R.J.V.

It Rains Sometimes in Juneau

This is the soft-spoken rain
of another country.
Somewhere I remember
Thunder gives a different voice to rain
And lightning zags across a wider sky.

I'm sheltered now
Far from those fevered gods
Who'd call the rain
Some other name than peace.

Here the only name for rain
Is rain...
A satin word upon the tongue
Gliding sleekly from the throat
Like lullabies or psalms.

Billie Wilson

CONTENTS

PAGE

ONE

WHAT HAPPENED

It all started on Sunday morning, July 9, 1972, at Powerhouse #2 known as Upper Salmon. Most of the roughly 14,000 residents in Alaska's capital city of Juneau were still asleep. The plant wasn't yet on line, only putting out about 100 KWs of electrical power. It was idling, generating just enough to keep it and the surrounding houses at Upper Salmon lighted and heated. The man running the powerhouse at night is not so much an operator as he is a custodian. There's just not that much work to do from midnight on. The only thing that's really required is that he stays awake and, hopefully, alert.

Chad Winkler was the lone operator on duty. It was almost 8:00 a.m., near the end of his graveyard shift. He was nodding a little – it had been a long night. He says that he was really looking forward to the arrival of the day shift operator - his relief. Well, he evidently woke up pretty fast because his co-worker, Rex Franz, came running up to the plant, threw open the door, and yelled, "My wife's been shot – back there on the flume."

Normally, Rex would have been his relief, but when Chad saw Rex's blood soaked clothing he realized that the man was in no condition to relieve anyone. As he picked up the phone to call authorities he muttered to himself that there wasn't going to be anything normal about this day.

It wasn't going to be a normal day for quite a few other Juneau folks as well. John Santori was one of those people. Shortly after arriving at work that morning he was told that he would be investigating a shooting that had just occurred at Upper Salmon. John no sooner walked into the locker room at Police Headquarters when Chief Parker stuck his head in the door and called to him, "Santori, in my office right now."

Once inside he began, "Your friend, Chad Winkler, just telephoned from Upper Salmon. He said that Mary Franz, the

1

wife of one of the operators up there, has been shot. You worked at Upper Salmon for a couple of years and you know the people and the area. So, check out a tape recorder and whatever else you might need and get up there right away. Take one of Lorenzen's choppers. I'll phone them and let them know you're coming. I'll also take care of sending you some help, but I want you up there right now. I'll tell whoever we send up there that you'll be in charge and that they are to follow your lead. From what Winkler told me the husband also got hit, but evidently his condition isn't serious. He said something about it being a deer hunter that did the shooting. It might just be an accident, but check it out thoroughly. Let's be sure that it's no more than that. In fact, bring along a test kit. Swab the husband's hands while you're there. If there's no showing of gunpowder residue on him or his clothes we can probably rule him out as the shooter. As you well know, John, anytime anything happens to the wife the husband is usually involved. So, be very thorough and assure yourself and me that Rex Franz is in the clear in this thing."

"Did Chad say anything about her condition?" Santori asked.

His answer was short: "She's dead."

A few minutes later Santori busied himself gathering the tools he would need in his investigation. He thought, "It's terrible that I'll be looking into the shooting of someone I know personally, but this is what I asked for when I got into this business. I need to find out what happened and then go after the bad guy. That's the routine. That's what police work is all about." It would turn out, however, that there would be nothing routine about this case.

When the pilot landed his helicopter on the pad in front of the two story house at Upper Salmon, he unloaded his only passenger and immediately took off. As the craft neared the nearby treetops it hovered a few moments. Santori looked up and returned the pilot's goodbye wave and then walked down and into the Upper Salmon powerhouse. There, his friend Chad Winkler filled him in with what little he had learned about the incident. Santori taped all of their conversation on his hand held recorder same as he did later when he interviewed Rex Franz. Upon finishing with Winkler he told him that he was now going to get Rex's account of what had happened.

Chad said, "I don't think you'll find him at his house. He went back out on the flume to be with Mary. He said they were shot at post #32."

Santori checked Rex's house and satisfied himself that no one was there. So, he started toward the flume intending to walk out to the victims. He stopped, however, when he heard the beat of rotors and then saw the large chopper begin its descent onto the nearby pad. It discharged its three passengers and a stretcher. This time the pilot was told to stand by. One additional Juneau officer and two Alaska State Troopers were now on scene. One of the men carried a body bag, and another carried a camera and the stretcher. All had notepads in addition to their other regular issue. Santori told one trooper to go into the powerhouse to further interview Chad Winkler and to wait in the area until he returned with Rex Franz. That same trooper later interviewed Franz, but that was after Santori's session with the man. The two interviews were later compared and found to be consistent.

As the three men walked along the flume toward post #32, Santori told the other two what he expected them to do. He also told them that he would be walking with the husband back to the man's house where he could interview him without any outside noises or interference. He said that he would then return alone to help them continue the investigation.

When they reached post #32, Rex Franz was sitting on the flume cradling his dead wife in his arms. It was readily apparent that the man was terribly distraught. Santori tried his best to first console him and then to separate him from his last tender embrace of his dead wife. It was a very tense and uncomfortable few minutes but, finally, Franz did let go. If Rex and John had been strangers it might have gone a little easier for both of them. But, they knew each other. They had worked together a few years ago right there at Upper Salmon, and they had always gotten along well. Now, however, Santori knew that both of them were wishing that this wasn't happening.

As the two men started to walk back along the flume Santori told Rex that he wanted to know exactly what had happened and that he would be taping all of their conversation. In between sobs, Franz started explaining. He tried to relate the actual chain of events that occurred just minutes prior to the shooting and the subsequent happenings. It was clear that the man was still in shock as he sobbed, "We were walking along toward Upper Salmon. She was going to spend the day with me while I was on shift. I told her I wanted to take her picture. So, we stopped and she sat down there on the platform while I climbed up on the hillside. I was going to snap the picture from up above. I leaned against that big tree up there and focused in on her. It was like an eerie blur. It went something like: 'SMILE, CLICK, BANG, THUD', and 'OH MY GOD.' I fell. No, maybe I didn't fall. I don't know, John, it all happened so fast."

Rex struggled with his recounting, sometimes repeating and other times ranting and crying uncontrollably. When he was able to continue he said, "Yes, I did fall. I can't remember exactly what I did first after that. I know the shot and the sharp pain in my butt caused me to drop the camera. It's probably still up there on the hillside above the flume. I don't really remember if I even took the picture. I do remember yelling something like 'No, No' and throwing off my backpack."

"Was there only the one shot?" Santori asked.

"I only heard one shot. So, that bullet that got me must be the same one that hit Mary. I'm sure I jumped down to her. Her head was a mess. I tried to feel for a pulse, but the way so much of the back of her skull was gone I knew she must be dead. I don't know why but I think I may have..... No, I'm sure. Yes, now I remember, I jumped back up on the hillside toward where I thought the shot came from. I was yelling, yelling - maybe thinking I could find the guy who shot us. I scrambled up past bushes and trees, fell down, climbed higher, fell down again, and then gave up and came back down to the flume. I held her in my arms. Her blood got all over me and my clothes, and the flume. I laid her back down and then I ran like hell to the plant. I don't know, John, it's all a blur," he said again. "I think that's how it

4

went. God, it was our anniversary," he sobbed. "Why'd she have to suggest her coming to Upper Salmon? I just wanted to go out to dinner at Mike's Place after my shift."

When they reached Franz's house they went inside and continued their conversation and the taping. Santori asked him if he could swab his hands and his shirt to see if there was any evidence of powder residue. Franz acquiesced without even the slightest hesitation or protest. Santori also asked him if he was the one carrying the knapsack and the significance of the wooden dowels. Franz replied that it was on his back and that he was bringing the dowels up to the workshop where he was building a coat rack that he intended to install in his porch. As Santori watched him applying a bandage to his injured buttocks, and still sobbing, he really felt sorry for the man.

Later, as Franz started to get out of his bloody clothing, Santori commented, "You were lucky to have been behind that tree or the shot might have been fatal to you as well." Franz made a convincing reply, "I wanted to get her looking up and smiling at me, so I got up off the flume and maybe leaned over to take the picture. I guess my butt was sticking out from behind the tree. Yeah, I could have gotten it right square in the back if I'd been over just a little to the right. Instead, he just got a piece of the meaty part of my rear end." As Santori looked into the man's piercing blue eyes (Rex's only real distinguishing feature of an otherwise average looking countenance) he could see they were now rimmed in red, evidently from the extended bout of crying which he was now still doing. Both men were more than glad when the questioning ended.

TWO

THE INVESTIGATION

When his talk with Rex Franz ended, Santori walked back out on the flume to post #32 where he joined the other two men in finishing up. They had already done most of the necessary work of picture taking and preparing the body for removal from the scene. With his own camera he took more pictures of the area including a few of the upright post that appeared to have a small bloody nick on its top. It looked like the fatal bullet might have grazed the post after exiting Mary's nape. After taking one additional picture of the now zipped up body bag atop the stretcher, he told the two men to take her to the waiting helicopter and transport her to Bartlett Hospital. Before their departure all three men discussed what they had found. They were in total agreement that it seemed to have all the earmarks of an accidental shooting – certainly nothing more.

The remaining trooper, after finishing with his interview of Rex Franz, walked out to the shooting scene where he joined Santori in some additional and, it turned out, fruitless searching. They took a few more photographs - one picture of the post with its blood spatter, one of the abandoned backpack that Rex had been carrying, one photo of the flume from above, and another from slightly below the flume. Santori also took a picture of Rex's camera where he evidently dropped it when he was hit. When he again looked at the top of the upright post #32 and the small nick where it had been grazed by the bullet, he observed that had the shot been just an inch or two lower it might have caused the bullet to be imbedded in the post. Now, it was probably gone forever and thus would never help determine the identity or type of weapon that fired it. He took one more picture of the grazed post from both sides and then started to gather the remaining evidence prior to departing. First, however, Santori decided to hike up the mountain far enough to see and to satisfy himself that

6

it was possible for a bullet to have traveled that far without hitting anything other than Rex's protruding rear end and Mary's face. He carried only the tape recorder and the pocket sized camera with him that morning and now wished that he had also brought along a tape measure and colored surveyors' tape to mark the possible bullet path.

From the long gentle slope of the mountainside it did seem possible for someone at the top of the mountain hundreds of yards away to have mistaken Rex Franz for a buck. The backpack that Rex carried with two wooden dowels sticking out from its top could possibly resemble a deer with antlers especially if the shooter were, say, a thousand yards away. In view of the large amount of foliage between the supposed shooter and the people on the flume, he could have been only four or five hundred yards away and still have thought he was shooting at a deer. Hunters had made similar mistakes in the past. One such incident happened to one of the owners of the grocery store in town just a few years before. He was hiking out of the woods with the buck he had killed stretched across his shoulders. Fortunately, the shot hit the dead deer first before ending up in the man's shoulder causing him and his prize to fall to the ground. It was only a scratch compared to what this shot did to Mary Franz.

After reaching an area that he felt was near 100 yards above the flume, Santori could still see a clear line of sight but he wanted to go to the top of the ridge for two reasons. First, he hoped to find the exact spot where the line of sight no longer allowed a clear shot to the target that could include hitting Rex as well. Secondly, from there down the mountain to the target he wanted to make a concentrated if not impossible search for a shell casing. He knew it would be like finding a needle in a haystack, but he was going to give it a try. In the end, he decided not to hike the additional distance to the top of the ridge. Instead, it seemed better to return the next day with all the right tools. He was sure he had to have a metal detector, some surveyors' tape, and a long measuring tape. Between now and then he would decide what else was needed to allow him to conclude his report on the shooting. Right now he felt certain, as did the other officers who had been with him at the scene, that this was an accidental death. Granted, there was a hunter out there somewhere who should have a guilty conscience. The question was whether he would ever come forward. Finding him otherwise would be very difficult. In Santori's mind, the only two obvious witnesses to a hunter's errant shot would never be able to identify him. One witness had his back to him and the other was dead. While Santori felt good about the thoroughness of his investigation, he still had that empty feeling in his gut that suggested the person who did this terrible thing might never be found.

The afternoon of the shooting Rex Franz asked for and was granted a leave of absence from his job at Upper Salmon. He explained to his superiors at Alaska Electric Light & Power Company that he needed to see to the funeral arrangements for his wife and to other personal business. He was told to take all the time he needed. He departed Upper Salmon early the next morning.

Santori, instead, decided to do just a little bit more searching. So, that same morning, he told Chief Parker that he would take one more trip to Upper Salmon simply to dot every 'i' and to cross every 't'. The Chief looked slightly puzzled as he asked, "Is there something bothering you?"

Santori replied, "No, I'm quite certain that it was an accident, but I just want to see if I can find exactly where the shot came from. I hiked up about 100 yards yesterday and from there it was easy to see the line of sight, the flume, and any people that would have been on the flume. There was plenty of foliage in the way, but the shooter, unless he had real bad eyesight, could have seen that it was people, not a buck."

The Chief was mulling over what he had just heard, and he asked, "What are you thinking?"

"Well, I'm gonna go up the mountain to the ridge to see if he still had a shot from, say, 200 or 300 yards or more. If so, I'll scout around to see if there's any evidence of anyone having been there. If he was that far away, with all the trees and bushes possibly in his line of sight, then it was almost certainly an accident. But, if he was only 100 yards away, it could have been intentional. I've probably seen too many TV whodunits, but one more day of hiking in the woods won't hurt. Then I'll feel comfortable when my report concludes that it was a hunting accident by an unknown shooter," he replied.

Later that morning, with the help of another Juneau police officer, Santori stretched a tape from post #32 up the mountain to the top of the ridge for a distance of almost 400 yards. From there, using a spotting scope, he was barely able to see post #32 through the trees and the leaves. He saw enough, however, to satisfy himself that the shot could well have been fired successfully from that spot. He concluded that it also could have been fired from anywhere in between along the path of the stretched tape. He added that fact to his report. With the aid of the metal detector, he also did a thorough sweep at the top of the ridge. He was hoping to find a spent shell casing. That effort proved fruitless. The two men then started back down the hill. With his helper holding back the branches and bushes as they went Santori swept the metal detector back and forth until they reached the edge of the flume. The path of the sweep was alongside and beneath the tape. Their search down the mountain found nothing. "So," Santori suggested, "let's take our stuff and go home." That afternoon he turned in his report saying it was a hunting accident by an unknown shooter.

The Monday night newspaper carried an account of the shooting as did the next morning's radio news. Both quoted Chief of Police Parker's statement wherein he requested help from the public. Anyone knowing of a hunter being in the area on that Sunday was asked to call the department. No such calls were ever received. Thus, the official investigation ended. Santori, however, wanted to do a little more searching. He asked the Chief if he could continue and even volunteered to do some of it on his own time. Appreciative of his thoroughness, Parker told John to continue with his investigation, "Just don't let it interfere with more pressing police business!"

Santori had a lengthy talk with his friend Chad Winkler after handing in his report. He intended to fill Chad in with what took place on the flume rather than to question him. At least, that's how it started out later that evening when the two were having a few beers at the local Elks Club. As they talked, John asked Chad about Rex's behavior in the months before the shooting: "I guess he took it pretty hard when his wife lost their second baby, huh? I remember him telling me, after she miscarried with their first son, how he had been so looking forward to the day when he would be holding his 'new hunting partner' in his arms."

Chad responded candidly, "He became a different person after that, John. It must have taken a real toll on him. He was always rather quiet, but then he became almost reclusive. Now, he rarely talked when he came to relieve me or the other operators, and it almost seemed like he was in another world with another agenda. He seemed to spend an awful lot of time rummaging in the woods. You remember - he was an avid mushroom hunter. Maybe he started eating some of those odd mushrooms - the inedible ones." Both men chuckled, but it sparked just a tiny bit of suspicion in John's psyche.

Santori interviewed all the other operators at Upper and Lower Salmon in the days following his conversation with Chad. They all more or less came up with the same observation - Rex had changed. Chad also told him later that same morning that he noticed Rex spent a lot of time in the workshop near the powerhouse prior to the shooting. Since little if any time was ever spent in the workshop by any of the operators other than to retrieve a tool or material for use in the powerhouse, this caused Santori to ask if he knew what Rex was working on out there. Chad replied, "No, whatever it was he must have kept it in the gym locker there in the workshop."

When he was pressed further, Chad answered that when he went to the workshop the day of the shooting he saw nothing peculiar inside. "In fact," he said, "the place was clean as a whistle except for a little bit of sawdust on the floor. I'd have looked in the locker, but there was a combination lock on it."

Santori's tinge of suspicion increased just a tiny bit more. He thought, "Why would he keep a coat rack locked up? Nobody ever locks anything up at Upper Salmon. Could there be something more involved here than just a hunting accident?"

While Rex was on his leave of absence and occupied with his business, Santori got busy with a little of his own business. After his recent talks with Chad Winkler he had become considerably more suspicious. He now felt that he might have more than just one 't' that had to be crossed. He wondered about what might be in that gym locker at Upper Salmon. Rex had told the operator at Lower Salmon and John, as well as others, that he was building a coat rack in the workshop at Upper Salmon. If the contents of the locker did in fact support his statement, then Santori really had nowhere else to go. So, the next morning he again walked up to visit his friend at Upper Salmon. Chad was doing a double shift – his own graveyard shift as well as Rex's day shift. When he entered the little office in the powerhouse where Chad was sitting, Santori confided in him that, "I'm just gonna check out what Rex keeps in that locker." At the same time he swore his friend to absolute secrecy as to his visit and his suspicions.

Once inside the workshop he copied on to his notepad the serial number and the make on the back of the combination lock.
He then returned to the powerhouse and telephoned Chief Parker. Earlier that morning he had explained his intentions to the Chief. So, when he telephoned him with the serial number information, it took only a few minutes to obtain the combination from the local locksmith.

After opening the locker he found very little evidence therein connecting it to a coat rack. There was only a screw eye, a U-bolt, and a scrap of 1x8 sugar pine about 20 or 21 inches long. It appeared to have been cut at an angle possibly from a longer piece. He snapped a picture of the locker's contents with a small pocket size camera that he had brought along just for that purpose. He then replaced the combination lock again showing the same number in the same position as he found it and walked back into the plant.

Chad sat there behind his desk looking like a little kid ready to open his Christmas presents. He immediately wanted to know what John had found. After reminding him how serious this was and the importance of complete secrecy, he told Chad that he really didn't find much at all – just a screw eye, a U-bolt and a piece of scrap 1x8. If John could find out what Rex was building and how these three things fit into that project, it might tell him something. Right now he still had nothing but suspicions. He asked Chad to question Rex the next time he relieved him (or vice versa) as to whether he ever finished his little project out in the workshop.

"I hope you understand, Chad. I probably have told you too much already. The less you know, the less chance that you might blurt out something that might let on to anyone, especially Rex, that he is under even the slightest suspicion."

Chad then suggested, "Speaking of suspicion, if you let me do some investigating up here whenever he's gone it would cause less suspicion than you being up here nosing around."

There was a lot of truth in Chad's idea. So, John laughingly asked him if he wanted to be his Dr. Watson.

Chad replied, "Elementary, Mr. Holmes!"

"Ok, you're hired," John answered with a grin. "You know that you have to play this real close to the vest and you'll tell no one, not even your family, right?"

Chad nodded his assent.

"And, if he questions why you're asking about what he was working on out there in the workshop, simply tell him that you've seen him in there a couple of times and you just wondered what he was building - that's all. I've already turned in my report calling it a hunting accident by an unknown shooter - and that's all it probably is. Rex couldn't possibly have a monetary motive in harming Mary because he was already able to share in any money she might have. There's no insurance on her life – at least not with any local agency. I've already checked on that. None of us have ever seen him even talking to another woman. So, what possible reason could he have? He'd have to be crazy, and right now he sure doesn't appear that way to me – strange, perhaps, but not crazy. I just have a suspicious nature about me, Chad. You have to be when you're in my line of work. So, bear with me and please keep my confidence until we conclude this thing. You have to promise me to be just a curious, but dumb, good old boy around Rex. It shouldn't be too hard for you to do – look dumb."

Chad's reply was a big "Ha, Ha, Ha," with a smirk on the end. Then he added, "While he's on leave I think I should look around in his house up here. He, like the rest of us, never locks the door to his place. Who knows, I might find something real interesting."

John was reluctant to agree to this last gambit of his, but he did see its merits. Chad could get away with it. And even if he was caught in the house red-handed he would be able to give a more innocent excuse than John could if found in the same predicament. So, John agreed to turn him loose. As he was almost out the door of the powerhouse, Chad hollered, "Hey, what kind of pay should I expect from JPD for this detective work of mine?" John answered with only a laugh.

The rest of the day and all of that night, John pondered his dilemma. He had all kinds of suspicions and no evidence to support them. The problem even carried into his sleep that night. He awoke with a start, and he was sweating. He had been having a terrible nightmare about a sniper, and he described it to his wife the next morning over breakfast. Rex Franz was not part of the dream, but in it this bad guy was shooting at people as they drove along Glacier Highway. It turned out that John was one of the intended victims. In the dream, he was driving his patrol car toward town when a rifle bullet crashed through the driver side window narrowly missing his head. When he described that part of the dream to Liz she laughed, "Well, at least you didn't get killed, honey. I'm glad he was such a poor shot." They both enjoyed a hearty laugh, but it got him to thinking about his real problem – the actual shooting – the one that took place at Upper Salmon. Later, while driving to work, he again went over in his mind his suspicions about Rex and what happened at Upper Salmon. In his dream he was the investigating officer and he studied some of the shootings and their line of fire to the targets. During the dream he was able to find the shooter's perch in each and every case. Now, fully awake, he remembered that in his real investigation of Mary's shooting he only checked on the line of sight from shooter's perch to target. He didn't look thoroughly beyond the target. He decided right then and there that he would go back up the mountain. He would plot a line from where the bullet hit Rex in the rear to where it nicked the upright 4x4 post #32 and beyond to where it might still be lodged in a tree.

The next morning John and another officer hiked up the steps and on to the flume to post #32. This time they brought with them a surveyors' telescope and tripod, more surveyors' tape, and the previously used metal detector. They set up the scope adjacent to the obstacle tree that Rex had earlier described to John as being the spot where he stood to take Mary's picture. They estimated the height where Rex was hit in the buttocks, and from there John sighted the crosshairs of the scope on the notch on post #32 that was grazed by the same bullet. With surveyors' tape in hand, his partner got down off the flume and worked his way down to Salmon Creek. Once across the creek, he climbed up the other side of the valley to a stand of trees, approximating the area where the bullet finally should have come to rest. From his perch, and with the telescope now focused on that area, John pointed out the five or six possible trees where the bullet could have impacted. These were then all marked with the surveyors' tape.

After his partner finished wrapping the suspect trees, John took the scope back down to the flume. He picked up the metal detector and then proceeded to hike the same path at least another few hundred feet across the valley to help inspect each marked tree. The two men scanned all of them, first with their eyes and then with the metal detector, but they found nothing. They concluded that the bullet probably missed all the trees and simply imbedded itself in the soil somewhere beyond.

They were about to give up the search when John thought to swing the instrument a little to the right to two or three additional trees. He thought maybe the bullet grazing the 4x4 post might have caused a slight deflection. On the last and the largest of the three trees the device let out a ping. As he looked closely at the tree's surface in the involved spot he saw the spent bullet. There was enough of it sticking out to allow him to remove it with a pair of pliers but he decided against that method for fear of damaging it. Instead, he scrambled up onto the trail and headed for the workshop. As he walked through the woods he commented to himself, "If you did this thing, Rex, you're sure making me work hard to nail your ass."

John returned to the identified tree with chisel and mallet and chipped away until a chunk with the bullet inside was removed. Later, after replacing the tools in the workshop, removing the tape from around all the marked trees, and after cleaning up the area, the two men retrieved their equipment and walked back down to their car at the lower Salmon parking lot. When the bullet was later extracted at police headquarters, they had their first tiny bit of solid evidence. Even though damaged from impacting the tree, there was still sufficient rifling that should allow its comparison to another spent bullet. If he could now find the owner of the rifle that fired that bullet he might well have the shooter. He thought back to his questioning of Rex Franz on the day of the shooting and realized that he had not even asked the man if he owned a rifle. He concluded that he would have to do that the next time they talked.

"How he could shoot himself in the ass with the same bullet with which he killed Mary is beyond me right now," John told himself. "Perhaps somebody helped him but, if so, who?"

The next few days John was back behind the wheel of a patrol car while some of the other regulars were at the Sitka Police Academy taking some refresher courses. During those few days, either while driving or sitting with radar gun pointed toward possible speeders, he pondered over and over all the different possible scenarios involving Rex and the shooting of his wife. He always ended up getting nowhere because he couldn't come up with any kind of motive, and there still was little or no conclusive evidence. There were only his damn suspicions, and even those weren't worth much.

THREE

THE POLICEMAN

John Santori was born and raised in San Francisco, went to grade school, high school, and City College all within walking distance from home. He served in the Navy during World War II, and reenlisted after the war, retiring after twenty years with the rank of Lieutenant. Most of his time in the service, especially the last part of it, was spent in the offices of the Provost Marshall. He liked the police type work in the Navy. So, just before retirement, he applied for temporary office work with the San Francisco Police Department.

In September of 1946, he married his high school sweetheart, Liz (nee Elizabeth Patricia Ryan), and they raised three children together.

After graduating from the Police Academy, John started full time as a patrolman in the downtown Union Square area - an upscale part of San Francisco full of exclusive shops, hotels, and high-rise office complexes. The work was enjoyable. In fact, he actually looked forward to going to work each morning. His real aim, however, was to make detective grade. So, while working, he also took some night classes in criminology studies with the thought that they would help him to that end all the sooner. All was going well both at work and at home. The couple's two daughters were now grown and gone from under wing and Andrew, their son, was doing well in school and was a joy to be around. Their eldest, Megan, was married and living in Arizona with her husband, Mel; and their youngest daughter, Paula, had just been hired as a stewardess with a charter airline.

Shortly after his arrival in Alaska, John was asked by one of his co-workers, Gary Felts, "If everything was going so well, what brought you from San Francisco all the way up here to Juneau?" And, almost in the same breath, "What caused you to give up such a plum of a job in the first place?"

16

"Well, it's like this," he explained, "I said I liked my work, but the truth is I quit liking it when the brass decided to transfer me to a beat in the Haight-Ashbury District. That area had been made famous, or infamous, by the influx of flower children (hippies). Unfortunately, too many of them had no regard for flowers, cleanliness, order, or a landlord's property. So, much of my on duty time was now spent not so much enforcing the law and protecting the city's citizens but, instead, rousting out unkempt, worthless beings from drug filled love-ins or from feces covered dwellings, most of which these people were occupying illegally. What a contrast – from the calmness and order of watching out for the welfare of the Union Square businesses frequented by neatly dressed men in their double-breasted suits and long legged women in their miniskirts to confronting the chaos and threats of bodily harm from the rebellious youth in their dirty surplus store khakis that was Haight-Ashbury. On my first beat I was always being greeted with warm words and friendly smiles. Now, there in what I and others called the jungle, I could be greeted with anything from bottles to spoiled food and worse."

When John stopped to take a breath he noticed his friend trying to stifle a yawn. He assumed that Gary was probably sorry that he had asked the question in the first place. But, since Gary had asked it, he decided to continue with his answer:

"It was after almost two years of this – bringing home the strain of the workday and the stench of that work - that I suggested to my wife, Liz, there just had to be a better place. I was fixing myself a martini as I waited for her reply. When she suggested that we might try going to American Samoa, I figured there was no use pursuing the subject with her. I decided to make it a 'double' which didn't help much either. Little did I know then that we would find that better place in a completely different direction than the South Pacific. One day in November of 1967, while at our local post office, I saw a poster reading 'JOBS IN ALASKA.' When I got home I told Liz about it. Knowing of my frustrations with my present job she said, "Well, let's go see what Alaska has to offer."

When John saw that his co-worker was no longer holding

back on his yawning he realized that he probably had overdone his reply to a simple question. So, he quickly sought to cut off his answer with, "So, the rest is history."

Felts made the mistake of adding his own footnote, "Instead, my wife came up here with me kicking and screaming all the way."

Both men laughed, and John was invigorated. So, he went on with his tale, "I couldn't believe what I had just heard my wife say. Liz has never been known as an adventurous soul. She's not really an outdoor person. She'd much rather be shopping at either I. Magnin's or Nordstrom's in downtown San Francisco than roughing it in a Forest Service cabin out in the wilds. When Andrew and I walk with her, men turn around to look at her. Just being with her makes us look good, but on a fishing trip she's just a real pain in the butt. Regardless, I still called her 'MRS. WONDERFUL.' I even call her that to this day. In fact, I've often told her I'd like to inscribe that on her tombstone if she goes before me. So far, she hasn't embraced that idea. Anyhow, I was pleasantly surprised when she suggested that I take a week off from work so that we could check out Alaska. Since Liz indicated her willingness, I wasn't going to look a gift horse in the mouth. Instead, I got busy making the necessary arrangements. I got permission for a seven day leave of absence from the police department, and I made the necessary airplane and hotel reservations. In another few days we were on our way – we were going to explore Alaska."

Both men laughed when John asked, "Does that answer your question?"

Gary Felts summed up John's answer in a slightly more pointed vein, "Yes, but remind me the next time to ask you those questions that can only have a 'yes or no' answer."

Both men laughed, but Gary thus missed hearing the rest of the story which was considerably more exciting.

FOUR

THE FIRST VISIT TO ALASKA

The sun was shining brightly in a cloudless sky, and it was unseasonably warm in both San Francisco and Seattle as John and Liz flew north that November morning in 1967. However, by the time they neared Ketchikan, Alaska, some 200 plus miles south of Juneau, clouds had begun to obscure the awesome scenery below. John had a window seat and had been enjoying the view of snow-capped mountains along the British Columbia Coast as well as the islands dotted deep blue waters of the Inside Passage that stretches from near Prince Rupert in Canada on the south all the way to Skagway in Alaska on the north. A short time later, as the pilot began his descent into Juneau, they were completely engulfed by those clouds. John leaned over the empty seat between them, saying to Liz, "You know, no matter how often I fly and whether it's on a sunlit day, a moonless night, or along a thick fog filled path, I never cease to marvel at the ability of those driving this huge monstrosity of a bus with wings. How they can guide it through the sky to its ultimate and successful touchdown is downright amazing." Liz simply nodded her head in agreement and closed her eyes.

This day, after having seen so many mountain tops from thousands of feet above, John wondered – actually he prayed that the man in charge of this airplane knew exactly where he was in relation to every one of those menacing white pinnacles. Earlier, just before the stewardess announced that they had begun their gradual descent and approach into Juneau, John felt the engines lose a bit of power and the nose of the airplane tilt down slightly. Now, after almost an interminable and agonizingly twenty minute-long very bumpy stretch of what appeared to be a downward blind flight through the soup thick clouds, he worried that they could well be getting much too close to some trees. In addition, during some of the worst of the turbulence, the airplane's fuselage was

19

actually making creaking noises. When one of the doors of an overhead bin popped open, John looked over at Liz who was sitting on the aisle, but she still had her eyes closed. He decided that this was not the right time to say anything to her – she wouldn't be much help anyhow. So, he just went back to holding on to each of his arm rests and looking out the window hoping to help the pilot find his way. Actually, all he could see was a solid grey mass of clouds or fog, and he wondered if the pilot had a better view.

Suddenly, and without any announcement from the pilot, his crew, or any of the flight attendants, the engines roared back into full throttle and the nose of the airplane tilted upward at an abrupt angle. This caused John to again look over at Liz. This time she had her eyes wide open. Hoping to calm any anxiety on her part, he said, "I suspect that we might not be landing in Juneau just yet." His suspicions were soon confirmed by the Captain who announced that Juneau had now fallen below the safe limits for landing, and they were going to circle above for a while to see if the weather would clear. He said further that should they not be able to land they would go on to Anchorage almost 600 more miles to the northwest where his people would put all the passengers up for the night after first treating everyone to a nice dinner with beverages. Then, in the morning after another free meal, they would all return to Juneau.

The Santoris didn't know it at the time, but Juneau was actually experiencing the last two days of a weeklong snowstorm. Unfortunately, John hadn't looked at any weather predictions before making their plans, and the Alaska Airlines people gave him no such warnings. To them, bad weather is the norm in this part of Alaska no matter what time of year. And, even if they had given a warning, John probably would have ignored it – he was anxious to see this 'New Frontier.'

So, they circled and circled in the warm sunshine above Juneau and the storm that surrounded it. Finally, after another wasted twenty minutes they were told that they were going on to Anchorage. Almost two hours later, after flying through more turbulent and cloud filled skies, the airplane thudded down onto the runway at Anchorage International. Liz told John later that she overheard a woman in the seat in front of her ask her companion if they had landed, or crashed. One additional bit of humor followed when one of the flight attendants later answered a question about the landing. She replied simply, "No, that was a routine one, and really not too bad for a youngster who only learned to fly a week and a half ago."

When they flew south the next morning the pilot didn't even bother to circle hoping for a break in the storm. It wasn't going to happen, and a few hours later they found themselves back in the Seattle airport. At that moment, John was feeling pretty low. Liz didn't make it any less painful when she suggested, "We can always try again later, maybe in summertime." So, reluctantly, he sought out the Alaska Airlines station manager there in Seattle. He showed him their tickets, and said, "You folks and the weather have already eaten up two days of our seven day vacation. So, how about flying us back to San Francisco, and we'll try again some other day."

The man made a convincing plea when he answered, "Enjoy your evening at the hotel, the fine meal as well as breakfast tomorrow morning all on us same as we did for you in Anchorage Then come fly with us one more time, Mr. Santori. We'll get you there tomorrow morning – I promise." After that appeal, there was no way John could refuse the man's offer. So, they accepted another free lodging with meals, albeit apprehensively, as they wondered what the next morning would bring. To help alleviate their concern, John even accepted another cocktail for each of them.

FIVE

ARRIVAL IN PARADISE

When the Alaska jet did finally land in Juneau that next afternoon it had stopped snowing, the sun was shining, and the area with its more than two or three feet of fresh snow from the recent storm looked like a picture post card. The Santoris were more than impressed and marveling at its awesome beauty.

They shared a shuttle ride into town to their hotel with the flight crew of the Alaska Airlines jet that brought them into Juneau and that gave John the opportunity to chat with its pilot. He told him of their harrowing landing attempt of a few days previously as compared to the smooth and uneventful flight that they had just enjoyed with him. The only irregularity in this latter flight, and John asked him about it, was that the airplane seemed to change direction just a few hundred yards before touchdown.

The man explained that the runway at JIA (Juneau International Airport) is set at an angle that makes a straight line approach impossible. "Coming in from the west as we just did we have to first navigate around or over numerous mountains with heights up to over 4,000 feet. Then, on our final approach, we still need to clear the imposing 573 foot high Mendenhall Peninsula that's a little less than two miles from the start of the runway. The Peninsula sits perpendicular to our flight path and in order to avoid having to drop suddenly in elevation after crossing over it we fly over its lowest point and then make a left turn, then a right turn to line up with the runway,"

"Wow, sounds like you really need to know what you're doing," John commented.

"No, it's a piece of cake after you've done it a few times. And, with our modern technology, I'm sure it won't be long before electronics actually land the plane for us – even here in Juneau," he replied confidently.

Remembering their earlier and unsuccessful approach to

the socked in Juneau airport, John asked the man what instrumentation they have in the airplane to help them navigate in the thick fog. His self-assured response was, "We have radar and there are beacons along the line of flight to compliment our onboard equipment." John felt certain that the man had oversimplified it because there certainly must be more to knowing where they are in the sky at any given moment than just radar and a few beacons. He sure did hope so.

Notwithstanding the man's reassuring words, John was glad that they had today landed in Juneau on a beautiful sunlit day. It turned out that just a few years later a scheduled flight into Juneau miscalculated the location of one of those beacon indicators with disastrous results. After that ride into town with their flight crew John never did see that Captain again and often wondered if he was aboard that ill-fated flight.

Juneau lies alongside the shore of the Gastineau Channel nestled in between and at the foot of Mount Juneau and Mount Roberts. Liz wondered and commented on how they came to build the town here. It seemed that everywhere they looked the mountains appeared to go from the water straight up to where they touched the clouds. Even the buildings housing the now abandoned gold mine were built right into the mountainside. What little flat land can be found is along the shoreline, and even there many businesses and dwellings sit on streets constructed atop pilings.

The next morning the Santoris began their inspection of Juneau and the promises that it might hold for them. They found that some housing was available, and most of it seemed reasonably priced. Jobs, too, were plentiful. So, at first glance, Juneau looked real good to John. Liz, on the other hand, wanted to see more. Not being the most trusting soul, she wanted to know if the town also had some not so good features.

"Better to know about it now rather than when we're living here permanently," was her more than keen observation.

John thought, "I guess I shouldn't fault her for that." So, for the next few days they rode everywhere and they walked everywhere. They talked to everyone who would talk to them, and still everything looked good. They rented a car and drove out to the end of the road – not much more than 30 miles and some of it topped only with gravel. They found the end of the road meant exactly that. There is no road in or out of Juneau. The town is surrounded by water on one side and 1500 square miles of ice fields on the other. They stopped at Tee Harbor and they visited the Shrine of St. Therese – two very unique places. They drove by Auke Lake, and even visited Chapel by the Lake. There, in that beautiful and peaceful setting, they held hands and stood in awe of still another spectacular vista. Behind the altar were floor to ceiling windows that allowed a view of the lake with the Mendenhall Glacier in the background. Liz whispered, "If we someday think of renewing our vows, this would be the place I would choose to do it."

John answered simply, "Yes."

He even gave her a little kiss, right there at the altar. Why not – they were alone.

A uniformed Forest Service Ranger gave them a tour of the Mendenhall Glacier Visitors Center later that same morning, He even hiked with them out to view the glacier up close along the ice covered lake fronting it. Fortunately, they didn't go up too close to its face. The Ranger warned them: "The glacier will calve occasionally since it advances or recedes as much as fifty feet a year. The resulting movement can cause a rift in the ice on the lake and possible injury or death to anyone nearby."

They topped off the morning with a piece of apple pie, freshly brewed coffee, and some conversation with a nice couple, Paul and Betty, in their little coffee shop within the Visitors Center. Before departing, they asked Paul to suggest a good place for lunch.

"The City Café down on Franklin Street in town is a good place for food and conversation. Lot of the old timers congregate there. You won't be disappointed," he replied.

"I'm sure we won't, Paul, if the food is as good as Betty's pie," replied Liz appreciatively.

"Hey, never mind about Betty – all she does is count the money. I bake the pies!" As John handed the tab and money to Betty, he smiled at her and asked, "I bet he also makes all the big decisions at your house same as I do at ours?"

Betty looked over at Liz, and they both just smiled knowingly.

A warm feeling surrounded them as they got back into their rental car for the drive back to town. It had so far been quite a morning.

Lunch at the City Café turned out to be exactly what Paul had promised – good food and plenty of friendly conversation. They arrived there after most of the lunch crowd was gone. So, the fellow behind the counter had a little more freedom to chat with them. They found out a few days later that he was the owner – he waited on the customers while his brother did the cooking. It all went well - talking to him and a few town characters including a salty old retired ferry boat captain. In the middle of their special of the day – corned beef and cabbage – Liz asked a question that she regrets to this day, "What's the elevation here in Juneau?" Unfortunately for Liz everyone there heard her and John almost fell off his stool. Not wanting to embarrass her, he kept quiet. However, the old sea dog wasn't going to let it pass. He answered with a smile, "If you and your fella finish up your meal and come with me down to Gastineau Channel we can watch the 2:00 o'clock ferry come in. The elevation there and most of the rest of Juneau, at high tide, is probably forty-eight inches at most." Well, that brought the house down. Liz did the right thing – with a slightly red face she joined in with the laughter.

They were staying at the Baranof Hotel on North Franklin Street, and on their last night in Juneau they decided to take a walk eastward down the hill. They had been there earlier in the day in their rental car and it had appeared to be just another city street. But, in the dark of night all streets seem to have a more threatening aura to them. The farther they walked down Franklin the more suspect it looked. Liz held on to John a little tighter and said, "Do you think we're safe down here?"

Historically, it seems, Lower Franklin Street was always a

rather seedy area. In the early days of the gold mines it housed mostly saloons and brothels. Juneau's red light district was purported to be Alaska's largest and longest running and it did so until circa 1954. Once the mines closed, those businesses went with them. Most were replaced by sometimes less profitable endeavors but certainly with fewer problems for the Juneau Police Department.

As they walked, John concluded that the area did indeed appear to be one of the not so good things about Juneau. So, he was more than glad when he saw a patrol car coming toward them. He waved it down. As he walked up to the passenger side, the lone officer driving the vehicle rolled down the window. When John told him of Liz's concerns the officer said emphatically, "Sir, you are as safe here as if you were in your mother's arms."

They thanked the policeman for his reassuring words and continued their walk with smiles on their faces and a little more warmth in their hearts. They knew that this was looking more and more like 'the better place.' If a rundown area like Lower Franklin could be free of crime while upscale neighborhoods in San Francisco had plenty of muggings, robberies, and worse, then Juneau is where they should be.

A few weeks after returning to San Francisco they placed their house on the market. It sold shortly thereafter and at a surprisingly good price. So, as soon as the sale closed and just before they had to give occupancy to the new owners, John handed his letter of resignation to his precinct captain. The man's only comment was, "Alaska – are you nuts?"

They told Andrew of their plans early on and he was thrilled at the idea of living in Alaska and the prospect of being able to fish and hunt with his Dad. Two weeks later they headed north.

There were no openings in the Juneau Police Department upon their arrival in Juneau. So, John applied for work at the next best place – Alaska Department of Fish and Game. They had no openings in their Protection Division but they offered him work as a file clerk until a Protection Officer (another name for Game Warden) spot became available. Liz also found work with the

State, so they were both at least putting bread on the table. Both jobs offered anything but excitement, and, like so many government office jobs, putting in your hours without falling asleep doing it was their biggest challenge. On the bright side, they now had plenty of leisure time in the evenings and during weekends. So, it didn't take long for Andrew to suggest, "Let's start doing some of the things that we came here for, Dad – let's go fishing!"

SIX

THE EXCITEMENT BEGINS

Their first few months in Juneau, while the Santoris searched for the just right permanent residence, were spent in the confines of a small apartment at the Airport Motel located about ten miles outside of downtown. This was not a four star motel – probably more like a one star or maybe an asterisk. It was simply that, while a few homes were available for purchase, rentals were at an absolute premium. No matter. They were thankful for what little they had – it kept them warm and dry.

When Andrew suggested to his Dad that they should go fishing he didn't have to do much arm twisting. One of John's co-workers at Fish and Game had earlier described the great fishing available at nearby Salmon Creek Reservoir. "It's an easy two mile walk on a wooden flume to the Upper Salmon Creek Powerhouse and then another mile along the trail to the dam," he said. What he didn't tell John was that it was straight up hill from the parking area near the highway to where the flume begins and straight uphill again for part of that last mile to the dam. John and Andrew found that out for themselves that next Saturday morning.

John breathed a sigh of relief when they stepped off the end of the flume and onto the path leading to the powerhouse.

"Yes," he said later, "it was an easy two mile walk on a wooden flume, but what my co-worker didn't tell me was that some of that two miles would feel like it was on a tightrope. That damn flume was too narrow and way up off the ground in too many places for my liking."

A short respite, maybe a cup of coffee, and some additional information such as best lures to use, and where to stand along the banks of the lake seemed like something they should explore with the operator inside. As they entered the building and walked toward the small enclosure where the lone operator was sitting, he stood up to welcome them. He was a most pleasant man named

Chad Winkler who turned out to be still another living example of the friendliness of the people of this 'Great Land.'

"Just about any lure you toss out there will catch fish," he said. "They're all Eastern Brook Trout and one's hungrier than the next. They'll almost jump up into your creel if you're not careful." Andrew looked at his Dad with eyes sparkling. He could hardly wait to get started.

"You could walk over to the trail to get up to the dam, but the short way is to walk the pipe. The trail passes through dense foliage and it has some sharp turns where you could surprise a bear or even a wolverine. Instead, the pipe is out in the open for the entire mile of its length - so you're able to see a long way ahead. Whichever one you choose, the trail or the pipe, going up or coming back, consider singing 'Old McDonald Had a Farm' good and loud. Let those pesky fellows know you're coming," Chad added, grinning.

"The pipe?" asked Andrew, now a little wary.

"Yeah, it's four foot diameter wrought iron and a little slippery in spots when it's wet. However, we haven't had any rain yet today so it shouldn't be a problem. It's partially buried in some areas and not too high off the ground in most of the others. There's just one place where it's maybe ten or so feet above the rocks – so be careful there." This time, when John looked over at his son, his eyes were open wide as was his mouth. Regardless, he was still anxious to get started and began exiting the small enclosure. Later, when John became one of the operators there, he called it his little reading room.

They were just about out the door of the plant when Chad called to them, "Don't forget what I said about watching out for bear. We have a few of them in this valley. They usually will not bother you unless you encounter a sow with cub – then it might get a little touchy." Now, when John and Andrew looked at each other, they were both wide-eyed.

They walked around to the back of the powerhouse intending to start along the top of the pipe toward the dam when they heard Chad Winkler calling to them again, "Be sure to start back down this way before it starts getting dark." He had opened one of the back windows and as he leaned out he added, "We're having tacos for dinner. So, if you get back around five, you're invited to join us. Ours is the bottom unit of the house over there."

John's boisterous young son answered for him, "We'll be there!"

Whether John would have accepted the invite or not was now moot. All he could do was to wave, nod his head approvingly, and yell, "Thanks." At the same time he glared disapprovingly at his young son and later admonished him to remember that he was the parent in this group and that he should be the one to make those kinds of important decisions. As a matter of fact, that's the way it had always been at their house. Liz and John agreed, many years ago when they first got married, that he would always handle the big decisions and she would take care of the small ones. Strangely, he admits, "We have had almost no big decisions to confront all these years."

So, the rest of the day now having been planned for them, they resumed their hike toward the dam. As they walked, John commented to Andrew that he was glad they had stopped at the powerhouse, that he looked forward to the meal, and meeting the rest of Chad's family. "We will need to telephone Mom when we get back here to tell her that we will not be home for dinner. Best not to have her worry about where we are," he added.

It turned out that the fishing was exactly as it had been described. It was almost a fish every cast and it seemed the trout liked just about everything they had in their tackle box. There is heavy foliage along the edge of the lake and that makes it difficult to walk its perimeter, so they simply fished from the most accessible spot at the end of a short trail leading down to near the face of the dam. Only later, after they had departed the area, did they learn that there was a trail high above the lake level that wound its way right up to the headwaters of Salmon Creek. For years after their initial visit to the dam they would traverse that trail all the way to where the creek enters the lake. There, in the winter, they would drill holes in the ice and again yard out those tasty little 'brookies'. Thanks to Andrew's enthusiasm for the sport of trout fishing, the Santori's freezer would always be well stocked. That day in the Spring of 1968 was only the first of many exciting times that they would experience in the wilds of Alaska. What they did not realize at the time was that this adventure was only half over. John thought it would be a leisurely walk back down along the top of the pipe topped off with a nice hot meal at the home of the powerhouse operator there at Upper Salmon. It did not go exactly that way. They started back early enough. They were almost tired of catching fish which is hard to believe, but John felt that starting back a little before 4:00 o'clock would easily get them there in time. So, with both of their creels full of fish – the legal limit at that time was an unbelievable 30 per day per angler – they started to walk. Contrary to Chad Winkler's warning, they weren't singing about McDonald and his farm. Perhaps they might have thought that it wasn't macho. Or, they might have been reliving those first exciting moments when they caught their first 'trophy' brook trout. The fish were actually no more than nine or ten inches in length – a few might have stretched to 12 inches. They learned later that there was simply too little feed in the lake to sustain its large population.

They were roughly 500 yards away from the dam and Andrew was in the lead on the pipe. John had warned him to be careful and to keep his footing near as possible to the top of the pipe and away from its downward curved slope to avoid slipping off into the bushes below, but the warning probably fell on deaf ears. They had just walked past a long grassy stretch where the pipe was almost entirely buried in the dirt for at least a hundred feet. Now, however, the pipe was again elevated a few feet above the ground. At the moment that it happened, John was looking down at the pipe in anticipation of his next two or three steps. He was looking for and hoping to avoid any wet spots. Evidently, Andrew, who had been walking a little too fast and without looking carefully for those slick areas, found one of them. His yell that sounded much like a long drawn out 'OOOOW' caused John to look up just in time to see Andrew's almost horizontal feet first flight off the pipe. When he disappeared into the bushes below, John was almost certain that he had lost his only son. In almost that entire area there are rocks under all that foliage alongside the pipe. If Andrew were to land atop one or more of the larger rocks with either his back or his head, it could be very serious or even fatal.

Stupid as it might sound, while John hurried to reach the spot where Andrew had slipped off the pipe, he began singing loudly that, 'Old McDonald Had a Farm.' He opined later that people probably sometimes do strange things in moments of panic. A second later he heard the sweetest sound, 'E, I, E, I, O,' and a tousled head of hair with a face full of smiles emerged from the green mass of leaves. In his right hand he held his creel full of fish which evidently had broken loose from its hold around his waist. John sat down on the pipe straddling it as if he was riding a bull and reached his arm down to help his son back up onto the pipe. Andrew, instead, stood up and horsed himself up on to the pipe without any help. Luckily, he had landed on a soft dirt mound that was hidden under the foliage and he suffered not even a scratch.

As John stood up to embrace him, Andrew yelled, "DAD, BEHIND YOU." At the same instant he threw his creel full of fish back over his dad's head. When John looked around he saw that it had landed and spilled some of its contents at the feet (or paws) of one big black ugly bear. God! He looked big as a horse. To make it even worse, he was now menacingly growling as he sniffed at half of their catch of brook trout. What to do? John now concludes that he did the right thing. He turned to face the bear, and, standing as tall as he could and with arms outstretched so as to appear even larger, he hollered as loud as he could, using every swear word that he could think of, "GET THE &@#$% OUT OF HERE YOU MISERABLE #+@#$%#&." Whether he scared it or it simply decided to take the tasty snack somewhere away from those loud humans will never be known. Thankfully, the animal casually picked up the creel in his teeth, turned, walked away down into the heavy foliage, and soon was out of sight.

Needless to say, the two wasted no time in walking the rest of the way to the powerhouse, and they sang in almost perfect harmony all the way. From there they walked to the nearby house and presented themselves to the Winkler family. After introductions all around, John asked if he could use their phone to call his wife to tell her that they would not be home for dinner. When he was connected, the conversation was short and to the point – they had been invited to dinner there at Upper Salmon and they would be home a little late.   John felt it would be best not to mention the bear incident until they were home together where it could be talked about in a calm and less worrisome atmosphere. After hanging up the phone, he did reveal to the Winklers what had transpired along the pipe. All of them laughed at how silly they must have looked and sounded as they sang about Old McDonald. Andrew added to the humor when he opined that it was a good thing his Dad swore at the bear instead of singing to him. "We might still be up there as the big fella's dinner," he laughed. All, again, joined him in laughter.

Their dinner and the time spent with the Winkler family was most enjoyable. They were very gracious hosts and, as the two Santoris were ready to head for home, they were shown even more of what they would soon learn was typical Alaska hospitality. It was now dark outside. So, Chad and his son, Marc, offered to walk with them along the flume not only to the penstock but all the way down to their car parked at Lower Salmon.   John accepted their kind offer, again thanked Laura Winkler for the nice dinner, bid her goodbye, and even insisted that she have some of their remaining catch. Both she and Chad declined the offer with thanks, saying that they already had a plentiful supply in their freezer both there at Upper Salmon as well as at their home in downtown Juneau. Chad asked that they not reveal a truth to anyone when he said that he and Marc had spots along the creek just a few yards from the house where they could catch all the brook trout they wanted.

Chad grabbed a couple of large flashlights, gave one to Marc, and the four started out along the flume toward the penstock. As they walked, John commented that the Winklers really had themselves an ideal family residence – a short walk from Chad's work, and in a most beautiful setting. He asked Marc if he home schooled and he replied negatively, that he instead went in and out from and to school during his Dad's ten days on shift. His revelation that he drove his Dad's trail bike along the top of the flume each school day caused Andrew to suggest, "Dad, you ought to get a job working up here." They all laughed heartily; and John quickly steered the conversation on to other things. When they reached the penstock, John told Chad that they didn't need to escort them all the way down the steps, but the man was insistent. Finally, after a little more back and forth, he relented and handed them the two flashlights.

"Drop them off with the operator at Lower Salmon and Marc can pick them up on his return from school on Monday."

Just before they parted company, Chad said that one of the other two full time operators there at Upper Salmon was going to be retiring in a few months. "If you might be interested in the job, I'd be glad to recommend you."

John thanked him, but expressed doubt that he had the necessary knowledge and electronics experience to warrant his being hired.

"Oh, there's nothing much to the job except to watch the gauges and open and close a few valves. It's not rocket science. It won't take more than a few days of training that they'll give you at the Lower Salmon Powerhouse, and you'll know all there is to handling the job up here. If you want, I'll compose some fancy resume and let you see what it looks like before I mention your name to the bigshots," he replied. John didn't answer him – just letting the question hang there – but Chad wasn't going to let it rest.

"Hell, if you did come to work up here you could even have our unit here. Laura is going back to her old job at the State, and Marc is so busy with his baseball and football, neither of them will be coming back up here anymore. I'd move upstairs to the little apartment. That way, you could have your family here with you. Ours is a two bedroom unit. So, your boy could have his own room. It's a pretty nice way to live, John. I think I already told you, didn't I, that it's all rent free up here. And, as I'm sure you've already noticed, the house is only forty or fifty yards from the powerhouse, so it's an easy walk to work except, maybe, in the winter when you might need to shovel your way there."

The man sure made a convincing argument. Regardless, as good as all of it sounded, John was not going to commit to anything right then and there. So, he closed it off with words that usually work when one tries to end a conversation, "I'll get back to you."

Andrew and John shook hands all around and they thanked Chad again and again for his and Laura's hospitality. Just before starting down the steps to Lower Salmon John turned to Chad one last time and said, "As I told you and your Laura at dinner, my work for many years has been in law enforcement and I really do hope to get on with either the City as a policeman or with the State as a protection officer. Maybe, you shouldn't try too hard to influence your people in my behalf."

Chad persisted, "John, what you're doing now as a file clerk with the State is only temporary. So, why waste your time there in a low pay grade when you can come work up here where the pay is almost double. You can also make this job temporary until the one you really want comes along. There's no need to tell the brass here that you don't intend to make this your life work."

They were about half a dozen steps down from the penstock when they heard Chad holler, "Do you folks have a dog?"

Andrew yelled back, "No, but we're talking about getting one."

"You should. When you're living up here it can chase off the bears."

Andrew looked back at his Dad wide-eyed and began, "Old McDonald Had a Farm ….."

They both laughed when John chorused in, "E, I, E, I, O"

What Chad said about the advantages of family living at Upper Salmon made sense, but John really didn't want to encourage him further. He simply decided that what would happen would happen. However, just in case, a few weeks later he did go into the main office of Juneau Hydroelectric and he did fill out a job application. Why not? What harm could it do?

SEVEN

THE WORK AT UPPER SALMON

Well, it did happen, and John Santori's family says that they will be forever grateful for the adventure that followed. A few months after their first trip to Upper Salmon and the visit with Chad Winkler, the call came from the people at Juneau Hydroelectric offering John the job of powerhouse operator at Upper Salmon. He stretched the truth in his application, as Chad had suggested, telling his future employer that he had high school and military experience with electronics. Actually, he knew little more about electricity than the fact that one side of the switch said ON and usually that lit up the room while the other side of the switch said OFF and that darkened it. His electronics background or lack of it didn't seem to matter. So, two weeks later he became their newest employee.

John was given about a day and a half of training at Lower Salmon and, a little more than two and a half years later, he bragged that he had become a veteran operator. He did learn most of what went on and what had to be done there and he could say, truthfully, that the plant had never been knocked off line while he was on duty.

During the winter, electrical transmission lines often sag from the weight of snow and ice that collects on them. They sometimes can touch the ground, a tree or some other projection and that might cause an outage. Falling trees or limbs will also short out the circuitry. When that happens, quick action by all the operators at all of the facilities is mandatory.

The machinery actually warns the operator that something is wrong. It starts to groan like a person would if he was carrying a load on his back and was starting up a steep grade. In the powerhouse much more water is needed immediately. The plant operator has to run quickly to the valves in front of the Pelton wheels and turn them wide open. More water means the wheels move the generators faster and thus more electricity is produced. Hopefully, a shutdown of the entire system is thus avoided.

Juneau's history of harsh winter winds coupled with many miles of exposed transmission lines often contributed to more than a few outages each year. So, during those times, the operators had to be even more diligent in preventing any interruption in their electrical system output. In Alaska it could be critical.

Almost three years had passed since John and Liz had first visited Alaska and he still had not been able to get on with the Juneau Police Department nor with the State in their Protection Division at Fish and Game. He was still working at Upper Salmon, but he admits that he was enjoying every minute of it.

His workplace at Upper Salmon was located one mile below the Salmon Creek Dam. Water from the outlet at the bottom of the dam ran through a four-foot diameter wrought iron pipe into the Upper Salmon powerhouse. There it flowed into Pelton wheels which in turn ran the generators that produced the output of electricity. The powerhouse was ninety five percent power generating equipment. The rest was personal accommodations. There was a toilet, a small two-burner stove, a sink, a refrigerator, and a small cubicle (or office) in an opposite corner of the plant where the operator sat during his shift.

There was no road into Upper Salmon – only a trail and the flume. Hikers used the trail that wound its way up the heavily forested mountainside through the skunk cabbage and devil's club past the powerhouse and on up to the dam. The powerhouse operators, instead, used the flume because it was the more direct route, albeit more dangerous.

The flume carried part of the spent water from Upper Salmon Powerhouse together with water from an arm of Salmon Creek into the penstock a little more than two miles down the valley. The penstock consisted of a small cabin with a wooden plank floor covering the top of a very large storage tank. The water from that tank then flowed through a similar wrought iron pipe almost straight downhill into Lower Salmon Powerhouse where it was again used to generate more electricity.

THE PENSTOCK AT TOP OF THE STEPS

**LOOKING DOWN AT LOWER SALMON
POWERHOUSE FROM TOP OF STEPS**

Upper Salmon operators parked their cars at Lower Salmon which was located just off Glacier Highway. They then had to walk up 876 steps to the penstock. The steps consisted of wood cleats nailed crosswise to planks anchored lengthwise up the mountain to the penstock. From there it was another two plus miles in on the flume to their temporary living quarters near the Upper Salmon powerhouse. Most of the men traveled in and out along the top of the flume on motorbikes that they stored in a corner section of the penstock.

Millions of people throughout the world drive similar vehicles from and to work, but it is doubtful that many of them do it on top of a six-foot wide wooden structure sans side rails that is sometimes suspended 20 or 30 feet above the ground.

In addition to the powerhouse, the Upper Salmon complex included living quarters in the form of an old two-story house with a two-bedroom apartment downstairs where Chad and his family stayed and a studio apartment upstairs that John used during his first few months on the job. Then, when Laura Winkler and her son moved back to their home in town, Chad made good on his promise by moving upstairs to the studio apartment and allowing John and his family to occupy the larger quarters downstairs.

During the summers, the Santoris lived the good life together at Upper Salmon. In the winter, Liz and Andrew stayed in their home in town while John went in and out to work each day up the 876 steps and along the snow covered flume. He felt that the steps kept his body in shape and the days or nights at home kept the marriage in good shape as well. When the weather was real bad or when the flume was covered with ice, John might spend his entire ten day work period there at Upper Salmon. Rain and snow on the flume called for caution, but ice made it downright treacherous and danger filled. During the winter, work crews did their best to keep the top of the flume cleared of snow, but an overnight storm could make it very difficult for the operator coming in to work the next morning. It was lonely for John during those periods when he stayed at Upper Salmon the entire ten days but considerably less risky.

At Upper Salmon there was also a small cabin where work

crews could sleep when long lasting repairs to flume or machinery were necessary.   In a clearing near the two-story house there was a wooden platform with what looked like half of a fat lady's torn silk stocking for a windsock.   That was their helicopter pad where food and supplies were offloaded for use of the operators and their families if and when they actually lived there during their ten-day work period.   In the middle of the complex near the crew cabin was a smaller building that served as a combination storage/workshop. The only other building in the area was a house on the other side of the flume where Rex Franz lived.

**POWERHOUSE #2 AND WORKSHOP WITH
SALMON CREEK IN FOREGROUND**

**UPPER SALMON COMPLEX WITH
BATCHELOR SHED AND FLUME ON
RIGHT AND LIVING QUARTERS ON
LEFT**

EIGHT

THE PEOPLE AT UPPER SALMON

Rex Franz started with the company only a few weeks after John did, but he was at Powerhouse #1 (known as Lower Salmon). When Boyd Hendricks, the other regular operator at Upper Salmon retired, Rex moved to Upper Salmon. So, Chad, Rex, and John were then the three regulars usually on duty up there. Each man worked eight-hour shifts alternating day, swing, and graveyard in sequences of ten days on and four days off.

Rex was married but he and his wife, Mary, had no children. She had two complicated pregnancies and had lost both children. She miscarried with the first and the second was stillborn. Since it was a sore subject with Rex, few of the men ever talked about it with him. As a matter of fact, few of the operators spoke much to Rex - period. He was just a little different - quiet to a fault. He didn't swear. He, supposedly, didn't smoke or drink. He didn't tell dirty jokes or even want to listen to them. He just was not one of the guys. After one of their union meetings in town when most of the group headed for the nearby tavern, Rex begged out saying he was going home – explaining that he had a project to complete. After he was out of earshot one of the men commented, He's sort of a 'Casper Milktoast' isn't he?" No one answered him.

Chad Winkler, unlike his co-worker, was usually the life of the party – the guy that always kept it interesting. He could never be described as a quiet man. Regardless, he was good people – big, tough, the kind of fellow you'd like to have had as a big brother when you were going to school. His son, Marc, and John Santori's boy, Andrew, became real good buddies. They spent a lot of their free time together – mostly fishing or hunting. Chad and John got to be pretty good buddies, too – mostly drinking buddies. Their wives (John's Liz and Chad's Laura), fortunately, liked each other, as well. They were shopping buddies.

The house at Upper Salmon where Rex spent so much of his

time had, years before, been occupied by a bachelor operator who was his exact opposite. That fellow, they say, often encouraged one or more ladies from town to visit him during his off days. To most of the young women it was an exciting and anticipated adventure. Needless to say, the happy bachelor (the guys all called him 'Stud') did all he could to reward the girls once they arrived. If the visitors brought along some alcoholic beverages it usually added quite a bit more warmth to the occasion. The resulting revelry and the noisy outbursts from the gathering could then be heard echoing across the small valley that surrounded the complex.

One time, two more than slightly soused ladies departed Stud's house in the middle of the night and were later brought into the emergency room at Bartlett Hospital after having fallen off the flume. Day or night, in the light or in darkness, and whether the flume was wet or dry, it was not a sidewalk or a roadway. It was a path that needed to be used carefully if one was sober and not at all if he or she was drunk. The bachelor remained a happy camper another two years. Then, one enterprising young woman walked him to the altar and finally made him an 'honest man.' After the marriage the visits and partying ended but the house's notoriety lasted. Boyd Hendricks was its next occupant, and he was a man that everybody liked.

Boyd's full time job was with the electric company, but his main effort in life was more spiritual. He was also pastor of a newly formed church group whose Sunday services were conducted in a rented hall in town. He began his mission for Jesus along Lower Franklin Street where he preached to exiting and usually inebriated bar patrons about the folly of their drunken existence. He would try to encourage them to forego their wasteful ways and instead join him on the 'Way of the Lord.'

Boyd's trail bike was the oldest and slowest of all those stored in the penstock, but it was dependable enough to always get him to work on time. There was one occurrence, however, when its dependability did get a real test – a life-saving one.

On his way into work early one morning, Boyd encountered two black bear cubs frolicking atop the flume. It was in an area where the flume rounded a promontory, ducked into a short indentation in the mountain, curled around still another promontory, and then continued on toward the powerhouse on a long straightaway. If one, either walking or riding, was on the flume in the indentation in the mountain he or she could not see for any distance either ahead or behind. Boyd was on his trail bike and moving at a reasonably high rate of speed - it being one of those rare sunny days when the flume was dry on its top surface.

On that Monday morning as Boyd rounded that last promontory before the straightaway he was immediately confronted with the need for a split second decision. The two cubs were directly in front of him. What to do? Should he attempt to stop and avoid hitting the cubs or should he accelerate and try to go between them. Either choice was risky. It was almost certain that the mother sow was foraging nearby. If he attempted to stop and turn around she would probably be up on the flume and atop him before he could escape back from where he had come. So, there being no other option, he stomped down on the gas and hurled himself and the bike as fast as it would go between the cubs who squealed as they jumped off the flume. He looked back for an instant and saw the sow giving chase. It was then that he pleaded with 'Nellie Bell,' as he fondly referred to his old bike, "Please don't fail me now." It didn't. Fortunately for Boyd, the sow soon gave up her revengeful pursuit and returned to her unharmed but frightened cubs. Boyd, instead, sped on thanking his Maker all the way to the powerhouse. From that day on Boyd began carrying a sidearm, and later became known by his co-workers as the 'Pistol Packing Pentecostal Preacher.'

The house that Rex inherited from Boyd Hendricks was the perfect place for someone like Rex. It was more or less secluded in amongst the trees away from the other buildings in the complex. In fact, if one were walking along the flume toward the powerhouse, day or night, the house wouldn't be noticed unless its outside lights were lit.

NINE

AN EASY RIDE TO WORK

Some of John Santori's ten days on shifts during the winter months were spent alone at Upper Salmon. But, when the flume was not covered with ice or snow, Liz and Andrew would join him. If she could walk in or out atop the flume without the fear of falling off she would welcome the opportunity to share those serenely uncomplicated hours with him. If he was on shift she would bring their meals from the apartment and they would eat together there in his little cubbyhole in the powerhouse. When he wasn't at work, and Andrew was away at school, they spent those hours enjoying each other's company away from the burdens of parenthood that had previously taken up almost all of their twenty three plus years of married life. Andrew especially treasured those ten day periods in that he, like his new found friend Marc, was able to use his father's trail bike to go in and out to school each day. Andrew missed only one day of school those almost three years that they lived at Upper Salmon. It was not because he fell off the flume – even though he even once did that – but rather due to a large mud slide that blew out a small section of the wooden pathway to the penstock. John, too, had his troubles on the flume. He skidded off the flume one snowy night on his way into Upper Salmon for his graveyard shift. Luckily, he and the bike landed in a snow bank just a few feet below the top of the flume. Miraculously, no harm was done to either machine or human. His only suffering came when he tried to lift the bike back onto the flume and forgot that one should never grab the exhaust manifold of a motorbike. This is especially true if the bike's motor has been running for any length of time.

Even Chad Winkler fell off the flume one day during John's time at Upper Salmon. His fall was considerably more complicated and life threatening than John's or Andrew's. Juneau had just experienced one of their prolonged rainy spells, and now the sun had finally appeared. The few remaining early morning clouds were dissipating, and one could feel that it was going to be a warm sunny day. The rain can be very depressing especially when it continues day after day. However, when the sun finally comes out, it makes it all worthwhile. This day was one of those beautiful exceptions when everyone is happy with their existence. Chad and John were walking up the steps together. Chad was returning from his four days off while John was going back for his regular swing shift. Each of them, as per their usual, carried a backpack filled with a few necessities. John didn't realize it at the time, but Chad's also contained a six pack of their favorite beverage. There was no wind – not even a cool breeze as they neared the top of the steps causing Chad to suggest that they should stop and enjoy the sunshine and a brew. Hearing not a hint of an objection he reached into his backpack and retrieved a bottle for each of them. They sat on the steps and looked out toward Gastineau Channel as they downed their drinks. Neither one said anything for quite a while. They were both caught up in their own thoughts and each was more than content with the peaceful moment they were enjoying. Chad finally broke the silence, saying, "You know, I could sit here all day."

John happily agreed, "Yeah, this is living."

Chad reached around to his backpack that he had placed on the steps above him and asked, "How about one more brew before we head in?"

John answered reluctantly, "No, I think I'll pass. It's hard enough to stay awake near the end of my swing shift without adding a couple of beers to it,"

Chad reply was loud and startling, "Look at that flock of goats."

John turned to look at what Chad was yelling about, but couldn't immediately see anything but trees. Chad pointed above the tree line on Blackerby Ridge - the mountain that borders the northwest side of the Salmon Creek Valley. Finally, John was able to see them - to the right on the mountain from where he had been looking. Sure enough, the green covered mountainside had a number of little white dots on it and they were all moving down the mountain. When the winter snows begin covering the local mountaintops one can often see animal life heading down into the valleys where the flora is still plentiful. This, apparently, was one of those events.

Chad jumped up, grabbed his backpack and started running up the remaining steps to the penstock. He turned and yelled, "Grab those empties please, John. I'm gonna go get me one of those big billies."

He was almost out of earshot when John yelled, "Hey, you better be back to relieve me tonight." Later, Chad would insist that he had hollered back, "No problem." If he said that, John never heard it.

It was still early afternoon - hours before John needed to be on shift. So, he leisurely picked up the two empty beer bottles, placed them into his backpack, retrieved from it his newly purchased transistor radio, and started up the steps. A few minutes later he was tooling his little Yamaha along the flume toward Upper Salmon. He was truly at peace with the world, with earphones in place, listening to Aker Bilk's beautiful rendition of 'Stranger on the Shore.' Upon arriving at his apartment and after closeting his bike he decided to take a nap – better to dull that sleep craving urge that always seemed to envelope him near the end of his swing shifts. He set his alarm for 3:00 pm and was soon off to dreamland.

When the ringing of bells at 2:45 pm permanently cut him off from Marilyn Monroe's embrace and the background music of Aker's clarinet, he was a little upset. First, he was almost certain that he had set the alarm for 3:00 pm – not 2:45 pm. Still not fully awake he reached for the clock to shut it off. When it wouldn't shut off no matter how many buttons he pushed, he began using some four letter words. They didn't seem to help either - other than to interrupt the ringing every few seconds. Only then did he realize that it was the telephone and not the alarm that had caused his blissful dream to disappear. He laughed at himself as he put the receiver to his ear and was pleasantly surprised when another sweet sounding feminine voice said, "Hi Handsome."

His own sexy and very suave reply was, "Uh, hello."

"John, this is Laura. Have you seen Chad? Do you know where he is?"

"Oh, I'm sorry, Laura. I was asleep," he replied, still somewhat confused and not fully awake.

"You know that Chad, like you, always phones home when he gets up there to let us know that he has arrived safely. He hasn't called, and I'm a little worried."

Now fully awake he replied, "Oh, I'm sure he's alright, Laura. I walked up the steps with him earlier. He saw a flock of goats on the mountain and ran off saying that he was going to shoot himself a big billy. He was in such a rush he probably forgot to call you. I'm sure the 'Great White Hunter' will phone you when he returns with his trophy."

When their conversation ended he felt that Laura had been reassured. However, to do the same for himself he felt it prudent to do a little bit of checking. He first telephoned downstairs thinking that Chad might have returned and taken his own little nap. When there was no answer he decided to go down to look for evidence that Chad had in fact gone off hunting. God forbid that anything else might have happened.

When he found Chad's rifle and his ammo still on his gun rack he knew there was a problem. And, when he looked in Chad's little shed, there was no trail bike. Now, it appeared to be more than a problem. It could well be an emergency. More than an hour had gone by since they had parted company, and Chad well could be off the flume somewhere either dead or seriously injured. John climbed aboard his bike and headed down the flume toward the penstock.

Since there were not many areas where the flume was suspended above the ground, John drove quickly to those areas, stopped, yelled Chad's name, looked down over the edge, and then continued on when no response came. Finally, after a few more fruitless stops, he came upon an almost humorous scene and was greeted with a most simple question: "Did you bring any beers?"

Over the years he would learn that his friend, Chad Winkler, was disposed to oversimplification. The events of that day, and his encounter with him in his then most untenable predicament, was a perfect example of how Chad always approached the vagaries of life.

He remembers that Chad later summed it up by saying, "Hey, good things happen and bad things happen and there's no use making a big fuss over those bad things – they've already happened. Just be a little more careful the next time." That was his philosophy.

When John looked down over the edge of the flume he saw that Chad was securely wedged between the very large trunk of a Sitka Spruce on one side and a sheer rock face on the other. He had an ugly lemon size knot on his forehead and his left arm appeared to be in a twisted and abnormal position behind his back. He had dropped only a few yards off the edge of the flume but far enough to be trapped and unable to free himself. His legs were dangling free and his right arm was also wedged tightly against the tree. So, he had no ability to free himself. Even if he had been able to unloosen himself, he was still almost ten feet above the jagged rocks below. It was apparent that Chad's only avenue of escape without assistance - if there was one - was up and not down. John answered as smartly as he felt the situation demanded, "No, I didn't bring any brews, and you're not gonna find any goats down there."

Later, when they talked about the incident, John asked, "Did you try to yell to me when I drove by on my bike? If you did, the noise from my bike coupled with me wearing earphones probably drowned you out."

"Hell, I don't remember hearing you or calling out to you. I think I was just coming to when you looked down at me from up on the flume."

Chad suffered only a broken arm, some bruised ribs, and a few scratches and bruises in addition to the bump on his head. He also could have suffered a concussion, but neither Chad nor anyone else ever mentioned that he was diagnosed with same. His bike had gone off the flume on the other side and, luckily, was undamaged. He was carefully removed from his precarious entrapment with the help of the Juneau Fire Department and then hoisted up onto the flume. Later, he was evacuated by helicopter to Bartlett Hospital. Two weeks later he was back to work in spite of the aches and pains, the cast on his left arm, and a still somewhat swollen and discolored forehead.

When Chad entered the powerhouse to relieve John after his time off, he was greeted warmly. As John looked at the cast he joked, "Good thing you're right-handed. Otherwise, I'd probably have to stay here to turn the valves for you." They both laughed about it, but John was really glad to see his friend back at work and he told him so. As for the goats, the flock survived another winter without Chad doing any culling.

TEN

A MORE NORMAL WORK DAY

The fall months of October and November in Southeast Alaska are sometimes the most pleasant. Before the snows begin to spoil it, the days are often sunny and cold. It's a good time to get out the snow tires, clean the leaves from the rain gutters, check all the heat tapes within and near those same gutters, and to get out the wool clothing. Conversely, August and September are usually rain filled but still warm and fairly pleasant. During those latter months before icy spots begin to form atop the flume it is still an easy ride into Upper Salmon.

This day, however, as John parked his car in the lot at Lower Salmon, he could see that he had a wet and uncomfortable walk ahead of him. That was nothing new – and it was raining steadily as he started his walk up the steps. Normally, the rain can be tolerated. It's usually a soft rain, but today was different. It was more like a gully washer – the kind of rain that spills over the tops of those rain gutters.

The rain didn't help his mood. It was already soured by the fact that this was a special day. It was September 4, 1970. Earlier that morning, Liz reminded him that 24 years ago they had walked down the aisle together. She felt strongly that they should be together this day to again celebrate the happy event.

"I don't see why you have to go to work today of all days," she moaned in disappointment.

John had told her the previous day that vacations and a few people off sick shortened the work force to the point that he just could not at this time get a day off. That excuse, although a hundred percent accurate, plus 25 cents would have gotten him a cup of coffee anywhere in town. However, it did little to pacify Liz. In fact, she added a little salt to the wound when, as he departed the house shortly after lunch, she yelled (with quite a bit of sarcasm), "Have a nice day at work, dear."

As John started up the steps to the penstock he started counting. If he had counted those steps once he'd counted them a hundred times over the past few years. The result at the top (or at the bottom) was always the same - 876. He would take an occasional rest stop part way up the mountain depending on the weather, the amount of weight in his backpack, the extent of his activities the night or the day before, or simply to have the opportunity to stop and smell the roses. It was a beautiful sight from those steps down to Gastineau Channel or across to Douglas Island. Often, when he would reach the top of the steps, he would again stop to look back. As he stared out at the distant landscape, he felt like he was standing at the top of the world. From there the view to the west includes the Juneau International Airport as well as the Mendenhall River and the tidal flats through which it flows. On a clear day even the Chilkat Mountain Range in the far distance is visible. The possible sighting of a bear or other Alaska wildlife also makes for an interesting climb up those steps. There were more than a few times when John simply stopped just to admire the view and to thank God for this beautiful and wonderful place.

When an old friend, Bud Howell, from the San Francisco Police Department telephoned John one day and asked how he was enjoying his new found vocation of powerhouse operation and what it was like going in and out to work, John replied, "It's really awe inspiring. The setting in this remote valley, the old powerhouse and the flume leading up to it, all the old buildings, even the people you work with makes you happy to be here. The work itself, on the other hand, is about as thrilling as watching grass grow." He went on to say, "In a way you can almost compare powerhouse operation at Upper Salmon to police work. You hope that it will always be peaceful, but when it goes wrong you know it can be exciting as hell. Then you try as fast and as hard as you can to make it go right again.

"You're making it sound like your work is real critical, John."

"It is, Bud. Picture this if you can. Here at Upper Salmon, in this little insignificant dot on a city map, we have a tiny source of

THE MENDENHALL FLATS WITH THE SNOWCAPPED CHILKAT RANGE IN THE BACKGROUND

JOHN SANTORI ON HIS BIKE BY THE BACHELOR SHED

ANDREW AND HIS PUPPY ON THE FLUME

electric power that probably generates no more than five to ten percent of the total energy needs of our entire area. However, if I were to somehow screw up and allow it to fail – get knocked off line – the entire grid could go with it. If, for some reason, the other ninety or ninety-five percent of our facilities could not quickly enough pick up the lost load the entire city would be in the dark. If it happened in winter time, that would be critical. So, one little old powerhouse operator like me is more important to our little town than twenty policemen in San Francisco are to their big metropolis. Now do you see what I mean, Bud?"

"Yeah, John, you're a real big potato! You are, without a doubt, indispensable."

Both men laughed, and John continued: "That's right, but not to glorify my importance, I must admit that the excitement and the uncertainty is not a major issue here. It can be dull as hell. Even if your eight-hour shift goes smoothly and nothing happens, the isolation and the monotony can still wear on you. Of course, if you have inner problems coupled with bitterness and even some hate, all of those little irritations become magnified as the hours and the generators keep grinding on. However, if you're happy with yourself, have a good outlook on life together with great family support, like I have, then it's just a long eight hours that you might use to study or do something else constructive. For me, it's been a great ride and I'm sure glad we made the move to Alaska. And, Bud, I'm still keeping my eyes open toward someday getting back into police work. I'm even taking a correspondence course on criminal investigations. I work on my lessons here at the plant. Why not – I have all the time in the world and rarely get interrupted. Nothing has opened up here in the Police Department or at the State in more than two years, but when it does I'll be ready. Fortunately, for me, my Liz spends a lot of time with me up here. When Andrew is at school and I'm not on shift, we spend a lot of quality time together. In fact, I think we've fallen in love all over again – we're acting like a couple of newlyweds."

As their phone conversation was ending Bud laughingly said: "Be sure to let me know when there is another open slot in your police department or your electric company, and I'll come to visit your little 'jerk-water' town." John gave him his standard reply, "I'll get back to you." Then he added, Oh, and to answer your earlier question about how I go in and out to work, I'll send you a picture of me on my 'hog' and one of Andrew with his puppy. We bring her up to Upper Salmon so she'll alert us if a bear is nearby. We call her 'Chicken' because she runs the other way whenever she gets anywhere near a bear. She usually runs ahead of us on the flume when we're walking in or out of Upper Salmon, but she comes running back if she even smells a bear. That's when we know it's time to start singing 'Old McDonald Had a Farm' good and loud"

"Old McDonald.......?"

"Yeah. I'll explain that some other day."

John, during his telephone conversation with his friend, might have gone a little overboard in extolling the virtues of Juneau, his work, and the surrounding area. He neglected to mention, or intentionally omitted the not so good features – like the rain. He decided he would let the man find out for himself if he ever did come to visit.

This day on his anniversary, when he should have been at home celebrating with his darling wife, John was instead walking briskly up the 876 steps. This wasn't a day to tarry or to stop for a rest. The rain was now coming down in sheets and as it chattered on his mackintosh he moved even faster, anxious to reach shelter and a warm shower. As he climbed the steps, his thoughts wandered aimlessly and then they somehow drifted to the poem entitled 'It Rains Sometimes in Juneau' written by a local lady named Billie Wilson. As he hurried up the steps, he laughingly muttered to himself that her poem should have been called 'It Rains ALL THE TIME in Juneau.' Since it does rain roughly 220 days a year here in the Juneau area his suggested title would have been much more accurate but certainly less seducing.

Today, however, was another story. He was now taking most of those steps two at a time. In spite of the fast pace, it still took him more than twenty minutes to reach the penstock and retrieve his motorbike. Then, because of the wet surface of the flume, it took him another very cautious twenty plus minutes to traverse the two or so miles along the top of the flume to the powerhouse. The top of the flume is covered by 2x12 inch planks running lengthwise as it meanders alongside the mountain above the rocks and Salmon Creek below. The flume is six feet wide but feels considerably narrower especially when it spans long stretches high above ground.

Forty minutes was not his best or even his average time. He had done it in thirty minutes, but that was on a warm sunny day when the top of the flume was completely dry. The record for the least amount of time from parking lot to living quarters was held by Andrew who made it once in 21 minutes. There are a few long straightaways on the flume and Andrew must have moved that trail bike at more than 25 mph in those areas. His mother never heard about that record trip. If she had, she might have threatened to kill him if he ever tried to improve on that record. Of course, Andrew's record trip was made on another warm sunny day. On a wet day, speed on the flume was out of the question because of the uneven surface areas where one often wet or snow covered wooden plank abuts another. Hitting one of those irregular spots even at a slower speed could easily cause one to lose control and possibly fall with the bike down to the water or rocks below. In some areas the flume is suspended high above ground. For most of the two plus miles, however, it hugs the mountain on the one side and lies along grassy, bush, or trees filled areas adjacent to the top of the flume on the other. So, caution is paramount only in a few spots where Andrew suggests, "You either slow down to a crawl or go like hell to get the scary part behind you as soon as possible."

This day, John's trip into Upper Salmon was uneventful except for the discomfort of the rain. He rode his little Yamaha to the door of his apartment, wheeled it inside the enclosed porch, threw off his backpack and rain clothes, removed the rest of his other somewhat damp garments, and headed for the bathroom and a much anticipated warm shower. He didn't quite make it. The ringing of the phone and the subsequent conversation finished the job of souring his day. It was Rex Franz and he was asking John to take his graveyard shift for him. This meant a workday of 16 hours and it wasn't a happy prospect. Rex said that his wife Mary was having premature labor pains. They would probably go to the hospital as soon as they talked to the doctor, and he really wanted to be with her during and after the delivery. John knew how the man would be so concerned. He remembered the bouts of depression that Rex exhibited after their first loss as well as his complete change of attitude more than a year later when he told his co-workers that his wife was pregnant again with, hopefully, their first child and his future hunting partner.

Since operators do occasionally trade shifts, John could do no less than agree to take on the extra eight hours, especially when there was so much at stake for Rex and his wife. After hanging up the phone he headed for the shower and then later took a nap hoping to offset some of the fatigue that surely would set in during that 16-hour shift.

As he contemplated the next 16 hours he considered breaking out his real estate books. He had been studying for his real estate license the last few months thinking that he might someday go to work for his friend, Joe Shaw, who had a real estate brokerage firm out in the Mendenhall Valley. Joe had often asked him to consider working with him at least on a part time basis during his four days off. Joe was one of the first people that Liz and John met when they first came to Juneau back in 1967. He sold them their first home and he made Andrew his friend and admirer for life by buying him a fishing rod and reel and helping him catch his first ever King Salmon.

John shelved the real estate books idea because people in town were starting to come home from work, and he'd be busy for the next few hours increasing the power output of the plant. Later, when things calmed down again and people began retiring for the night, he could consider doing some reading and some studying.

Nowadays most hydroelectric plants are automated and only a few even need a caretaker operator. In Juneau, in 1970, very little was automated. Everything about Upper Salmon was old. In fact, the entire generating system of the area was antiquated and in need of some real updating.

There was a combination operator/dispatcher on shift at the Gold Creek facility in downtown Juneau who had control of all the plants. In his hydro-driven power plant he also had diesel power as a backup in case of emergency, but starting it up with the flip of a switch was not a luxury he could enjoy. He also had a console in front of him that showed him the amount of electricity being used throughout the Juneau area and how much was being generated by each facility. It was his job to instruct the operators at all of the other plants when to increase or reduce their production. Soon after 4:00 p.m. each day he would start phoning operators at the various plants telling them to 'up two' or 'up three' depending on gauges displayed on that console. The term 'up two' meant that the operator needed to go out into the plant and make two complete turns of the valve in front of the Pelton wheel running each generator. This would allow more water to hit the wheels and more KW's would thus be inducted into the transmission lines. When the power requirements subsided later in the evening the dispatcher would start reversing the process by telephoning with instructions such as 'down two' or 'down three,' etc.

When the phone rang again, John thought sure it was the dispatcher, so he answered in jest asking, "Up 15?" It wasn't the dispatcher. It was Rex, and he could tell immediately that it wasn't good news. The man was almost sobbing, "Mary is not in good shape. The baby was stillborn. Will you take over for me again tomorrow, John, so I can be with her? She's really down, and I know she needs me."

There was absolutely no way that he could refuse. All he could do was to offer his condolences and assure Rex that he would do his eight hours for him.

ELEVEN

A CHANGE OF SCENERY

Needless to say, John's next four days off were a welcome respite after all that happened the previous week. His next ten workdays were scheduled to be on the graveyard shift, and they passed with no problems. . When he came on shift at midnight the plant was already off line. During the night, when most people are sleeping, the plant is taken off line and it generates only enough electricity to keep it and the houses at Upper Salmon lighted and heated. Then, at about 6:00 a.m., when most people start awakening, turning on lights, heaters, and appliances, the operator begins his work getting back on line and upping the plant's electrical output. Eight nights of the shift went by without incident. At the end of the ninth, just a few minutes before 8:00 a.m., as he waited for his relief, John received an unexpected phone call:

"Hello, John, this is Chief Jim Parker."

It was so unexpected he was struck dumb for just a split second. He thought, "What does the Chief of Police want?" Then it all came back to him and he apologized. "I'm sorry for the hesitation, Chief. It's just that I wasn't expecting your call."

"I know," the Chief replied. "It's been a while, but we now have an opening in the Department and I wanted to talk to you about it if you're still interested."

"I sure am, Chief."

"Well, when could you come in to see me?"

"I'm just finishing up my graveyard shift. I'd like to get a little sleep and freshen up. Could I come in this afternoon, maybe, around four?"

"That will be fine, John. I'm usually here until six. So, no need to hurry."

John thanked Chief Parker for thinking of him and their call ended. He no sooner cradled the phone than it rang again. This time it was Liz, and she wanted to know what he had done to warrant a call from the Chief of Police. John suspected that the Chief tried to reach him at the house and she gave him the number there at Upper Salmon. He answered smartly, "The Chief said that he received a report that I had been beating my wife and neighbors were complaining."

Liz snapped back, "Ok, wise guy, what did he really want?"

When he told her the real reason for the Chief's call, he asked what she thought he should do. She had always supported him in past decisions and it would be no different this day. She encouraged him to follow his instincts especially since she knew that police work was what he enjoyed most.

Coincidentally, John had heard rumors that A. J. Mining was going to divest itself of its electrical generating systems in the Juneau area. If it came to pass, Alaska Electric Light & Power Company would surely be the new owner of Juneau Hydroelectric and that would mean a consolidation of work forces and layoffs of those operators with the least seniority. Since John was one of the last hired, he would be one of the first fired.

So, his answer to Chief Parker as they sat at Police Headquarters later that day was, "I would very much appreciate the opportunity, Chief, and thank you again for remembering me."

"Well, John, we gave you a pretty good looking over before I called you. The people in San Francisco were good enough to send us a copy of your work record and it was rather impressive even for the short time you were with them. However, I am curious as to why you left there."

John gave him a truthful answer together with a few of his thoughts regarding urban crime problems, hippies, drugs, the anti-war movement, etc. He felt that the Chief shared some of those same feelings even though all he did was listen. He did talk a little about the 'good old days' in Juneau by confiding that, "Just a few years ago, the troopers here used to meet every ferry boat when it docked. If they spied someone they thought might be an undesirable, they handed him a free ticket back to Seattle."

"Back to where they came from, huh?" John asked.

"Exactly, and as they escorted them back onto the ferry, they would tell them to: 'Have a nice day.' Yes, we had a quiet, safe little town. Of course, it's still a safe town. We still rarely lock our doors or take our keys out of the ignition. But, the town is growing and we now have a few more problems."

As they parted company, Chief Parker asked John when he could start, and John answered that he would give the electric company his two weeks notice the very next day. The next morning he did just that and two weeks later he was being fitted for his new uniform – that of a Juneau Police Officer.

The first few months on the job he spent in the office getting acquainted with his fellow officers, his superiors, department staff, fire department officers and staff, dispatchers, procedures, rules and regulations, etc., etc. Just about everyone he met made him feel more than welcome, and he again was most appreciative. After a while he was driving a patrol car and doing some of the major police work of Juneau officers, namely, pulling over drunk drivers, citing them, and then jailing them. Nothing much more serious ever happened in Juneau in those days, except maybe a domestic disturbance where again alcohol and too much consumption of it was usually involved. This police work, however, was heaven compared to his previous beat in the big metropolitan City by the Bay.

There was even a bank robbery in Juneau during his early days with the Department, and he was one of the first officers on the scene. John was quick to admit, however, that he didn't solve the crime or catch the culprit. That was done not too many days later and the guy was arrested because a local attorney remembered that the robber, an eccentric old timer with possibly less than a full deck, had bragged to him only weeks before that it would be real easy to rob a bank in Juneau.

When the attorney phoned Chief Parker a few days after the robbery suggesting the possible connection, two officers were sent out to the suspect's home. Upon being invited into the residence, the officers were almost immediately handed the man's verbal confession. He gleefully admitted the theft, and even showed them the stash of bills together with the threatening note all still in the paper bag with which he had exited the bank. They, in turn, showed him the way to their patrol car and then to the front door of the Lemon Creek Jail.

There also had been a murder or two committed in Juneau over the years but they were few and far between. Robert Stroud, the Birdman of Alcatraz, got his start in Juneau in the early 1900's. He wasn't famous for being born in Juneau or for having done anything to benefit its people. Instead, he killed a man for messing with his girlfriend. There are different versions of the killing. One is that the girl was a prostitute and that Stroud was her pimp. Evidently, the victim had roughed her up and refused to pay her. So, Stroud confronted the man and a heated argument ensued. It ended when Stroud fired a bullet into the man's head. Stroud, then only 19 years of age, was sent to McNeill Federal Prison in Washington. Later, because of his continued violence toward guards and prisoners alike, he was transferred to Leavenworth Federal Prison in Kansas where he was again anything but a model prisoner.

During still another violent argument, he stabbed a prison guard to death. That action caused him to land on Death Row at Alcatraz. The movie about Stroud that starred Burt Lancaster made him out as a bird lover and an expert on the diseases of canaries and birds in general. Many felt that because of his work in that field he warranted a pardon. After the movie aired, the hue and cry for Stroud's release was long and loud. It is said that the star of the movie even went so far as to offer to take him in, if and when he received his parole. Burt evidently forgot or decided to ignore the fact that the man viciously murdered two people including a federal officer.

Crime, other than alcohol related, was not a real problem in Juneau during John's early days with the department. As the months passed he continued to be assigned additional responsibilities, all of which he attempted to perform as completely and as professionally as possible. He especially tried to do his job without rancor whether the duties were enjoyable or otherwise, even though cleaning vomit from the back of his patrol car after delivering a drunken driver to the Lemon Creek Jail was not at the top of his list of pleasant duties. His performance reports continued good and if his salary boosts had increased accordingly, he would have been an even happier fellow. Regardless, he was more than content in his work.

All was going well at home and on the job. Unfortunately, with highs must come lows. One of them came in early July of 1972, when the call about a shooting at Upper Salmon came in. John was the officer who was dispatched to the scene, and he remembered the stern admonition from Chief Parker: "It's probably an accidental shooting, but make sure that it isn't anything more than that."

Earlier, during his last two weeks at Upper Salmon, John met his soon to be replacement. Aloysius P. McInerney was his name. He was a huge hulk of a man whose scarred face suggested that he might have been in a few scrapes during his youth. John helped break him in on the job, and later admitted that in spite of his looks and his demeanor he enjoyed the man's company.

In addition to all his other 'fine' qualities McInerney had a keen sense of humor and a vast knowledge in the study of etymology. John learned more new swear words than he ever thought existed in just two short weeks in his company. John's replacement to be also had an extensive knowledge of early Irish history even though John doubted many of his salty words even existed that far back.

It was readily apparent that he didn't like to be called 'Aloysius' or even 'Al.' He was known to friend and foe alike as 'Pinky' which was short for his middle name, 'Pinkton.' If someone made the mistake of calling him by his given name he would respectfully correct him or her and say, "My friends call me 'Pinky.' I prefer that name."

If the recipient of that advice took it as Bible, then all was well. Anyone who didn't heed it usually paid a painful price. When a man standing at least 6'5" and weighing more than 270 lbs., with a leathery and unclean face asks you to not call him by his given name, it should be taken as a reasonable request.

One happy drunk standing next to him at the bar in one of Pinky's usual haunts expressed an inciting thought one evening when he said that anybody with the name 'Aloysius' had to be a sissy no matter what his size. That unlucky fellow didn't show up at his place of work the next morning or for quite a few mornings. He was instead housed at Bartlett Hospital. Later, that same poor soul visited his dentist for some major dental work.

Pinky started his first few days at Lower Salmon getting acquainted with the machinery and his fellow workers. He did well with both. He was already an experienced powerhouse operator, and his laughing and boisterous personality went well with everyone. When he arrived at Upper Salmon a few days later one could quickly tell that all would not go well there. Rex Franz started it by saying something uncomplimentary about parents who saddle their children with strange monikers. When Pinky took exception to the slight, Rex laughed. Their association went downhill from there. They never would like each other.

Pinky and John, instead, clicked from the very beginning. John saw right away that the man liked to get along with people. He was a happy man and he usually made those around him just as happy. It became evident months later, however, that a few too many alcoholic drinks could adversely affect his demeanor.

Since John was only going to be at Upper Salmon two more weeks, he asked Pinky to share his digs there at the house. Liz and Andrew, together with some of their furniture, had already moved back to their home in town. So, it seemed only proper that he should make the offer for Pinky to move in with him. When he explained that he would have his own bedroom, his own bed, and that he could do the cooking while John did the dishes, he accepted the invite.

Those last two weeks at Upper Salmon went by too fast. John was excited and looking forward to getting into his new work as a Juneau police officer, but he knew that the great experience up there in those mountains was now going to end. It had been a great ride, and he would miss it.

The day before his departure he had a heart to heart talk with Pinky. He felt that since he was probably a few weeks his senior he could take the liberty of cautioning Pinky about a few things.

"First, to start off on the right foot up here, Pinky, I would suggest that you offer to trade residences with Chad. He has seniority over you. He has a family who might like to visit him up here occasionally, and that offer to him would certainly cement your new relationship with your fellow worker. He gave me this unit years ago so that my family could live up here with me. That's just a little studio apartment upstairs where he is now, and you certainly don't need anything bigger than that. Chad is good people and you should do all you can to cultivate his friendship. You can always trust him to do right by you. Secondly, if I were you I would give Rex Franz a wide berth. You've already seen that he is not the friendliest of people, and antagonizing him will not help the situation. Finally, to show my affection for you and the enjoyable two weeks that we have spent together, I am herewith bequeathing to you our cat. He or she is a great mouser and invaluable to have policing the premises."

Pinky took John's first two pieces of advice with all seriousness and he assured him that he would act accordingly toward both men. It turned out later that he did not follow John's suggestion about how to treat Rex Franz, and his actions toward the man did later come back to haunt him.

As for his gift of the housecat, Pinky accepted it with his usual Irish colloquialisms, "Faith and Begorrah, what a wonderful gesture. And what, pray tell, is its name?"

"I don't know that it has a name. We just called it 'Hey Cat.' It comes in to the house once a day to be fed and then disappears until the next day at the same time. So, you'll need to keep well stocked with cat food," John answered

"So be it! 'Hey Cat' I shall know him as," laughed Pinky.

TWELVE

ANOTHER KIND OF CHANGE

Chad and John didn't talk as often now that they were working in different fields. It was only when the two families got together that they would bring each other up to date on what was happening at AEL&P and at the Juneau Police Department. Both men did also meet occasionally at the Elks Club. There they could be more explicit about subjects of interest. Chad, when asked about Rex Franz, said that the man changed dramatically after his wife's stillbirth episode that September of 1970, and that the change was not for the better. He described how Rex had become even more quiet and withdrawn - not that he was ever very verbose when things went well for him. The opportunities for operators to talk to each other during working hours were slim and none in those days because orders were that telephones should be used only for calls from dispatcher to operators. Face to face pleasantries might be exchanged during shift breaks, but rarely did those involve Rex. According to Chad, the man now walked in or out of the plant quickly and with head and eyes down. If he spoke at all it had to do with work done or work that needed to be done. The only people he did talk to regularly were the poker players in the back room of the downtown Horseshoe Saloon that he began frequenting during his four days off. There he found receptive ears to his tirades against women in general and bad cards in particular. Of course, they probably only tolerated his gripes because they saw he was a poor poker player and he seemed to have plenty of money to waste.

Unbeknownst to anyone, Rex was beginning to fall into a very deep and sinister abyss and even he didn't realize that he would never climb out. Like the old saying: 'If you find yourself in a hole, the first thing you need to do is to stop digging.' Well, Rex didn't come near to heeding that advice. He just kept digging deeper and deeper. It would overcome him.

Rex's wife was an only child. When her wealthy widowed mother died of pancreatic cancer shortly before Mary lost the second baby all the family treasure willed to her became evident. She asked Rex, "Why don't you quit your job? Let's just cruise the world for a few years."

"No, not now," was his reply.

Later, when she asked again, he used the excuse, "You know how I hate to travel."

Actually, he looked forward to someday traveling to some distant and exotic island - but not with Mary. He now had other plans for her – murderous ones. Those plans started to germinate soon after the loss of their second child. Their lonely and separate environments coupled with her seemingly reluctant attitude of not wanting to share his sexual attempts for one more try at a baby's birth only fomented his evil plan.

Early on, during his four days off, he would spend time with her at their home in town. As will happen, even in the best of families, they often argued. Most of the time it was over the slightest of things. Other days there were heated confrontations over Mary's refusal to accept even a hug or a kiss. Any warm gesture on his part was usually rebuffed.

Soon, name-calling followed. He accused her of being 'a cold fish' and she retaliated calling him 'selfish, unfeeling and unsympathetic.' During one heated encounter when he bemoaned the loss of his sons during her pregnancies she suggested that his was probably an imperfect or contaminated seed. A germ of hate started to grow in his soul when she uttered those hurtful words.

Their latest differences were over his continued and large financial losses at the downtown poker tables. After too many of these exchanges Rex decided to spend more and more of his four days off right there in the comfort of his little house at Upper Salmon. Now, he no longer went to his home in town. Instead, he used the free time to plan.

The solitary work at Upper Salmon aided his preparations. In fact, it was in the Salmon Creek Valley that he planned to rid himself of this now unwanted burden – Mary. He continually told himself, "I don't need her. What I really need is her money."

Facing a continued lonely and uninteresting union, Mary told Rex one day that she was going to do something worthwhile and productive to occupy her time. Tourism was beginning to be more and more of an influence in Alaska, especially in Juneau and the towns of the Inside Passage. So, in December of 1970 when Mary came up with the idea to open a gift shop, Rex encouraged her to do so.

In the late Sixties and early Seventies many changes were actually taking place on lower Franklin Street. Many more businesses were locating there with one or two gift shops here, a café there, a grocery store, a taxi stand and even a real estate office. Property values were still at a reasonably low level and it wasn't until the mid Seventies that prices began to skyrocket. By that time Mary Franz had purchased two old buildings side by side on the north side of lower Franklin. After extensive remodeling, inside and out, both became gift shops and for her huge successes.

Mary began to see less and less of Rex. He was spending more and more of his on and off time at Upper Salmon. She, meanwhile, was devoting almost all of her waking hours either at the two gift shops or on the road. In the summertime, from May through September of 1971, she was at her gift shops. Then, later, during that following winter when there were no more tourists she closed her shops and she traveled   It seemed she was always traveling either to native villages throughout Alaska or to the Lower 48 looking for more items for her gift shops. She tried to buy mostly Alaskan made goods, but almost everything she purchased seemed to sell.

Rex, at Upper Salmon, spent his idle hours reading on the inclement days and hiking or hunting for either mushrooms or game on the sunny days. Rain or shine, however, he was always planning on how to devise and execute the perfect crime. His reading material consisted mostly of murder mysteries, and that's probably where he solidified a warped belief that he could execute the worst of all sins without being caught.

Over the many months of his bitterness over the loss of his so much desired hunting partners there did come a few tender interludes when he actually had some misgivings. There were even a few times when he questioned himself by asking, "What the hell am I doing?"

Sometimes weeks would pass, even a month or more, when he would forget about his deadly plan. One day, however, all thought of changing his mind quickly faded for good when the on duty dispatcher, during one of their short telephone exchanges, said that on his next four days off he would be flying into Cache Lake in British Columbia with his youngest son for the boy's first ever fishing trip. That particular lake is loaded with trophy size rainbows, and Rex had often dreamed of standing on the bank watching his son reel in one of those big fish. When Rex put the phone down it felt like he'd been stabbed right in the heart.

During his next four days off Mary again rebuffed his sexual advances. Instead, she again brought up the subject of their savings account that continued to shrink because of his constant poker losses. When he suggested that her recent inheritance could easily cover his small and temporary financial setbacks, she replied that she would never let her parents' hard work and frugality get squandered on a poker table. Rex was becoming a man with less and less financial freedom and more and more sexual emptiness. It made for a terrible combination. The die was now cast. His maddening resolve increased and it would continue to final fruition. Nothing would reverse it.

THIRTEEN

BEGINNING OF THE PLAN

"My plan must be perfect," Rex said to himself. "So, the first thing I need is a checklist. But, since it will be lengthy, it needs to be on paper. There's no way I can possibly remember it all in my head. Where can I keep it to prevent someone accidentally finding it? It needs to be somewhere close so I can add or delete when necessary but still be completely hidden. In fact, it really needs to always be within easy reach so it will be available to me when I am at work, in the house, or walking in the woods or in town. Where can I possibly hide it?" he mused.

His plan had not even begun to take shape except for the actual intent. The checklist had not even been started and already he was stumped. It took a few more days before the answer finally came to him. He was getting into his jeans preparing to head across the flume to the powerhouse for his day shift. As he slipped the wide western style leather belt into the loops of his jeans, an idea came to him.

Later, when his shift ended at 4:00 p.m., he didn't immediately walk out the door as was his usual. Instead, he stopped for a minute to talk shop with his relief and to express the thought that today because it was so unusually sunny and warm he would go to town for dinner with the missus. Once out the door, however, he lost no time climbing aboard his motorized bike and racing off down the flume. If the door to the powerhouse had been open his relief might have seen Rex tearing down the straightaway on his bike and wondered why he was in such a rush. Instead, no one noticed. No one else was around. Upon reaching the penstock he closeted the bike and hurried down the steps to Lower Salmon and his parked car. In town he left the car more than two blocks from his intended destination and began walking toward the only shoe repair shop probably in all of Southeast Alaska. As he turned off Seward onto Second Street he was

74

pleased to see that the shop was still open and the owner was its only occupant.

"Can you sew a strip of thin leather about 9 or 10 inches long to the inside of this belt leaving both ends open so I can slip paper money in there when I travel? Last time I was in Mexico some guy picked my pocket while I was in a crowd and got away with my wallet, all my money and airline tickets plus my I.D." The cobbler assured him that the task was not a difficult one, that it was a great idea, and that he could have it for him by the next evening.

The first part of Rex's plan was now underway and all of it, from the plant to the parking lot, to the shoe repair shop, was done with not even the slightest suspicions being aroused. Now he could add or delete items on his checklist and it would always be in his possession. It would not be subject to being seen accidentally or otherwise. Soon, the checklist started to take shape.

The first item listed which needed no further written explanation simply said 'AROUSE NO SUSPICION.' He had already done that and would continue to do it to the nth degree. The next few items and those following changed from day to day and from sequence to sequence depending on new or discarded ideas. Among them, for instance, the item: 'SELECT WEAPON' had beneath it the sub-headings: 'a - my rifle' and 'b - other.' Under those were other items such as 'BUILD CONTRAPTION' and 'REPORT RIFLE STOLEN.'

He saw early on that the checklist needed to be written in pencil so that any corrections could easily be done with a rubber eraser. If a listed item was already accomplished it could be circled. In this way there would be no need to destroy the list or to worry that a copy of it had been lost somewhere. The one and only copy would always remain with him, safely tucked into his belt around his waist. Rex decided that the deed would be done with his own rifle and that the subject firearm should be reported to the police as stolen. This he would do some time during the weeks before Mary's 'unfortunate accident.' In order to completely discourage any thought of his culpability, a rifle must be shown as having shot him, too, and all with the same bullet that killed Mary. If he could accomplish that tricky feat it would be the ultimate, the clincher, and further proof that he was in no way involved in the shooting.

So, after circling the part about whose rifle, he went down the list to the how, when, and where to fire it. At the bottom of the list he added the words 'INCRIMINATE ALOYSIUS' in very large letters. He had a special hate for the man and he meant for him to suffer someday, somehow. He would figure that out later.

If Rex were to use an accomplice to kill Mary it would be much easier but considerably more risky. Secrets in the planning of a crime, as are secrets after the fact, are hard to keep even for a lone plotter. He would need to do it himself alone with no help from anyone and without anyone's knowledge. If he were to attempt to physically handle the weapon as it fired there could be incriminating powder residue on him and his clothing. He had to do it but without any contact with the weapon itself. He would need to devise something that would accomplish the job and it would have to be foolproof. He worked on this thought long and hard. One day it came to him. Soon thereafter he started work on his 'contraption.'

Early in his planning, Rex had envisioned simply pushing Mary off the flume during one of their leisurely walks into or out of Upper Salmon, but that would be too obvious and suspicious for one and not certain for the other. She might survive a fall into even the deepest of gullies, and that would result in failure of the plan and possibly many years in jail for him. No, if he could execute the current plan without a flaw it would be foolproof, as would be his alibi. In fact, he wouldn't even need an alibi since he would be a victim, too. So, for the next few weeks he searched the mountainsides above the flume for just the right spot, with the right vantage point and with enough foliage cover and with just the right tree or trees where he could securely attach his contraption of death. After much searching he found the ideal place in an area where the flume rounded a promontory, ducked into a short indentation in the mountain, curled around still another promontory, and then continued on toward the powerhouse on a fairly long straightaway. It was in an area very similar to where years before Boyd Hendricks had visited with two bear cubs and their mother. This spot that Rex found was, instead, near post #32 and adjacent to a storage platform. Not more than 50 yards above the flume he found his ideal spot from which to fire that special bullet.

THINGS TO DO	DATE DONE
1. AROUSE NO SUSPICION	
2. SELECT WEAPON	12-1-70
(a. my rifle) b. other	
3. BUILD CONTRAPTION	
(a. buy lock)	1-11-72
b. buy U-Bolts + Screw Eyes	1-25-72
4. SELECT SHOOTING SITE	
(a. flume) b. woods c. house	
5. HIDING PLACE FOR CONTRAPTION	
a. during construction (in gym locker)	
b. after shooting (in log)	
6. (TEST FIRE)	7-1-72
7. (REPORT RIFLE STOLEN)	7-2-72
8. DAY PRIOR TO SHOOTING	
(a. rig trigger pull)	7-8-72
9. DAY OF SHOOTING	
(a. load rifle)	7-9-72
(b. check entire setup)	7-9-72
(c. dismantle setup after shooting)	7-9-72
10. IMPLICATE ALOYSIUS	
11. DISPOSE OF CONTRAPTION	
a. in woods (b. in water)	7-26-72
12. REPAIR GUNWALE	
(a. get rid of orange paint)	8-1-72
13. (METAL RAKE FOR TYLER)	8-21-72

REX'S CHECKLIST

FOURTEEN

MORE OF THE PLAN

Rex calculated that the weapon that fired the fatal bullet would need to be at least 30 to 40 yards from him and Mary when discharged so that there would be no powder residue on either of them. It had to appear that it was fired from a great distance - a hunting accident - and that an unknowing stranger probably caused it. He wanted the rifle to be set up in heavy foliage with only the front sight of the barrel peeking out so as not to be seen by anyone prior to its ugly deed.

Dense vegetation is everywhere in Southeast Alaska and in the Juneau area in particular. The entire terrain is heavily forested, mostly with Sitka Spruce, Hemlock, and some Yellow Cedar. Hiking in the woods, except on maintained trails, is almost impossible because of the heavy undergrowth. So, while Rex had no problem with adequate cover, he now faced the task of constructing something that would hold the rifle and properly aim it at a critical spot on the flume below.

Every spare moment was now consumed with working on that contraption - but only on days when operator families were gone from the area. It must be constructed in such a way that the rifle would be firmly encased, insuring that it would neither fall, move, or even tremble. It must hit the target exactly where needed for a fatal shot. He did almost all his work in the company workshop where the windows faced both down the flume as well as back toward the powerhouse. So, as he worked, he checked every few minutes in both directions to see if anyone was coming. He attached the rifle to a length of 1x8 pine that he found in the workshop. He used a U-bolt to hold the front end of the barrel and a larger one to secure the stock. When the task was complete and the rifle firmly secured he placed the mount horizontally in the shop vise. When he tried to look through the sighting scope he found that he could not get his eye to it because part of the 1x8 board was in the way. So, he removed the rifle from its restraints, cut a piece from the board, and reattached the firearm. Now, it no longer looked like a trophy mount, but at least he could get his face close enough to the scope as needed to aim it properly.

He returned it to the vise and then attached a strong length of twine to the trigger. From there he ran the twine through several screw eyes placed strategically around the inside walls of the workshop. It was his intent to mirror as closely as possible the same setup that he would later arrange in the woods above the flume. With the crosshairs of the telescopic sight fixed on a nail head on a far wall of the shop he yanked on his end of the string, which in turn pulled the trigger (without a bullet in the chamber, of course). He then checked through the telescopic sight to insure that its crosshairs were still on the nail head. After a few more adjustments, increased tightening of the U-bolts, and after five or six more pulls of the trigger without the crosshairs moving even the slightest from the nail head target, the contraption was ready to be placed on a tree in the woods. With the success of a solid placement on the tree he could then circle that item as complete on his checklist.

The workshop where he toiled on his project contained a tall gym type locker where Rex was able to hide the rifle and its mount under lock and key. When, finally, it was ready he stored it for the last time knowing that the next time he removed it from the locker it would be on its way to the eventual launching site. The planning was progressing well. More and more items on the checklist were being circled, but he still had problems to overcome.   Now that the contraption was ready, he devoted almost all his free time searching the mountainsides for a place to hide the contraption after it had fired its fatal shot. Time, at least, was in his favor because this was early June and his plan was to wait until July when deer season opened in the Juneau area. An unidentified hunter mistaking Rex for a buck would cause the 'accident.'   Rex felt sure that the police would so conclude if all went as he planned. With the exception of the practicing he had done in the workshop and the lining up of the rifle sights once the mount was firmly attached to the tree there would be nothing left to trial and error. It must be right the first time. He was feeling confident that it would be.

Rex had always been an ardent mushroom hunter and he was often seen scrounging around on the hillsides above and below the flume around Upper and Lower Salmon searching for the elusive Morels, the rough stemmed Boletus or his favorite, the majestic King Boletus. Some days he might even be found on the few grassy areas on the banks of Salmon Creek below the flume seeking out the sharper tasting Shaggy Manes or their cousins, the Inky Caps. So, when in early June he spent most of his free time searching the area for the right tree and for the much needed hiding spot, no operators or any of their family members seeing him on the hillsides gave it a second thought because Rex was 'just doing his usual thing.' He had also thought fleetingly of feeding Mary a poisonous mushroom, but that idea was quickly discarded because he remembered that she did not share his passion for either hunting for mushrooms or eating them. It was certain, he concluded, that her death from eating poisoned mushrooms would only raise all kinds of suspicions.

It was almost the middle of June when Rex finally found the necessary hiding spot. Since the mount and its attached rifle, the spent cartridge shell, the string, even the screw eyes had to be removed from the scene and hidden immediately after the shooting this seemed to be exactly what was needed. All the items had to stay concealed until long after everything calmed down. Then he would recover them from their hiding place, after his shift at midnight, and take them aboard his boat to be dumped somewhere in the deepest part of Lynn Canal or Icy Strait.

The hiding place he found was an old deadfall possibly from the early construction days. As he searched among the moss covered stumps and logs he stumbled upon one that was quite large in diameter. It had been partially hollowed out possibly by animals, insects, or maybe just by rotting from old age. One end of the old log looked like it had been sawn and seemed solid. The other end was jagged but open enough to accommodate the contraption, especially after Rex did a little more hollowing out of his own. He did this with an old hoe and a spade that he found early on when he first moved into his house by the flume. These two items had been stored behind the electric water heater together with some other gardening tools. He had never been into gardening himself, but some past occupant must have tried growing a few vegetables because Rex had seen some evidence of that in the form of a few cabbage plants that sprouted up near the back of the house. From a smaller diameter and much shorter log he fashioned a plug that he felt was necessary to completely seal and hide everything inside the big log that might ever possibly implicate him in the shooting.

During the initial construction of the flume, special platforms were built and permanently attached alongside the structure, approximately one platform at each half-mile. Their purpose was for storing lumber during the flume's continued construction from the penstock to Upper Salmon. In this way, workers wouldn't need to walk or ride back to the staging area to pick up more lumber. Additionally, the platforms when spaced at intervals alongside the flume would be used upon its completion to store planks and supports that might later be used for maintenance and repair. The tops and sides of the flume consisted of 2x12 boards, while the supports both on the outsides and underneath were 4x4s. In the early days, lumber treating methods either did not exist or if used at all were not very effective in preventing decay and destruction either by insects, water, or weather. Avalanches were the flume's greatest enemy, however, and when one occurred quick repairs were always necessary. Thus, work on the flume was almost always a yearlong task.

There were also extra 4x4 inch upright support posts attached alongside the flume all the way from the ground below to roughly four feet above the top of the flume at approximately every 100 yards. To the top of each post was affixed a metal number in consecutive order to help identify for a work crew the area that might be reported to them as needing repair. The numbering on the upright posts began with #1 near the entry door to the penstock ending with the highest number #46 near the crew cabin at Upper Salmon.

Inspections of the flume were done by a crew boss on a regular basis every three or four weeks, but casual inspections were made almost every day by the operators themselves as they walked or rode in and out. Along the flume there was also an occasional small doorway on the side of the structure that could be used as an entry when inspections or repairs needed to be made to the inside of the flume. Of course, the doorways had to be located near the top of the side of the flume so that the opening was above the flow of water on the inside. As it was, the old structure leaked considerably without further openings being built into it. The doorways were kept locked to prevent any unwanted entry by either animals or humans. In fact, the sluice gate at the initial opening of the flume was protected from entry by a wire grate that also kept any floating debris from Salmon Creek entering the structure. Rex hadn't even given a first or second thought to throwing the contraption in the flume because it could be discovered there, or it might even be carried down by a sudden surge of water into the penstock holding tank where a work crew might find it during routine maintenance. No, this was too important an item on the checklist. Hiding and later disposing of the mount and the other items in the right place was not only necessary, it was absolutely critical.

As time passed more and more items on the checklist were circled. The hiding place was now secured as was the firing place. Fortunately, both sites were close to each other, no more than 100 yards apart. The hiding place was on the opposite side and lower down the mountain and a ways below the flume where Rex felt little or no investigation would be made after the 'accident.' According to his plan, the shot was supposed to have been fired from the top of the mountain down toward the flume. So, why would anyone look below the flume for clues as to what happened.

He visited the site again a few days later to thoroughly check the line of sight from firing point to target. He was pleased to see that a tree he had earlier observed during the initial find was, luckily, just about where it had to be to fit into his plan. He was concerned about this tree at first because it might be in the way, but now he saw that the mount could be adjusted when he nailed it to the other important tree or trees above in such a way that this tree would shelter him from the bullet as it passed by on its way to the target. Of course, it was not going to shelter him completely, and that was good because it was such an important part of the plan.

At the end of the line of sight there was the upright post #32 which was also in his plans. If he could line up the rifle so that it fired its projectile directly into the middle of that post, he would use it as a marker where he would suggest to Mary that she should sit and rest for a few minutes while he climbed up a ways to take her picture.

"Move a little to the left, honey. That's it, a little more. Rest against that post and smile," he planned to say to her as he leaned his back against the obstructing tree. There'd be just enough of his upper thigh and buttocks peeking out so as to be in the path of the arriving bullet.

"This is crazy," he said to himself, "but, risky or not, I can pull it off if I really set it up right."

While he was confident that it would work, still, he did not have the luxury of much of a trial run. He felt that he could safely have only one practice shot without arousing suspicion. One shot fired in the area on opening day would probably not even be heard by the operators in the powerhouses because of the noise of the rotating generators. If someone did hear it - so what? It's deer season. There had been some occasional shooting in the Salmon Creek Valley. A few ptarmigan were shot there over the years, but that was almost always done with a .22 rifle which makes considerably less noise than does a .30-06 - Rex's "stolen" weapon.

A large male black bear was killed there in the valley years before by one of the operators, but that was more of an accident than a planned hunt. The animal was trying to break into his house and the man inside simply shot the bear dead right there on the porch. Coincidentally, it was the same house that was now occupied by Rex Franz.

FIFTEEN

EVERYTHING'S READY

During the first week of July 1972, Rex took care of the few final but important items on his checklist. He first took the mount and its attached rifle to the shooting site above the flume and nailed it to the tree. There was an adjoining smaller tree close enough so that he was able to first attach one end of the mount to the large tree and the other end to the smaller tree. The space between the two trees was sufficient to allow him to get his eye near the spotting scope. Then, once he got the crosshairs aligned with the upright post #32 and high enough above the post to where Mary's head would be, he pounded in the nail to hold the mount securely on the smaller tree.

To be sure that the mount would not move he used two larger nails (one to each tree) and again sighted through the scope to the post target. The contraption was now ready for a test firing. First, however, he scrambled down to the flume and at the platform with its supply of planks and supports he picked up two short pieces of 4x4. From his pocket he removed a roll of duct tape that he had brought from the workshop. He taped the scrap pieces of 4x4 to the front of the upright post #32 intending that the extra pieces of wood would receive the bullet from the practice shot. Later he would dispose of those scraps, leaving no telltale mark on the upright to which they had been taped. These extra pieces served to protect the permanent upright post in case he had aimed his practice shot too low. He certainly did not want to damage it in any way. In addition, after the practice shot he could then measure the exact distance from the sitting surface of the platform to the bullet hole in the 4x4 scraps. That measurement had to be exact to the inch. If the rifle was aimed an inch or more too low the bullet might hit Mary in the neck and possibly only wound her. If aimed too high it could miss her entirely. Finally, he taped a piece of rigid clear and transparent plastic sheet to the

REX'S CONTRAPTION

obstructing tree making sure that some of it stuck out far enough for a portion of it to be in the line of fire. It was most important that he determine how close to the edge of the obstructing tree the bullet would pass. He had to know exactly how far out from behind that tree he could safely stick out his rear end when the real bullet came that way. Luckily, when he first positioned the mount he saw that with proper placement and adjustment the shot could be made to just barely miss the bark of that tree.

When all preparations had been made he went quickly back up the mountain to the tree and its mount. He checked the sight one more time and once satisfied as to its aim he placed a shell in the breech, slid the bolt closed, and fired. He removed and pocketed the spent cartridge, slid the bolt closed, and quickly covered the mount with some camouflage netting that he had found at his garage in town.

He then hurried down to the obstructing tree and the stiff plastic sheet affixed to it. He carefully positioned himself with his back to the tree and faced the flume below, putting to memory exactly where the bullet would have hit if it had been his buttocks rather than a piece of plastic that had been penetrated. If he stood perfectly still at just the right spot when the real shot was fired it would clip his trousers and a little bit of flesh causing him to be a lucky victim who received only a scratch rather than a bullet right between the eyes as was supposed to happen to Mary.

Satisfied that this part of his plan was ready, he removed the plastic sheet and tape from the obstructing tree and carried them down to the flume. He sat down in front of the post to see where the bullet hole in the scrap 4x4 lined up with his face. Again, it was perfect. If he had been sitting there, the test shot would have hit him in the chin. From past observations he knew that Mary, when sitting down next to him, was roughly four inches shorter than he was. So, when the real shooting was going to take place and he was positioning her on the platform, he would need to tell her to look up at him while he took the picture. The result should be a hit right between her eyes. He now was certain that a second practice shot was not necessary. So, he gathered up all the testing material and then walked at a leisurely pace back along the flume to his house. There he placed all the items in the fireplace, lit them, and settled back to enjoy the fire and to reflect on his progress.

The next day he drove out to the head of the Herbert River Trail to where another important part of his plan would soon unfold.

"I parked my car and hiked in a few miles along the trail to some of my favorite spots to search for mushrooms and afterwards I was gonna stop at the rifle range with my .30-06."

That is what he said to the trooper when later in the day he showed him the broken passenger window on his car and aided in the filing of his stolen property report. As the trooper started filling in the report Rex commented, "It used to be that in the good old days we never locked the doors of our homes or our cars. If I hadn't locked the car I might still have lost the rifle, but at least I would still have a passenger side window."

The Trooper didn't comment. He simply asked his next question: "Do you have the registration?"

"No," replied Rex.

"Do you have record of the serial number?"

"No, I bought the rifle from a guy at a garage sale in Seattle four or five years ago. I don't remember getting any paperwork from him. Hell, it was such a good deal at the time, I didn't quibble."

The truth of the matter was that a friend of his had actually stolen it from a pickup truck at a rest stop near Spokane, Washington. The thief had in turn traded it to Rex for his crop of marijuana plants when Rex was pulling up stakes to head for life in Alaska.

"What kind of weapon was it?"

"It was a Remington .30-06 with scope."

Actually, it was a Winchester rifle, but Rex was making sure that the real rifle would never be traced back to him.

"What make scope?"

Rex simply groaned and shook his head.

"Well, Mr. Franz, you don't give us much to go on. I don't hold out much hope that we'll find it."

Very little of what he told the Trooper about where and when he bought the weapon was the truth including the part about the scope. It had no scope when he traded his weed for it. Instead, he purchased one for the rifle in a Seattle sporting goods store days before he boarded the ferry for Alaska. He knew the make of the scope. He just didn't tell the Trooper. When he was asked if the rifle had any distinguishing marks or if it had the leather sling attached to it, Rex again lied and answered, "No." Actually, the sling was attached and it now hung from the rifle on the contraption nailed to the tree.

Rex looked pained and remorseful because he could give the man so little concrete information. But, it was exactly the way he had planned it. He felt that there would be no way the rifle could ever be traced back to him even if it was found some day. And, he would make damn sure it would never be found. The lies he told the Trooper that day did more to implicate another than they ever did to protect him, but Rex didn't know that at the time.

Almost all the items on the checklist were now circled. Rex had still to rig the trigger pull that he planned to initiate as he leaned against the obstructing tree preparing to take Mary's picture. He had still to devise a ruse to get her to accompany him into Upper Salmon. He had still to prime the rifle for firing and he had still to plan what he would say and do for the days, weeks, and even months after the shooting to continue to avoid blame of any kind. His constant thought was always to do nothing that might arouse suspicion.

In that regard, he thought back to when Mary had first opened the gift shops. After it was clear that both shops were succeeding financially above and beyond their wildest imagination, she had suggested that they should probably take out a large benefit insurance policy on her life. At the time he had already begun making his nefarious plans and he had quickly and tactfully squelched the idea of insurance because he knew suspicions would arise after her 'accidental death.' His plans did not call for anything that might even smell suspicious. She had already inherited millions and, soon, all of it would be his. There were no other heirs. So, why even risk it? Would eleven million be that much better than ten million? Of course not.

The day after he reported his car broken into and his rifle stolen Rex again walked out to the shooting site. This time it was to place the screw eyes and affix the long twine to the trigger. From the trigger the twine first went up the mountainside to a nearby tree where it passed through the first screw eye. It then spanned across an opening to another tree closer to the direction of the powerhouse through another screw eye and then back down to the foot of the obstructing tree. There Rex wrapped the end of the pull string securely this way and that way around a large, almost round rock. To insure that the string would not slip off the rock he wrapped duct tape around it crosswise in two directions. He planned to kick that rock at just the right moment as he snapped the photo of the smiling Mary.

First, he went through a half dozen dry runs. After the first and the second tries he concluded that the twine should have some slack in it so that kicking the rock would then cause a jerking motion to the twine, thus insuring the trigger would be pulled. The next four kicks proved him right, and another item was circled.

While things were going well for Rex, insofar as his checklist was concerned, they were not going as well between him and his fellow worker, Pinky McInerney. They often clashed over trivial work matters. They had nothing else in common other than their work. Pinky was a drinking man and he made no excuses for it. He would often relieve Rex, after four days off, still hung over from the night before. On those occasions, and there were many, he would revel in greeting Rex up close with a big 'HOWDY' at the same time that he exhaled a sour breath in the man's face. There was never so much as a shoving match, but the air of tension between the two men could be cut with a knife.

Finally, Rex mentioned his problem to his union rep. Fortunately, and with results benefiting both men, it came to pass that Pinky was able to transfer to Lower Salmon. The man he replaced wanted to be at Upper Salmon, as did his family and they especially liked the idea that work at this facility included free housing. Pinky no longer had to worry about those 'miserable 876 steps,' and Rex was now free of his nemesis.

There were company owned houses at Lower Salmon, too. However, they were not rent free as they were at Upper Salmon. Pinky was able to rent part of one of those Lower Salmon houses – the one of the three closest to the powerhouse. He boasted that he could now almost roll out of bed right into work. This house, too, had a studio apartment upstairs and it suited Pinky just fine, except for the nights when he came home drunk. When he still lived and worked at Upper Salmon, he had severely curtailed his drinking. He found that navigating 876 steps in a drunken stupor was not only dangerous but downright stupid. Now, living and working at Lower Salmon he drifted back into his old ways which while still unwise no longer involved the danger factor of those 876 steps and the two plus miles of usually wet and slippery flume.

On a few of those recent occasions after four days and nights of bodily neglect and serious drinking he was found the next morning still passed out face down and spread-eagled on the stairs leading to his new residence. His next eight-hour shift after each of those incidents was always painful. After each of them he had vowed to change his ways. Unfortunately for Pinky, the habit always seemed to overwhelm the good intentions.

SIXTEEN

THE SHOOTING

July 9, 1972, would mark ten years of marriage for Mary and Rex and because they had always been together on each anniversary it was not difficult for Rex to convince Mary that she should come in to Upper Salmon to share that work day with him.

"Then, we can walk out together and go to Mike's Place for dinner," was the last part of his suggestion to which she readily agreed.

This appeared to Rex to have been one of the easiest to overcome of all the obstacles on his list. Everything seemed to be falling into place.

"You'll have to get up early Sunday, but don't stop to fix breakfast. I'll whip up something for us at the plant. Let's meet at Lower Salmon at 6:30 a.m., if you want to walk in, or at 7:00 if you're willing to ride in with me on the back of the bike."

Mary had only ridden in on the flume one time previously, and it was such a scary experience that she vowed to never again take such a risk. She said, "I'll meet you at 6:15. I would prefer a nice leisurely walk, especially since the weatherman says we will continue to have sunshine for the next week."

When their conversation ended Mary was pleased that they would be getting together on this special upcoming day. They were not seeing much of each other lately - she with her gift shops and he with his job and its isolation. This day could possibly start a rekindling of their, presently, rather stagnant relationship. It sure was lacking, she thought. Perhaps, if all went well, she might even relent on her stubborn unwillingness to try for another child. This thought warmed her even more.

"Maybe we could skip Mike's Place and have a cozy dinner with wine right there at his little house at Upper Salmon," she commented to herself.

As the day grew nearer she even searched for and found her

old backpack into which she placed two well-wrapped and insulated bottles of their special Charles Krug burgundy. She also threw in a silk negligee that hadn't seen the light of day in many months.

Early, on the morning of July 9, Rex rode his bike out toward the penstock and his meeting with Mary at Lower Salmon. On the way, however, he stopped at post #32, parked the bike, and climbed up the hillside to the rifle.   There he removed the protective netting, placed a live round in the chamber, and slid and closed the bolt into the firing position. He took one more look through the telescopic sight to satisfy himself that it was still properly aimed. It was, of course.

So, he next checked the twine to see that it was securely tied to the trigger and that it was not snagged near or between the affixed screw eyes. He saw that the rock was still securely tied, so he again positioned it in just the right spot where he felt sure that one slight kick would send it down a short incline, thus pulling the trigger. Satisfied that all was in order he again covered the mount with the netting, returned to his bike, and continued on to the penstock.

He arrived at Lower Salmon a little early so he could spend a few minutes talking to the operator on duty. He mentioned that his wife was coming in to spend the day with him at work so that they could celebrate their wedding anniversary together. This was just another part of the plan to cement a story that would later need to be told. It would also include the part about their intended dinner at Mike's Place where he had earlier already made reservations for two.

The Lower Salmon operator, Ed Sloan, listened with interest and then, when Mary arrived at the plant, he offered his congratulations on the event of their tenth anniversary. After a little more small talk Rex announced that it was time for him to go to work.   As they departed the plant Rex took Mary's knapsack from her and placed it on his back. He then stopped at his car, opened the trunk, and removed two lengths of wooden dowels. He handed them to Mary asking her to slip them in the backpack.

Sloan, still standing in the doorway of the plant and seeing the dowel material protruding from the pack, asked, "What are you building now, Rex?" If a script had been written for Rex, it couldn't have been more perfect. He answered, "Oh, I'm just building a coat rack for my house up above."

The truth of the matter was that he purchased the dowels some days ago intending to bring them up to the house this very day but not for the purpose of building a coat rack. Hopefully, after the accident someone might conclude that with the sticks jutting out from the pack on his back he might have been mistaken for a buck. He also reached into the glove compartment of his car and retrieved their 35mm camera suggesting that they might take some snapshots during their walk.

As they hiked up the long stretch of steps Mary commented innocently to Rex that she certainly understood why he would not want to walk in and out of Upper Salmon every day. They stopped for two short rest periods and to enjoy the view. Then, at the top of the stairs in front of the penstock, Rex asked Mary again if she would want to ride in on the bike.

"No, let's just walk and enjoy the beautiful morning," was her reply. Little did she realize that the only advantage to a walk rather than the ride would be the extension of her time on earth by only a few extra minutes.

Upon nearing upright post #32, Rex suggested that they should stop so he could take her picture sitting on the platform aside the flume with the trees in the background. She complied and sat down on the edge of the platform with her back resting on the upright post. Rex scrambled up off the flume and looked down at her through the viewfinder. She did exactly what he instructed her to do. She moved a little to the right and she smiled up at him.

What happened next was exactly as Rex had planned. With Mary properly positioned with her head resting against the post, and with only a small portion of his buttocks protruding from behind the tree, he'd dislodged the triggering rock. The shot was aligned perfectly and did its terrible deeds. One was a minor scratch and the other a deadly face shot. The bullet entered her left eye and took part of her brain through the back of her neck.

Rex immediately dropped the camera and his backpack, picked up the rock and the twine, gathered all the screw eyes and carried everything to the base of the trees where the mount was nailed. With a claw hammer that he had earlier stashed nearby, he removed the four nails and placed all the loose materials (the twine, the rock, the screw eyes, the nails, the hammer, and the netting) into a plastic bag that he had also hidden in the same proximity. Then with the bag and its contents securely in hand he picked up the mount with its rifle still attached and hurried down to the hollow log. He placed all the lethal and incriminating evidence in the log, inserted the prepared plug, covered much of the plug area with leaves and debris, and then scrambled up onto the flume.

He stood for a moment looking down at Mary. The plan was that he would now run to the plant to call for help. It didn't happen exactly that way. Instead, the adrenalin rush began to subside and remorse and tears started to replace the high. It was then that he realized the enormity of what he had done. He knelt down beside her, and took her lifeless body in his arms. He kissed her as he sobbed uncontrollably. After a few more agonizing moments he again took control. He stood up, looked down at her one more time, and then ran along the top of the flume into Upper Salmon. There, at the door of the powerhouse, is where he made his first and most convincing display of terrible heart-wrenching grief.

SEVENTEEN

THE AFTERMATH

During his leave of absence, Rex Franz buried his wife in a short and private ceremony. The next day he met with Jane Whitney, the manager of Mary's gift shops. He asked her to hire the necessary person or persons to fully staff both units until the end of the tourist season. Then, as did almost all other gift shops in Juneau, they would close their doors for the winter.

After he and Jane had considerable discussion about employees, merchandise that still needed to be ordered, inventory, sources of supply, etc., Rex made a startling suggestion. He asked her if she felt she could handle full control of both shops would she consider accepting a partnership in the business. He went on to say that it would be with the understanding that it would be her full responsibility to operate and manage. He would want only his fifty percent of the yearly net earnings – nothing more and nothing less. He even suggested that, if she could run the shops as efficiently and as profitably as Mary had, she might later consider buying him out completely. Jane assured him that she would take care of the business to his complete satisfaction and she thanked him profusely for his generous offer.

Before their meeting ended he told Jane that, if she could later purchase the shops, he would probably leave Juneau. For now and for the next year or two he would continue to work at Upper Salmon. When she asked him why he would want to continue with his job at Upper Salmon he answered simply that he needed time and tranquility to plan the rest of his life. "There is no more tranquil place in the world than at Upper Salmon," he confided. In the days and weeks that followed, his fellow operators and others asked him the same question and to each he gave that same reply.

To Rex it now appeared that he had relieved himself of still another burden. He felt that this latest action of his would, again,

'AROUSE NO SUSPICION.'   Now, however, there was no longer the excitement of the planning and the execution. Instead, there was more of the same deep gloom that had haunted him for weeks and months after Mary's miscarriage and again later after the stillbirth.   There now followed more extended bouts of depression and more sleepless nights. He had long ago fallen into this deep abyss, but now he was still inside and digging it deeper.

A little more than a week after the shooting the now widower, Rex Franz, returned to work at Upper Salmon. The case, for all intents and purposes, was closed. Co-workers and friends alike offered   their   condolences,   and   they   were   all   gratefully acknowledged.   Life went on and at Upper Salmon all was tranquil. Days later, Rex walked into the powerhouse ready to relieve Chad from his just completed day shift. Rex seemed to be a little more verbose this particular day – mostly small talk – so Chad switched the conversation to the more important subject when he innocently asked, "Did you ever finish that project you were working on in the workshop?"

Just as innocently, Rex said, "No, I didn't. I was building a coat rack but I never finished it. After what happened to Mary, I lost interest. I used it for kindling."

That ended their short conversation, but Rex's few words were what Chad repeated to John Santori later that day.

"Give me that again, Chad. He said what?"

"He said that he gave up on the coat rack project and used it for kindling."

He thanked Chad for his report but was disappointed because it really proved nothing. John was still faced with the same problem - there was no motive and there was still no evidence. The case was closed. It was ruled an accidental death and his report to the Chief did more than anything else to contribute to that conclusion. Regardless, he was still suspicious about what Rex was doing in the workshop in spite of what Chad told him that Rex had said. On the other hand, he might not have been lying. It could be that he was so distraught over what happened to Mary that he did give up on constructing a coat rack. Or, he might instead have finished with a different project and what John saw in the gym locker could have been the leftovers from it.

Unfortunately, what John found really didn't prove too much. One might not use a U-bolt to construct a coat rack but the other items could have been so intended. However, if perchance Rex was not constructing a coat rack, on what other project could he have been working? The right-angled, triangular 20 inch long piece of wood appeared to have been cut with a handsaw, but that again proved little or nothing unless he could find the larger piece from which it was cut. Why would he cut a triangular piece off of a coat rack? It just didn't figure. So, his suspicions continued.

The next morning John received another bit of disconcerting news. Chad telephoned him to say that he went to the workshop and found the locker was now empty. The combination lock was gone, and the floor had been swept clean. Now, John didn't know what to think. It revealed one thing, however. Rex might be starting to feel the heat. Then and there John decided to enlist Chad's additional help. He told him, "Telephone me, day or night if you see Rex leaving Upper Salmon. Secondly, do not question him anymore about anything. Again, just play dumb."

Chad promised that he would do nothing to compromise the investigation. He did, however, say that he would start leaving the front door to the plant ajar so he could see the flume from his office cubicle. He wanted to be able to alert John if he saw Rex departing the area.

Whether Rex noticed the constantly open door of the powerhouse or not, he certainly was not going to do anything during the day from now on. He would wait, preferably for a rainy weeknight after his shift before he'd venture out to dispose of the incriminating evidence that was stored in the hollow log. Hopefully, it would be when everyone was asleep.

The opportunity came very early on a Wednesday morning just after midnight in late July. He was walking out of the powerhouse, having finished his ten days on swing shift. As he headed toward his house he could feel the weather was worsening. It was starting to rain and it was getting quite windy. Few people would be out on such a miserable night. No lights were on in the other house at Upper Salmon. "This will be the night to do it," he concluded.

Upon entering his house he immediately began getting ready. He prepared a lunch and placed it in his knapsack. Next he readied his rain gear. He felt certain that no other operator, except the one now on duty in the plant, was in the area. If anyone was, they should be asleep. He grabbed a flashlight and the roll of duct tape, donned his rain clothes, and with knapsack on his back started to walk out.

He stopped, however, when he remembered the items that he recently cleared out of the gym locker in the workshop. So, he went back in and retrieved them. As for the piece of scrap wood, he had already thrown it on his woodpile to be burned later in his fireplace. Actually, while he threw it onto the woodpile, it did not come to rest there. It fell behind the pile without Rex noticing it, and it lay hidden there out of sight and out of mind. He pocketed the screw eyes and the U-bolt intending that they too would join the other very incriminating and worrisome evidence. All of it would soon be dumped somewhere in the deep. Secure that he now had it all, he was about to exit the house. Then he remembered the .30-06 ammo. Why keep it? He no longer possessed a rifle. So, he took the ammo along with the other items and departed. He didn't use his flashlight until he was out of sight of the powerhouse. When he reached post #32 he climbed down off the flume to his hiding spot. He took the plug from the fallen log and pulled out everything he had earlier placed inside. Opening the plastic bag he added the screw eyes, the U-bolt, and the box of ammo. He then placed as much of the contraption as would fit inside the bag and sealed it shut with several layers of duct tape. Only a few inches of the barrel of the rifle protruded from the plastic bag.

He then climbed back up on to the flume, placed the bag in his knapsack, and continued his walk out to the penstock. The steps down the mountain to his car at Lower Salmon were negotiated carefully and with little problem with the aid of the flashlight. Fortunately for Rex, no one saw the beam of light on the flume or on the stairway. The people that were in the area (the plant operators) were both unaware of his departure.

Rex drove to Auke Bay at a leisurely pace, never exceeding the speed limit. There was no reason to rush or to arouse any suspicion. He parked his car and walked down to the marina with knapsack on his back to his moored 22-foot Bayliner. He was glad to see that he was the only person on the dock and was even more pleased by the fact that the rain and the wind seemed to have subsided.

He thought fleetingly of simply dropping the entire package into the waters of the marina but decided against it. There was a houseboat moored nearby with lights on inside. "So," he said to himself, "let's just take a boat ride. Any of these boats, whether there are lights on inside or not, could have people in them looking out. The boat ride will be safer and smarter."

EIGHTEEN

A VISIT TO GLACIER BAY

Rex decided wisely that he should not attempt his venture out of Auke Bay in the middle of the night. He felt that it would be better to traverse a route to the ultimate dumping spot during the day when he could see where he was going. He had no radar aboard his small vessel and he was not that much of a sailor that he could confidently navigate with compass and maps. So, he slept in the cabin of his boat dockside until the next morning and then made the rest of his plans. He first walked up the ramp to Tony's Deli where he bought another sandwich and a couple six packs of beer. He decided that since he had never been to Glacier Bay National Park, this would be a good time to visit there. He earlier checked the cruise lines schedule and saw that there would be no ships coming to the area for the next two days. This, coupled with the upcoming Salmon Derby on the weekend, would mean few if any people would be in the area of Icy Strait. The limits for the Derby fishing grounds were restricted to waters east of Point Retreat. So, his plans were to go west of that area.

Here, locally, there were always people and boats on the waters. Also, on the land there were often telescopes in living room windows. Conversely, there were few if any people along Icy Strait and certainly no people or dwellings on the shores inside Glacier Bay. The only humans within miles were either at Bartlett Cove or in Gustavus. Dumping his evidence in Glacier Bay would not only be a safe move, it would be a wise move. The Bay, because its waters are glacier fed, is heavily silted and anything dropped into the water there cannot be seen - no matter how shallow the bottom. As it is, Glacier Bay is actually an area of very deep waters because it was hollowed out eons ago by more than ten advancing and later receding glaciers.

Rex departed Auke Bay in the late morning and moved at a leisurely pace feeling that there was no reason to hurry. He encountered a few vessels, but they were always a safe distance away and most appeared to be fishing boats. Those boats might be interested in another fishing vessel, but they would care little about a small pleasure craft.

Once he passed Point Retreat, he saw only one more boat. A few hours later, when he finally anchored in Mud Bay across from the opening into Glacier Bay, he felt quite confident that no one recognized him or his boat. He decided to stay anchored until near nightfall. Then, he would head into the Bay and dump his package during the darkest part of the night. The next morning he would act like a tourist and motor his boat among the recently calved icebergs dislodged by the glaciers.

As for now, he would wait. Fortunately, there was only a small crescent of the moon on display in the sky above as day started turning into night, and it would shed no light on the waters below. The rain had now stopped completely. The clouds had lifted and there was only a small amount of fog on the water in the Bay and outside.

As Rex waited for full darkness he had a sudden thought about the plastic bag and its contents and wondered if it would be heavy enough to sink to the bottom. He also thought about whether the bag might have been torn while being stuffed into the fallen hollowed out log or during its transport to his boat. He certainly didn't want to have the rock slip out of the bag and thus reduce its weight to little or nothing. To make sure and since there was still plenty of time, he decided that it might be better to add something, perhaps his boat anchor. Presently, there was only the rock and the rifle that made for true ballast. He also retrieved another plastic garbage bag from the cabin and started undoing the duct tape from around the rifle and its surrounding single plastic bag. First, though, a few hunger pangs told him to have a snack – a sandwich and a bottle of beer – maybe two bottles. He was not usually a drinker, but this night was different. When he was finished removing the tape he now decided, "Oh, hell, that's pretty heavy. It won't need any more weight." So, he just placed the entire package inside the second bag and laid it all aside. He ate half of another sandwich and drank another bottle of beer and then contemplated a nap. "Why not," he said to himself, a little snooze won't hurt, and by then it should be getting dark."

When he woke it was just that – almost dark and quite late. In addition, large patches of fog now surrounded him. He pulled his anchor and was about to set out. He was turning the key to start the boat motor, but he reconsidered when he saw he was already drifting out into the Strait. He was being taken out of Mud Bay by wind and tide and the boat was heading in the direction he wanted to go, toward the entrance to Glacier Bay. So, he sucked on another bottle of beer as he drifted and all was calm for almost two hours.

The still of the peaceful night was suddenly broken by the sound of a boat motor. Rex panicked. He and his boat were now completely engulfed by the fog and he could not tell for sure from where the other boat noise was coming. He reached down and pulled the mount from the plastic bags, holding the attached rifle at the ready. As the approaching motor drew nearer it was accompanied by a voice through a bullhorn and then a bright light. He did not wait. He acted. It was a foolish act, but it was more than effective.

NINETEEN

ANOTHER SHOOTING

Stationed at Bartlett Cove, U.S. Fish and Wildlife Service Officer Aubrey Hutchison was near the end of his routine patrol in his zodiac when he spied Rex's boat. It was more than a couple miles away. Because of the low lying fog and the approaching darkness he could not immediately make out if it was a commercial fishing vessel or a pleasure craft.

He reached for his field glasses, but by the time he got them up to his face the fog had now completely covered the target boat. It didn't matter. If it was a commercial vessel and it was heading into Glacier Bay he would check to see that the skipper had all his necessary paperwork. Salmon trollers were frequently coming into Glacier Bay during the open season, but at this time of year they were restricted to fishing only in certain areas of the Bay.

This boat had not yet reached any restricted area. In fact, it was not even in the Bay. It was actually outside of his jurisdiction and he very well could have allowed it to be checked later in the morning when and if it did enter the National Park boundary. However, it might just be a pleasure craft in need of help since it did not appear to have any running lights. Either way, he would investigate and then go home.

The thick fog and the increasing darkness necessitated his advancing toward the other boat at slow speed. He, too, had no radar in his small cabin. Almost immediately, the fog thickened as he moved out toward the entry to the Bay. As he passed the buoy marker near the entrance and drew closer, he slowed his boat almost to a crawl. Occasionally there would be an opening in the fog layer, and on one of those short respites from the bothersome curtain he saw that it was indeed a pleasure boat. Then in another minute he was back in the thick impenetrable fog. As soon as he felt that he was close enough for the other boat to hear him he used his bullhorn to identify himself and his mission. At the same time he turned on his powerful searchlight that was mounted on a standard in the bow. Because of the now heavy fog, the light beam only succeeded in blinding him as it bounced back toward him. He reached to turn it off but, before he could something more deadly also came toward him and at almost the same speed as the reflected light. He felt it before he heard it, but he did not feel or hear anything after that.

Rex Franz made another fateful decision that July night. This one was not based on any preconceived or written plan. Granted, he did not want a confrontation. But, if he had thought rationally about his predicament he'd have wisely concluded that the fog and the darkness would easily allow him time to finish taping the plastic bag – certainly enough time to throw it overboard. Even if the officer was alongside, which he was not, Rex could still have dropped the entire package into the water and been none the worse for it other than, perhaps, receiving a ticket for littering.

Instead, he reached into the bag and found the package of .30-06 cartridges. He ripped out three, and quickly inserted them into the magazine. In spite of the fact that the rifle was still attached to its wooden mount, he was still able to aim it at the piercing searchlight. He fired, ejected the shell, quickly slid the bolt forward, closed it, and fired again. He fired blindly once more after that.

He didn't know it at the time, but he could have saved the third bullet. The first one, a hurried but lucky shot, killed the officer and the second one extinguished the searchlight. Actually, both of the first two bullets found their way into the body of the officer. The first shot shattered the cabin window of the small zodiac, went through Hutchison's life jacket and into his upper chest severing his ascending aorta and part of his spinal column. It came to rest outside his rib cage but still in his body. The second, after it hit the searchlight, entered the officer's shoulder and would not have been fatal. It exited his body and was found in the back portion of his cork life jacket. The first shot caused the officer to bleed to death even before his zodiac rammed into the side of Rex's boat.

The collision knocked Rex to the deck. When he picked himself up and saw the stricken officer slumped over the wheel inside the cabin of the zodiac he breathed a large sigh of relief. As the pilotless zodiac with motor still running drifted away from him and in toward the opening to Glacier Bay Rex felt that there was now time to continue disposing of the package.

He replaced the contraption in the bag, retaped it securely, and threw it all into the water. He watched it sink and as it did he breathed still another long sigh.

He then remembered the empty shell casings. He found one on the deck and threw it overboard. He searched for the other two, and then remembered that after the last shot he didn't eject the shell. It was still in the rifle and safely at the bottom of the Strait. But, where was the other one? After a long and futile search with the aid of his flashlight, he concluded that the casing must have ejected out of the rifle directly into the water. He would make another thorough search tomorrow in the daylight just to be sure.

Now he slowly and cautiously eased the Bayliner farther out and away from the entrance to the Bay. With the aid of his maps, flashlight, compass, and the one-lighted buoy, he was able to inch his way out into the middle of the Strait and safety. He moved slowly in a southeasterly direction but then decided against any further advance. It was now pitch dark and he really did not know exactly how far out into the Strait he had moved. He was probably safe somewhere in the middle of the waterway, and he knew it was at least five miles across the Strait to Point Adolphus. On the other hand, if he continued moving and came close to either shore it would be quite dangerous to go on in the dark. So, he allowed the boat to simply drift with the tide, which happened to be in the direction he wanted to go – to the southeast toward Chatham Strait. In addition, the wind picked up slightly. It was now blowing in the same direction as the incoming tide, and this further assisted his movement toward home.

As the boat drifted so did Rex's thoughts and they were depressing to say the least. He knew what he had done. He had stupidly taken still another innocent life. Fortunately, he should still be in the clear. The bad news was that he would now be the object of a search and that was a worrisome prospect. The more he thought about it the more he realized that the nightmare might not be over.

As he worried he downed a few more beers, and that seemed to settle him slightly. He concluded that it didn't seem possible the two killings could ever be connected. Yet, he still was out here in the dark a long way from his warm and comfortable bed at Upper Salmon. He continued to drift aimlessly out in the Strait for hours aided by the tide and the wind. As the boat drifted he pondered his situation. If the dead officer were to be found in the next few hours and Rex was stopped anywhere short of Auke Bay he would need to explain what he was doing out in those waters at such an early morning hour. He reached the conclusion that, close shoreline or not, he should again start moving. At first, it was at a very slow speed. Then, as the hours passed and the morning light started to show itself, he was able to increase his speed.

As he drew near to Chatham Strait and saw Admiralty Island in the distance his confidence began to increase. Now, he considered his next move. If the officer he shot had been in radio contact with anyone, Rex felt that he would have heard something on his own marine radio. Since it had been silent he could well be home free. On the other hand, if the officer had been able to report to headquarters on some other radio frequency that he was heading out to investigate a vessel just south and west of the entrance to the Bay, then Rex could be in serious jeopardy. He definitely could not afford to be seen in these waters.

When he approached Admiralty Island and turned north toward Lynn Canal he looked in every direction for any sign of movement toward him and saw none. He did see a few seagulls and some porpoise but no vessels. He heard and then saw a floatplane in the distance, but it was heading south away from him, probably toward Angoon.

Later, as he made his turn around Point Retreat, Rex saw a few fishing vessels heading north toward Haines and Skagway, but they were miles away and soon behind Shelter Island. He felt confident that they either did not see him or they would never be

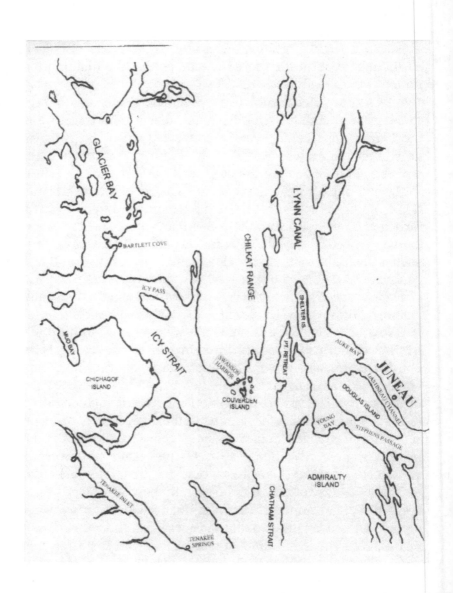

SKETCH OF THE AREA BETWEEN
GLACIER BAY AND JUNEAU

able to describe him or his boat.

Rex saw nothing else to alarm him as he later idled into Auke Bay. He moored his boat in its usual stall and felt he could now remove the checklist from its hiding place and circle that last item. First, however, he would satisfy his hunger and a little more of his thirst. He did that with the last of the lunch from his knapsack and a few more beers. Since he had only some intermittent sleep in the past 24 hours he decided to take a nap right then and there in the cabin of his boat. Opening his sleeping bag for the second time he crawled inside and was soon fast asleep. He slept soundly for the first time in days and probably would have been there for many more hours had he not been awakened and panicked from still another unnerving surprise.

Shortly after daybreak on Thursday, radio contact with Fish and Wildlife Officer Hutchison was again attempted by the dispatcher at Bartlett Cove, but proved unsuccessful. Efforts were made to reach him during the last part of his patrol, but nothing was heard from the officer. After initial attempts, calls were made outbound from the station approximately one every fifteen minutes. At first light another zodiac - this time with two men aboard - was sent out to search for the officer and his boat. The bow damaged zodiac with its dead occupant was finally located adrift in a cove miles inside Glacier Bay. By then it was late morning and Rex had already moored his boat in Auke Bay.

At the same time at Upper Salmon, Chad walked to the workshop and found no one inside and no indication that anyone had done any new carpentry work. He then walked to Rex's unlocked house and again found no one. So, now certain that Rex was gone from the area on his four days off, he concluded that this might be a good time to look around. He searched the small house with a fine toothcomb. He did it carefully and made sure to disturb nothing. He also found nothing. He stepped out into the partially enclosed porch and searched it as well. He saw only the firewood and did not notice the incriminating scrap piece of 1x8 pine that had fallen behind the stack of firewood. He entered Rex's house hoping to find conclusive evidence proving that the man had killed his own wife. Instead, he found nothing. Either the man was very clever or he and John had misjudged him. Was it possible that he really had been constructing a coat rack as Ed Sloan reported?

Back at the Auke Bay marina, Rex woke with a start when he felt the boat suddenly rock. He looked up to see a face staring down at him from outside the cabin door. As he wrestled to extricate himself from his sleeping bag he realized that the face belonged to Pete Tyler, owner of the marina.

"Rex, what are you doing down here asleep in the middle of the day? If you're going to fish the Derby tomorrow you're sure getting an early start."

"Damn, did I sleep that long? I guess I drank too many beers last night," answered Rex motioning to the empty beer bottles strewn about the cabin.

"Well, I was just gonna put this notice on your windshield. You haven't paid your moorage fee the last couple of months. Do you want to be evicted?"

"Hell no," answered Rex. "I'll be up to your office in a little while and write you a check.   It's just that life has been pretty unsettling for me this past month, and I've let quite a few things get away from me."

Pete replied with real sincerity when he said, "Believe me, Rex, I know. I lost my wife a while back. So, I feel for you. I'm really sorry for your loss."

After a few more friendly exchanges, Tyler climbed over the gunwale on to the dock. He was about to depart when he looked down and saw the damage to the side of Rex's boat. He turned and said, "Hey, what did you hit? You've got orange paint and a pretty bad scrape on the side here."   Rex did not realize the damage that was caused by the collision with the wildlife officer's zodiac. Still, he was able to answer without hesitation, "Just another one of my recent problems," he replied. "I bumped into the buoy out at Tee Harbor a while back while I was reeling in a fish. Didn't look where I was going." As Tyler walked along the
As Tyler walked along the dock and then up the ramp to his

110

office he thought that it seemed Rex had not moved his boat in quite a while. However, to give Rex the benefit of the doubt, he was not always down on the dock, and Rex could have slipped away in the early morning or in late afternoon and returned without his having noticed. Then he thought about the dent in the side of Rex's boat and wondered if the Tee Harbor buoy wasn't red rather than orange. Secondly, he wondered how fast Rex's boat was going to get that kind of a dent simply from hitting a buoy while reeling in a fish. "Oh well," he said to himself, "no use making a federal case out of nothing."

Actually, it was much more than nothing and it was now a federal case. The FBI would be fully involved and the airwaves would soon crackle with the news. Later, as Rex was sitting in Pete Tyler's office, they heard about it on the marine radio and a few minutes later on local radio Station KJNE.

TWENTY

LUCK OF THE IRISH

One of Pinky McInerney's drinking buddies, David Royce, lived on Thane Road near where Pinky once lived in a rented trailer. So, the two often drank together at one's home or the other. They had known each other for almost four years and Pinky had often served as a crewman on David's trolling vessel, often while both were under the influence. Pinky had cleaned up his act considerably after he went to work at the electric company's Upper Salmon plant. He had almost completely given up drinking. So, he and David didn't party much anymore after that. Then, when Pinky transferred to Lower Salmon and later when he lost his job because of the takeover by AEL&P, their partying resumed .

On his four days off, when he was still working at Lower Salmon, Pinky would occasionally crew for David. Now, without a job, he went out fishing with David as often as he could and they drank together or separately as often as money would allow. Pinky, on a few occasions, fished the boat alone because his friend was too drunk to even get aboard a boat, let alone fish it. It was not a wise thing to do because Pinky had no salmon-trolling permit. Regardless, when Pinky returned to town with a sizeable catch, he would awaken his friend and they would go together in David's boat to Southeast Cold Storage to offload.

This day, while Rex was wasting no time returning to Auke Bay, Pinky was on another one of his illegal fishing ventures in David's boat. If Pinky had only known. This was one time it would have been much better if he had enjoyed one or two more drinks and had, instead, gone to sleep alongside his friend.

As Pinky pulled another salmon from one of the lines being winched in and threw the fish into the hold of the boat he saw that one of the other lines appeared to be dragging a heavy weight. Since the trolling pole wasn't bouncing up and down, Pinky suspected that it might be a big lingcod. Trolling near the bottom will occasionally result in one of those ugly monsters taking the lure or the herring.

As he winched in this second line he saw that he had instead snagged a large black plastic garbage bag with what looked like the barrel of a gun protruding from it. He was at that moment in Icy Pass a few miles east of Glacier Bay between Gustavus and Pleasant Island. He did not see Rex or his boat as they passed on the other side of the island. It was too dark and too far away, and Pinky was occupied - intending to do some serious fishing. He was dropping his lines in the water as Rex was drifting past on the other side of Pleasant Island. Later in the morning the last of the incoming tide caused the recently jettisoned bag to drift a considerable distance from where Rex had dropped it in spite of the weight inside. There was still enough captured air inside the bag to make it somewhat buoyant. It may have drifted with the tide and perhaps even tumbled along the sandy bottom to where it snagged itself onto Pinky's line. Regardless, it was interrupting his fishing. So, Pinky now hurried to detach the bag from the hooks so that he could continue fishing. The tide now having turned from high to outgoing, he reversed direction and headed eastward trolling into the tide and toward Juneau. The fishing was good, and he was filling the hold with his catch as he went. Hours later, perhaps ten miles west of Pt. Couverden, he felt it was time to start for home. By now, the boat's hold was almost full of fish and he was anxious to see what was in the package that had mysteriously snagged itself on to his line. So, he pulled in his lines, secured the winches, closed the hold, washed down the deck, and started for Juneau. As he motored slowly along he started unwrapping the funny looking package. What he found inside puzzled him. Here was a perfectly good rifle attached to a board, and it had all just recently been dumped in the water. This was evident because there was no marine matter, not even a bit of slime, on either the rifle or its enclosing plastic bag. There was a rock in the bag, so it was clear to Pinky that someone wanted the package to remain hidden in the deep waters. He detached the rifle from its mount and looked through the scope. It, too, was clear of slime probably because that part of the rifle had been sealed within the plastic bag. He set everything aside just as a Coast Guard helicopter flew overhead. He could see it was heading for Bartlett Cove. It didn't stop at Gustavus, so Bartlett Cove was probably its destination.

He heard parts of radio communications between the chopper and people on the ground - references to passengers aboard from the FBI, Fish and Wildlife, Coast Guard, etc. - and he could feel that something major was going on. So, Pinky, in his wisdom, decided that this might be a good time to head for home at a little faster pace.

The boat he was fishing was not his own and the troll permit was not his either. There were already on his record too many scrapes in past years with the Feds and other police agencies to warrant still another confrontation. He would take the boat back to Juneau and its owner, get his share of the catch's worth, and then head for home at Lower Salmon. David Royce didn't know that Pinky had taken the boat – he was still passed out in his trailer on Thane Road. Earlier, while in a drunken stupor, he had suggested to Pinky that they should again go fishing together. A few more drinks after the suggestion was made, however, David was in no condition to do anything but sleep. So, Pinky simply took the man's keys to the boat and went off on another of his solo adventures. Pinky did plan to return to Juneau with the boat and its cargo. He had to. Once docked, he would telephone David to come down to the boat so they could proceed, as they had done in the past as captain and crew, to Southeast Cold Storage to sell their catch. Unfortunately for the two of them, Pinky got back to Juneau but the boat didn't.

When the Coast Guard helicopter touched down at Bartlett Cove and discharged its passengers it was immediately ordered to seek out any vessel within Glacier Bay. Finding none, it was then ordered to search the entire area just outside the entrance to the Bay. The only vessel they found was the one that was heading southeast in Icy Strait. It was identified as the fishing vessel "Royce's Girl" owned by David Royce of Juneau.

Pinky intended to take the same route back to Juneau as,

unbeknownst to him, Rex had taken - east in Icy Strait, north to Lynn Canal, and around Point Retreat to Juneau. It was by far the most direct route. Unfortunately for Pinky, another part of the United States Coast Guard other than the aforementioned helicopter would intercept him just before he passed between Couverden Island and the mainland. Had he been just another few miles to the east he would have been in the lee of the island and thus might not have been seen by the crew of the cutter as it passed into Icy Strait heading west to Glacier Bay. Instead, in spite of the fog between him and the cutter, a blip of his boat was seen on their radar. This was just not going to be Pinky's day.

The Coast Guard Cutter Intrepid had been on her regular tour of duty heading south in Chatham Strait on the west side of Admiralty Island when her captain was ordered to increase speed immediately and to divert to Glacier Bay. On the way, she was ordered to intercept any vessel leaving the area, especially the fishing vessel that the helicopter had seen a few minutes earlier. The cutter was warned that those on board might be armed and that all caution should be used in approaching her.

As the cutter appeared through the fog and hailed him, Pinky quickly concluded that the rifle might be involved in whatever was going on so he quickly dropped it overboard. Between him and the cutter was part of the boat's cabin. So, he felt that there was enough structure in the way that no one aboard the cutter could have seen what he had done. Hopefully, the thick fog hid the rest of him. He was almost one hundred percent right. Regardless, it was now in the deep. "They'll play hell connecting me to that thing," he said to himself confidently.

Unfortunately, there's a lot of truth in another old saying: 'When it goes bad, it goes bad in bunches,' because this day it would go exactly that way for Pinky. A sailor on the stern of the cutter was the only one of the crew of the cutter to have an unobstructed view of Pinky. He later reported to the captain that he saw the man throwing what appeared to be a rifle or a shotgun overboard.

As the cutter pulled alongside instructing him to: "Heave to, prepare to be boarded," Pinky knew immediately that he was now completely out of his element and in a world of hurt. Some of these people approaching him had weapons drawn. This, definitely, was not a good sign.

Upon being found to be without a permit and piloting a fishing boat that was not his own, Pinky was immediately arrested and taken aboard the cutter. The fishing boat was confiscated with all its cargo – including the plastic bags and all the remaining contents. The board and the loose U-bolt were also gathered up. All was taken aboard the Intrepid to join the reluctant, but submissive, Aloysius McInerney.

Pinky argued that his cargo had to be brought to Southeast Cold Storage to avoid spoilage. He, in turn, was informed that spoilage was the least of his worries. While admitting that he was not the owner of the vessel and that he had no permit, still, he continued to question why the boat was being towed back toward Glacier Bay instead of to Juneau. He was very much concerned about the possible worsening condition of his cargo, and he kept stressing the point. He was told 'flat out' that it was no longer his cargo and that the vessel was being towed to Sitka - Intrepid's home base. When he continued to protest, and when he correctly stated that Juneau was much closer than Sitka, he was rather forcefully placed in the cutter's brig. It was not so much because of his words or his actions. It was simply that it was the best place for him to be for all concerned – out of the way. None of the crew of the cutter, not even the captain, knew all the details as to why this man and the boat had been seized. Regardless, they now had orders to deliver him to Bartlett Cove, and the people there would know and they would take over. Later, the Intrepid would continue on to Sitka with the confiscated vessel in tow.

When the Intrepid arrived at the dock in Bartlett Cove and discharged its now manacled passenger, the captain of the cutter informed the FBI agent who greeted him that the man had been seen throwing something overboard. When asked if it might have been a firearm he replied that it was not clear as to what it was except that it had made a splash. "It could have been a shotgun or a rifle," he said, "but the fog was pretty thick so it would be only a guess as to what it really was." He did say that one crewman on the stern of the cutter thought he had seen the man throw a weapon overboard, but it was from a considerable distance. The sailor, too, said that there was fog in the area at that time that further hampered his view.

Regardless, the captain handed Agent Wolters a hand-written statement as to what he and his crew had observed together with the garbage bag with all of its contents - those previously inside and those collected from the deck of the confiscated fishing vessel. In addition, he also described the exact area where the vessel was intercepted. "We anchored a small buoy over the spot. It has the identifying number I-29 and the usual Coast Guard markings on it. The depth there was 15 fathoms and it shallows out a little more as you get closer in to Swanson Harbor. So, a diver shouldn't have too much trouble searching in that area." The Agent thanked him, saying, "Real professional, Captain. We'll get a diver right out there."

There being no further need for the cutter to tarry, it departed with the fishing vessel in tow. If the cargo in Royce's Girl's hold was still sufficiently cooled and in good condition once they reached the processing plant in Sitka, it would be sold and the proceeds later taken into the United States Treasury. Before departing, the captain of the Intrepid was finally briefed on what had taken place there near Glacier Bay. He was also asked to radio Bartlett Cove if he saw any other vessels either departing or coming toward the area so that they could be intercepted. The search continued for most of the day, but no other vessels appeared to have been anywhere near the shooting. The few that were stopped were apparently heading toward the Glacier Bay area rather than away from it. So, they were soon released and sent on their way.

The helicopter's search from the air had been much more encompassing and it was mostly in the direction of Juneau. This was due largely to fuel constraints. After identifying the troller, Royce's Girl, the chopper was ordered to return to Bartlett Cove. Hours later it would transport to Juneau the body of the slain officer, his probable shooter in the person of Aloysius P. McInerney, as well as its original inbound passengers. These men had with them all of the evidence that had been taken from the fishing vessel. They also had with them the slain officer's life jacket with the spent bullet still inside. It appeared that another bullet was still in the body, and this would be confirmed later at autopsy.

As the chopper flew toward Juneau there was little conversation other than from Pinky. He continually asked why he wasn't being told anything, and why all this federal brass was necessary for a little fishing violation. He also expressed considerable anger at being handcuffed, but again received no reply. They simply wouldn't talk to him.

In spite of his size and his bravado, down deep Pinky was now one very frightened man, especially since there had been very few words and not one question directed at him. He was still completely in the dark as to what was going on. The questions from the other side were bound to come sooner or later. Pinky knew it, and he was not excited about the prospect. He was right – the questions finally started. They went on and on, and the questioners were unrelenting.

Before the questioning of Pinky McInerney began in downtown Juneau, Rex Franz out in Auke Bay was fending off a slew of them, all posed by the marina owner, Pete Tyler. They were sitting in Pete's office and Rex was attempting to write the check that would bring his moorage fees up to date.

"I went down to put this notice on your boat yesterday, but it was gone. Were you out fishing then, too?"

"No," answered Rex, "I went mushroom hunting."

"No kidding? That's one of my secret passions – hunting mushrooms. The other, not so secret, is eating them," replied Tyler laughingly. "What kind do you look for, and where?"

"This time of year I look for Chicken of the Woods," replied Rex, "and surely you don't expect me to tell you or anyone where I find them."

The talk of mushrooms now set aside all else until the announcement of the shooting near Glacier Bay came across the airwaves. It was very brief – only that a Fish and Wildlife Officer had been killed, no names would be revealed until notification of next of kin, and that an investigation was ongoing. It caused the conversation between the two men to take a different turn. An almost immediate question from Pete Tyler noticeably shook Rex. "You weren't hunting mushrooms out near Glacier Bay were you," asked Tyler almost in jest.

"No," replied Rex. "I don't go that far to hunt anything."

Their friendly talk continued, as did the questioning even though Rex was trying as hard and as tactfully as he could to end it without causing suspicion. Finally, he came up with the right words when Pete asked him again, "Are you going to fish the Derby tomorrow?"

"No, I didn't buy a Derby ticket because I start my shift at Upper Salmon in a few hours. I've got to get going, but why don't we go out mushroom hunting some day. I'll show you where I look for the Chicken of the Woods and you can show me your spots where you find the King Boletus. That'll make for a fair trade. It might be a little early for the Boletus, but the Chicken of the Woods starts growing just about now."

"Good idea," said Tyler, and with that the visit ended.

As he departed Tyler's office Rex commented to himself that it had felt more like a grilling than a friendly conversation. "I'll make sure to avoid the man in the future, Boletus Edulis or not. I shouldn't have mentioned us going mushroom hunting together. He'll probably want to do just that."

TWENTY-ONE

THE INTERROGATION

On the ninth floor of the Federal Building in Juneau later that day the questioning began. Pinky McInerney sat on one side of a large oval table fielding the questions - most of them posed by FBI Agent Wolters who sat on the other side flanked by the previously mentioned representatives of the Coast Guard and the Fish and Wildlife Service. In front of all of them on the table was a tape recorder that received into it the following introduction:

"This recording begins today on Thursday, July 27, 1972. My name is Frederic G. Wolters, FBI Agent stationed in Juneau, Alaska. Questioning of Aloysius P. McInerney is being conducted here in the conference room on the ninth floor of the Federal Building at 709 W. 9th Street in Juneau. At my side are Coast Guard Lieutenant Melvin F. Lonard and Fish and Wildlife Juneau Field Office Chief Robert N. Gerdes. Mr. McInerney was apprehended today near Couverden Island in Icy Strait while he was piloting the vessel Royce's Girl, not his own. At the time that he was stopped, Mr. McInerney was the only person aboard. He has been advised of his rights and he will be questioned today about the shooting of Fish and Wildlife Officer Aubrey Hutchison."

At that moment, Pinky felt like he himself had just been shot. He yelled out, "I don't know anything about any shooting. So, this is what all the brass is about. I was fishing – nothing else. If your people had asked me early on I would have told them that."

It took a few minutes and a few stern words from the interrogator before Pinky calmed down. The questioning and the taping then resumed:

"Please state your full name."

"Aloysius Pinkton McInerney"

"Where do you live?"

"2153 Glacier Highway."

"What is your date of birth?"

"August 19, 1927."

"What is your occupation?"

"Powerhouse Operator."

"Where do you work?"

"I'm unemployed."

"Where was your previous place of employment?"

"At Lower Salmon Powerhouse."

"Who was your employer?"

"Juneau Hydroelectric."

"Why did you leave there?"

"I got let go. They were taken over by AEL&P and that outfit consolidated jobs and fired those with least seniority."

"Where did you work before that?"

"Coeur d'Alene, Idaho. I was a Powerhouse Operator there, too – for almost fifteen years."

"Was that your home?"

"Yes, I was born and raised there."

"How long have you lived in Juneau?"

"About four years."

"Do you have a salmon trolling permit?"

"No."

"Were you in Glacier Bay yesterday or today?"

"No."

"Were you in or near Glacier Bay at any time in the last month?"

"No."

"Where were you fishing today?"

"In Icy Pass east of Gustavus."

"Where were you fishing the day before?"

"I was in the same place."

"You were salmon fishing?"

"Yes."

"Where were you heading earlier today when the Coast Guard Cutter stopped you?"

"Juneau."

"What were you going to do there?"

"I was going to call David Royce so he could come with me and the boat to Cold Storage."

"Cold Storage?"

"Yes, Southeast Cold Storage, where we unload our catch."

"Why were you going to call David Royce?"

"He's the owner of the boat."

"Why wasn't he aboard?"

"He was sick. Actually, he was drunk. He was passed out."

"So, you took his boat?"

"No, while we were drinking at his place he said I could take it. He lent it to me. He's done that in the past."

"You said he was drunk?"

"Yes."

"If he was too drunk to man his boat, how could he be sober enough to lend it to you?"

"He did. He just told me to fish it and we'd split the proceeds. Then he passed out."

"Did he give you the keys first?"

"No, he was already passed out, so I took them out of his pocket."

"Now, let's get back to Glacier Bay."

"I said I was nowhere near Glacier Bay."

These first questions aimed at Pinky had all been asked by FBI Agent Wolters. Coast Guard Officer Lonard now began his own series of questions:

"When you were stopped by the Coast Guard Cutter Intrepid, where were you?"

"I was just west of Swanson Harbor."

"What were you doing there?"

"I was taking a short cut."

"A short cut? Or, were you attempting to hide?"

"No, it's just shorter to pass north of Couverden Island than it is to go around it."

"You were going to head north into Lynn Canal?"

"Yes."

"So, you know your way around in those waters, and in

Glacier Bay?"

"Yes, but I wasn't in Glacier Bay. I already told you that."

"Yes, you did. When was the last time you were in Glacier Bay?"

"I guess it was last year."

"Last year?"

"Yes."

"Why did you come back to the area?"

"It's a good place to fish."

"What about Glacier Bay?"

"It's a good place to fish, too, but I wasn't near Glacier Bay this time."

"When the cutter hailed you what did you throw overboard?"

"I didn't throw 'nuthin' overboard."

"You didn't? You didn't throw a rifle overboard?"

"A rifle? I didn't have a rifle to throw."

"Then what was it that you did throw? A shotgun?"

"No, I didn't have a shotgun either. All we ever use on the boat is a .22 pistol."

"So, what did you throw overboard? You were seen by several of the crew."

This now appeared to Pinky as the opportune time to use all his guile. He answered simply, and quite innocently, "Oh, yeah, I was throwing kelp overboard. A lot hangs up on the lines, and then it gets winched aboard with the hooks. That's probably what your guys saw."

Fish and Wildlife Chief Gerdes now started in on Pinky and this time with much more pointed questions:

"Were you concerned about being caught?"

"No, all that booze made me forget the consequences."

"Forget?"

"All I thought about was the money."

"No, I think you were worried about being caught!"

"I wasn't."

"I think you were concerned enough to even shoot someone

123

to avoid being caught."

"No, I wasn't, and I couldn't do anybody much harm with a 22 pistol."

"Oh, did you fire the .22?"

"No. I only use it on some of the bigger fish – mostly on big halibut. Why? Was your man shot with a .22?"

"We are asking the questions, Mr. McInerney!"

After that exchange Pinky started to feel a little better. They had nothing on him. There was no way they could prove otherwise, but it took just another few seconds before Pinky's confidence took a nosedive. It happened with the next series of questions and Pinky made the mistake of talking too much. Coast Guard Lieutenant Lonard started in with his second round of questions. He stood and leaned over the table, and was almost nose to nose with Pinky when he began. Pinky forced him to back up quickly, however, when he expelled a large still whiskey soured breath into the man's face. So, most of Lonard's next questions were issued from a more comfortable distance. The questions were short and they were mostly harmless. Pinky, in turn, made his answers rambling and overly descriptive. He figured the longer he talked, the less opportunity his questioners would have to pose theirs. Since the kelp excuse seemed to work well the first time, he brought it up again. He calmly and confidently remarked, "I'm sure if your young matey was paying attention, he'd have seen that what I threw overboard was really just a big piece of brown kelp."

That's when Lonard hit him with a zinger. It was a lie, but Pinky didn't know that:

"Did you know a crewman took a picture of you just as you threw the rifle overboard?"

This shook Pinky to the core. He started to reply with "uh…" and then remembered advice he'd received years before. A friend who had been interrogated in the past told him, "When you are cornered by a difficult question, weather it with complete silence." He figured correctly that the first one to talk could be in trouble. So, he kept quiet. It worked exactly that way because this time the FBI agent resumed the questioning, and it was now in a much less menacing tone:

"So, you hadn't been in Glacier Bay in months?"

"Right, it's been more than a year."

"Do you own a rifle?"

"No, not now."

"Do you own a shotgun?"

"Yes, I have a Model 1897 Winchester – 16 gauge."

"Those are rare."

"I know, but mine is not in too good of a shape."

"Did you have it with you?"

"No."

"What do you usually shoot with it?"

"Nowadays, nothing. I just keep it loaded with buckshot to protect against bears."

"Do you ever use it to shoot deer?"

"No, when I hunted deer in Washington I had a .30-06."

"What did you mean by 'not now' when I asked you if you owned a rifle?"

"It got stolen about five years ago."

"Did it have a scope?"

"No. It didn't have a scope."

"Where was it stolen?"

"At a rest stop on U.S.90 near Spokane."

"Did you report the theft to the authorities there?"

"Yes, and to my insurance man in Coeur d'Alene."

"Pretty convenient."

"Well, it's the truth."

"We will be able to check on that, Mr. McInerney."

"Yeah, I hope you do."

In spite of the fact that he was on solid ground on this latest part of the questioning, Pinky was starting to perspire. He thought to himself, "There is no way that could be the same rifle I threw overboard. That would be a zillion to one shot. Nobody could be that unlucky." Unfortunately, the luck of the Irish was not going to connect with Pinky this day.

All three Feds now moved their chairs a little closer when

they saw a bit of anxiety on his face. The three men and their questions had meshed beautifully together even without a prearranged plan. They had all done questioning in the past of innocent and guilty alike and this day that previous experience proved very beneficial. They were still without conclusive evidence – certainly not the weapon – but the probable shooter appeared to be before them and he was sweating. They had already softened Pinky up with their first set of questions, so Coast Guard Lieutenant Lonard hit him with another shocker. This one pained Pinky a lot more:

"There are divers on their way right now to where you threw the rifle overboard, Aloysius. What are you going to say when they recover it? It's not much deeper than 10 to 20 fathoms in that area outside Swanson Harbor. They should have it by tomorrow. What will you say when the bullets that killed Officer Hutchison are matched to that rifle?"

The only thing Pinky could do with that question was, again, to not answer it. Quite a few more questions were directed at him but Pinky denied any culpability in the shooting. He said one thing over and over again whether they asked the specific question or not: "I wasn't in or near Glacier Bay and I didn't shoot anybody."

At one point in the interview one of the questioners stated that the board with the smaller U-bolt still attached appeared to have held the rifle. Powder residue on that board, he told Pinky, would confirm that it had been involved in a shooting. It was not even mentioned or questioned that the rifle and the board had been in the water and that, possibly, the powder residue could have been diluted or completely washed away. That kind of evidence would surface in time one way or another:

"Why did you have the rifle attached to that board?"
"I didn't have a rifle."
"What about the board?"
"It was in the plastic bag that got hung up on one of my lines."
"How about the larger U-bolt? Was it also hung up on your

line?"

"No, it was in the bag."

"If it was in the bag, why did you pull it out of the bag?"

"I didn't pull it out. It just spilled out."

"You say it just spilled out. If it just spilled out why didn't the screw eyes also spill out, or the ammo?"

"I don't know."

"I think you detached the rifle from the board to be sure the evidence would sink."

Pinky's reply was his first of the day from any vestige of strength: "Well, Mister, if I was gonna use a rifle to shoot a Fed why would I attach it to a board in the first place?"

Since he felt he was on a roll Pinky again said, "I had no rifle. I wasn't near Glacier Bay and I sure as hell wouldn't shoot anybody especially a Fed over a missing permit. I might be dumb, but I'm not stupid."

TWENTY-TWO

THE SEARCH

Denny Gustafson, a local Juneau dentist, was also a certified scuba instructor and he often did underwater salvage and repair work in Juneau and the surrounding area. A Coast Guard Officer contacted him at his home the same evening that Pinky was being questioned. Denny was asked to assist in the recovery of a weapon that they suspected had been thrown into the water near Swanson Harbor.

Coincidentally, Denny and his wife Sue were close friends of the Santoris and had been invited for a crab cioppino dinner at their home the next night, Friday. When Denny agreed to assist in the search he asked his wife to call Liz with apologies and an explanation.

"You can go if you want, but they want me there early tomorrow at slack tide."

"No," replied Sue, "I'd like to go with you. So, I'll call Liz and cancel, and I'll ask her if they'll babysit the kids. That way we can take our boat and have a one or two day vacation."

Sue made the phone call to Liz and one to Denny's office receptionist with instructions to cancel all his appointments for the next day as well as those for the following Monday and part of Tuesday. The couple then set about gathering their gear, food, drink, and whatever else they felt necessary to take on this two or three day hiatus.

The next morning, near their moored pleasure boat in Auke Bay, they met with a Coast Guard officer. He told them that his boat, the Cutter Active, whose home station was also in Auke Bay, would escort them out to the area of the intended search.

They all arrived on scene a few hours later, and the underwater search began soon after.

While Denny Gustafson was in deep water and uncomfortably cold, Pinky McInerney was cozy warm in his cell in the Federal Building. Later in the day, however, he would be in hot water and also very uncomfortable. It turned out that his 'old friend' and drinking buddy, David Royce, had just hung Pinky out to dry. He was in FBI Agent Wolters' office just down the hall from Pinky's cell and he was denying that he had lent his boat to anyone.

David might be a drunk but he was smart enough to know he couldn't admit to being a part of any past endeavor that was being investigated by the FBI. He wisely concluded that he probably would be able to get his boat back if it was proven that it was stolen or taken without his permission. He had no illusions, however, of ever recovering its cargo. Only a miracle would make that happen.

All of the questions and answers between the two men were taken down by a secretary and later transcribed into written form. The document was then presented to David for his signature which he readily provided. The same secretary and another office employee then witnessed his signature. Soon afterwards David Royce departed the Federal Building safe in the belief that he would soon have returned to him his 'stolen' vessel.

A Coast Guard diver and Denny Gustafson worked together in the search near Swanson Harbor, but to no avail. They dove near the buoy left there by the Intrepid and they did more than a thorough search. Unfortunately, they found little other than plenty of halibut buried in the sandy bottom. At least three elements worked against them. The first two were the extreme depth and the cold. These two factors caused them to return to the surface more often and then again dive to continue the search. They staked off the bottom into a grid and, after being searched, each section was marked off on their clipboard. The third factor that made the search next to impossible was the strong tides that sweep the narrow areas between the islands in and around Point Couverden, Swanson Harbor, and most of Southeast Alaska for that matter. Granted, they were diving during low slack water, but the damage had been done during the almost 24 hours that had elapsed since the rifle had been dropped into the water. The previous day there had been a twenty foot difference in tides at Swanson Harbor from a high of plus 18 feet to a low of minus 2 feet in a little more than six hours. That was just the outgoing tide. In another six plus hours the incoming tidal action moved almost the same amount of water in the opposite direction.

While this kind of tidal movement might not be too apparent at the surface, if one were on the bottom it would feel like a fast flowing river. This has the effect of not only disturbing the sandy bottom but also causes objects on the bottom to be moved or buried.

In addition, but much less of a factor, the sandy bottom could easily have engulfed a rifle or any other heavy object simply from the movement of halibut. These fish catch their daily meal by burying themselves in the sand with little but their eyes showing. They remain motionless until smaller animal life drifts or swims by above them. Then, in a flurry of roiling water and sand, they are upon the unsuspecting prey. As they put away their meal they return to the bottom to prepare to repeat the stalking ritual.

The men also dove the next morning again at slack water and again they found nothing. They had only a small area where they could search. The rest of the area was simply too deep for scuba equipment. On their last rest period, Denny commented to the cutter's captain that they would go down one more time. "If we can't find it at a minus 2.6 foot slack tide, there is no use us continuing. You folks better bring in the navy divers with their sophisticated equipment."

On their last dive, Denny checked an area close to the buoy anchor where they had searched the first morning. There was a small sandy area between two outcroppings of rock where the Cutter's anchor had settled. There it was. The anchor had actually come to rest atop the stock of the rifle. It and the shifting sand had apparently obscured it from view on their initial dive the previous morning.

Now, the last tidal flow had uncovered it almost completely. It was a lucky break. Had any kind of metal detector been used in that area that first day, and any showing of metal revealed on the instrument, the diver might have considered it as being caused by the anchor and ignored it. This would have been almost a certainty if the sand still buried it. There were more than a few satisfied smiles when Denny surfaced with the rifle in hand.

The weapon was taken into the machine shop of the Coast Guard Cutter where it was first rinsed in fresh water and then oiled over all its metal surfaces. It was found to be without any corrosion. The fact that the actual owner of the rifle had also kept the weapon properly protected from moisture certainly contributed to its good condition. It also did not hurt that it was only in the salt water off and on for less than 48 hours.

This was most fortunate because it could now be test fired and the bullet could be compared to the one taken from the slain officer's body and the other one found in his life jacket. The weapon was handed to Agent Wolters that afternoon and within hours it and all the accompanying evidence, including even the plastic bags, was on its way to FBI Headquarters in Washington, D.C.

As the evidence headed east, Denny and Sue Gustafson headed south. After a job well done they would spend a few quiet days at Tenakee Hot Springs on Chichagof Island. Hours of cold in the deep of Icy Strait would soon be forgotten while he soaked in the 100 plus degree mineral waters of the bathhouse at Tenakee. A month later, when Denny received in the mail a check for his two days' work, he also received a Letter of Commendation from the Admiral of the Seventeenth Coast Guard District.

TWENTY-THREE

ANOTHER CHECKLIST

Up until he heard that the Gustafsons would not be coming to dinner John hadn't given much thought to or listened to any accounts of the happenings near Glacier Bay. Once he heard from Liz that Denny and Sue weren't coming and their reason for canceling, he decided to phone Fred Wolters. He was hoping to learn the details behind the search.

Not in his wildest imagination did he think that the weapon being sought by the Feds would also be the one at the center of his investigation. If they were looking for a pistol or a shotgun John never would have even considered making the call, but if it was a rifle he sure would like to be kept advised.

The FBI has always been known to keep things to themselves. They are prone to secrecy, probably more than any other agency. Fred Wolters was not one to stray from that reputation. He told John only that a Fish and Wildlife Officer had been shot, a fishing vessel had been seen leaving the area of the shooting, and the man piloting the boat appeared to have thrown something into the water just before being apprehended by the Coast Guard.

When John asked why the man was being held, Fred said only that he had no salmon troll permit, and that it appeared he had stolen the involved vessel. Fred didn't mention the evidence that had been collected from the vessel and John neglected to ask. In retrospect, he should have pressed him for more information, but it really didn't seem to be anything that would interest him or the Juneau Police Department.

If he had even the slightest suspicion that it was the rifle that Rex had reported stolen, John probably would have volunteered to dive with Denny even though he never had any scuba diving instructions, let alone much experience under water. If he had been told that the name of the suspect was Aloysius McInerney, then he for sure would have gotten involved even though there was not much that JPD or John could do. It would be a State or Federal matter. When he later received a call from Chad Winkler telling him, "Pinky is in the pokey," then he did decide to get involved.

At first, his involvement was anything but fruitful. He had no evidence, not even a suggestion as to how to absolve Pinky of blame in the shooting of the Fish and Wildlife Officer. Thankfully, he had his regular duties with JPD as his main focus. This latter work alternated from the patrol car to the office and sometimes even to the Police Academy in Sitka. No matter where his work took him, however, there tagged along in the back of his mind the nagging thought that Rex Franz could well have gotten away with murder. There were simply too many loose ends and too many small bits of evidence continuing to haunt him. What was even worse, they were all too darn small. He needed something big to tie it all together and he wasn't finding anything even resembling big.

Many nights while he tossed and turned in bed trying to sleep he would attempt to figure out just how Rex did it. This particular night he went over in his mind some of the different scenarios that he had previously thought about. It came to him that he should write some of his thoughts down on paper so that he could review ideas that might have been thrown out in past musings. To keep track of those discarded ideas as well as those that he did retain he decided that it would be wise to start a checklist. How ironic. If only he had known that another checklist was started months ago for a completely different and more sinister purpose.

John started his checklist the very next day as he sat having lunch downtown at the City Café. On the blank piece of paper on his clipboard he wrote down the first items. They were: "SCREW EYE, U-BOLT, and BOARD." Under that he wrote: "HOW USED and WHERE." He, too, used a pencil knowing that there would be plenty of erasures. The owner of the establishment, Sam Yamata, seeing him busily writing, jokingly

133

asked: "What are you working on there, John, your last will and testament?"

"No," he replied, "this is just a draft of my letter to the Health Department about this greasy spoon that you're running here." They both laughed as Sam yelled, "Get out of my restaurant."

While John was starting his checklist, his wife Liz was well into her own list. On one side of the paper she listed their monthly income, which consisted only of his paycheck and some interest and dividends from a few small investments. On the other side were all of their expenses. She confronted him with the list one night after dinner and suggested that perhaps she should go back to work.

"You can see that we aren't getting that far ahead. I know that police work is where you have always wanted to be, but you're now earning less than you did at Upper Salmon. If we want to buy a house on the beach one of these days, we better start building a better nest egg," she added. "My take home pay could go into a savings account solely for that purpose."

What she said made sense, but John couldn't just up and say, "Yes, do it." So, first he asked, "What about Andrew?"

He knew her answer before she came out with it:

"He graduates in June, and he already has a temporary job at the paint store. They want him there full time, and he'll want to be out on his own as soon as he graduates. You know that. Andrew won't be a problem and I'm sure you know that as well as I do. He's so involved in his after school athletic programs he often doesn't get home from school much earlier than I would coming from work."

Liz was working as a dental hygienist when they first met more than 25 years earlier and she filled in occasionally at various dental offices both in San Francisco early in their married life as well as here in Juneau at Denny Gustafson's office. Several times in these past few years Denny asked her to consider working for him full time. Each time she thanked him but she would always decline because, as she explained truthfully, "I still have a son to raise." Now, however, things were different. "I think I should accept his offer," she said with conviction.

"What can I say? If that's what you want to do, then go for it," he replied. John was one of those men who learned early on that women get their way whether you object or not. Little did he know that his agreeing to her request would someday bear more than monetary fruit.

A few days later, as John pondered his own still short checklist, he concentrated on the first item – 'SCREW EYE.' It seemed to him that a screw eye had few purposes. You either use it to hang something or you run something through it. Since he saw it in the locker with the piece of sugar pine it probably was used in conjunction with it, or maybe with the bigger piece that was never found. Since it was a large screw eye, it could   not be used to hang something as thin as that board. It could easily split the board. It had to have some other function.

The U-bolt could have been used to attach something to the larger board. "So," he said to himself, "let's take it a step further. Let's assume that what Rex was building out in the workshop was a killing device.   Then, let's also consider that it might be something that would allow him to commit murder without anyone's help – something to allow him to pull the trigger of a rifle without Mary suspecting what he was about to do."

He decided to put this theory to a test in his garage workshop. Before he even mounted his own rifle on a board he figured out the need for the screw eye. In order for him to be able to pull the trigger of a firearm that was pointed at him from behind, the pull would need to come from behind the rifle and farther away from him than the weapon. Yes, the screw eye would do it.

Since John had a vise in his workshop he decided to put it to use in his experiment. He first mounted the rifle on a long board with the use of U-bolts – a small one to hold the barrel and a larger one to hold the stock at its smallest circumference. He then placed the board in the jaws of the vise and tightened it therein. He tied a string to the trigger, ran it back in the workshop to a screw eye on the inner wall of the garage, and then back to where he would stand next to his 'contraption.' He pulled on the string and, *voila,* the rifle clicked. He noticed that his pull caused the weapon to move slightly. So, he tightened both U-bolts to the maximum and pulled the string again. This time it didn't work because the board moved slightly within the jaws of the vise. So, he tightened the vise on to the board with as much force as he could muster and pulled again. This time it worked. Now he could see that the pulling of the trigger in that manner would have fired a bullet if one were in the chamber.

When he took the mount from the vise he noticed that the jaws of the tool left an imprint on the soft wood both front and back. If he could find that larger piece of board, he thought, "I might be able to nail Rex with it." If there was any slight imperfection on the jaws of the vise in the workshop at Upper Salmon, that imperfection might have transferred its imprint on to that board. In that event John would have a big piece of evidence that he needed to start building his case.

When he lifted the mounted rifle toward his eye to sight on a target in his garage he saw that he couldn't get his eye close to the scope because the long piece of wood extended past the end of the rifle's stock. The board was in the way. "Aha," he said to himself. "That's why he cut a piece from that board." There was no question in his mind – he was getting closer.

TWENTY-FOUR

THE ARRAIGNMENT

Pinky McInerney, meanwhile, was cooling off in the Lemon Creek Jail. During his arraignment he pleaded not guilty to the theft of the fishing vessel Royce's Girl. When he was asked if he was represented by counsel he replied, "I'm not, Your Honor. I can't afford a lawyer."

"You're indigent?" asked the judge.

"No, I just don't have any money."

That bit of humor was enjoyed by everyone in the courtroom except Pinky who stood wondering what was so funny about being broke. It was the only respite from his very serious, but brief, court session. Days later a trial date was set and since Pinky could not afford to post bail he was handed over to the Alaska State Troopers who in turn escorted him back to jail. Not long after he was visited by a local Juneau attorney, Cameron Switzer, from the law firm of Fulmer & Bancroft. He told Pinky that he had been assigned by the court to represent him at trial.

Pinky's first words to the young man were, "You gotta get hold of David Royce and remind him that he told me I should use his boat."

The attorney replied that he would do so. He also told him he would be at work gathering all the evidence that he could between now and the trial date of November 15. It would be necessary to support Pinky's contention that he simply borrowed the boat - not that it was stolen. He reassured Pinky somewhat when he said, "This should boil down to a case of you said, he said."

As he was about to depart, Pinky stopped him:

"Do me one more favor, young fella."

"Sure, Mr. McInerney."

"Will you stop by my house and get something for me?"

"Sure, I'll do that, Mr. McInerney. What do you need?"

137

"Near the kitchen sink you should find a couple tins of Copenhagen. Will you get those and bring them to me? My apartment is upstairs at 2153 Glacier Highway. That's one of the Juneau Hydroelectric company houses. The door is unlocked."

"Okay, Mr. McInerney. I'll do that, but I can't get them for you today. I'll pick them up tomorrow on my way back. I'll plan to be here at 10:00 a.m."

"Great, I'll be here, and thanks," replied Pinky.

"Oh, and one more thing, Mr. McInerney. If, as you say, there have been times that you did fish David Royce's boat alone, were there any fishermen who saw you doing it?"

"Sure there was, and I can give you some names. There was Serafino Rio, Babe Gorman, and Christopher ...... somebody. I can't think of his last name. Maybe when you come back tomorrow I'll have remembered."

"Good, I'll see you tomorrow. Maybe you can come up with some more names by then. If you write them down for me, that will help. If you can remember the names of their boats, that would also help."

So, Pinky waited. While he enjoyed many sober days with good food and a comfortable bed in the Lemon Creek facility he wondered and waited to hear what the FBI had found. He feared that considerably more than the accusation about the fishing violations and the theft of David Royce's boat. If they found the rifle where he had dumped it and if they really did have a photo of him throwing it overboard he could be in serious trouble. "In that case, this young kid just out of law school better get me some big time help," he said to himself.

TWENTY-FIVE

THE WAITING

While the Juneau police were doing their best with what little they had to build a case against Mary Franz's killer, Rex was busy trying to prevent real evidence from being found that might implicate him in the second shooting. He felt certain that he was already home free on the first one. He waited for the right circumstances that would allow him to carry out the next part of his plan.

On another rainy and windy night (again with the hope that most people were indoors) he departed Upper Salmon heading for Auke Bay. This time he carried a piece of steel wool that he intended to use to remove the smudge of orange paint that Pete Tyler had seen on the side of his boat. He considered having the damage repaired professionally but then reconsidered based on the first item he had written on his checklist – 'AROUSE NO SUSPICION.'

Rex reached the side of his boat without being observed and using the steel wool he rubbed away the orange paint from the damaged area as best he could. He then headed back toward home feeling secure that he had tied up another loose end. While he wasn't seen that night, the following morning Pete Tyler noticed the attempted cleanup when he happened to walk by Rex's boat.

Upon seeing that the orange smudge was gone from the side of its gunwale, he chuckled to himself, "I'll needle Rex about it the next time I see him." Pete didn't know it, but he was about to wake a sleeping tiger.

While Pinky waited in his Lemon Creek jail cell, so did Fred Wolters wait in his office in the Federal Building. He felt certain that his people back east would soon return the evidence to him with a positive report of their matching of the rifle to the bullets that killed Fish and Wildlife Officer Hutchison.

As Pinky and Wolters waited, so did a few others. John Santori was waiting for Denny and Sue to return from their vacation so he could find out exactly what was recovered out at Swanson Harbor. Rex Franz returned from Auke Bay and was back at work. He waited for midnight and his relief to show up so he could go to sleep.

Pete Tyler was waiting to see Rex again because he wanted to ask him more about what happened to the side of his boat. In the meantime, however, he was waiting for his friend at Fish and Wildlife to return his call. He wanted to know more of the details about the shooting in Glacier Bay. He was especially interested to know if the zodiac the slain officer had been piloting had sustained any damage to its bow, and whether it was of the type that are painted orange. The thought of blackmail actually entered his thinking, but first he felt he needed more incriminating evidence.

Rex, meanwhile, thought about starting another checklist, and Pete Tyler was the single objective of that list. If he did go to hunt mushrooms with the man and Tyler again started questioning him about anything having to do with Glacier Bay or the shooting, or anything more about the damage to his boat, Rex felt that Tyler might need to be eliminated. If so, he already knew how he would accomplish it.

This one would not be near as complicated as the first one. If Pete Tyler made no more mention of his suspicions about the event at Glacier Bay, Rex considered discarding the checklist idea. If Tyler persisted he would act and deep down he almost welcomed it. He was now so far into the abyss that he was actually starting to like what he was doing.

Liz started work full time as hygienist in Doctor Gustafson's office on Monday, August 7, and she was waiting for her first patient of the day. The week before, when Denny and Sue returned from their short vacation, the doctor called Liz asking if she could start that very day. He said that his temporary help was flying south because of family problems, and he needed Liz's help immediately. When John heard that it was Denny she was talking to he quickly asked her to let him have the phone. He asked Denny, "Well, what did you find at Swanson Harbor?"

"We recovered a Winchester .30-06 rifle with scope but that's all I can tell you," he replied. "The Coast Guard guys thanked me and then took off like scared rabbits." When John questioned if Denny was kidding, the reply was, "No, they wanted to get the rifle back to Juneau as soon as possible and they didn't stick around to explain. I think it might be connected in some way to that shooting out in Glacier Bay last week. If it is they probably wanted to send it and any other evidence they have back to FBI headquarters in D.C., or Quantico. That's all I can tell you, John. Why are you interested?"

John replied honestly that he was involved in an investigation that might involve a .30-06 rifle, but he did not explain further. He promised to fill the good dentist in with all the details at a later date. After a few more pleasantries back and forth, their conversation ended.

After only a few days as the new and permanent hygienist in Denny Gustafson's dental offices, Liz was enjoying the new direction in her life. She was more than happy that she had accepted Denny's offer to join his staff. One of her first patients that next Thursday morning was a most unlikely one. It was Fred Wolters, the local FBI Agent.

She knew who he was, but he didn't know her. She introduced herself only by her first name and made only small talk. She cleaned and polished his teeth and then went on to her next patient while Denny took over her chair to more closely inspect Fred's teeth and gums.

While he worked, Denny was discussing more meaty subjects with the Agent. Liz did her best to hear what they were saying even though they were in the other room. Her patient was a gabby little old lady, so she quickly started to scrape away on the woman's heavy tartar buildup hoping to keep her silent. Unfortunately, Liz heard only pieces of the conversation. One piece was something about the rifle possibly having been attached to a board. The other little bit she was able to remember hearing was that they had the shooter in jail charged with stealing a boat.

All of this she told John over dinner that evening. Needless to say, that bit of news made his day. He later told Liz that this had been one of his most enjoyable dinners in quite a while.

"I don't see how you can get so excited over leftovers," was her reply.

TWENTY-SIX

THE INTERVIEW

The following morning, bright and early, John was at the Lemon Creek jail. He was still in his civilian clothes, having come direct from home to the jail. As a courtesy they allowed him to interview Pinky McInerney - just the two of them in a private room. John was wearing a hidden recording device, but he didn't volunteer that to Pinky. When the big Irishman was ushered into the room his eyes lit up and he had a big smile on his face. His first words were, "You're from the Government and you're here to help me!"

John didn't laugh. "No, I'm not with the Federal Government. I'm with the Juneau Police Department, and you darn well know that. It was a few years ago when you took over for me at Upper Salmon that we first met. And, I thought we understood each other."

"No, I know who you are, John, and I do appreciate you being here especially if you can help me."

"Well, Pinky, maybe I can help you, that is if you stop with the wise cracks and if you don't try to blow smoke up my ass."

Pinky got serious – he could tell John wasn't in a joking mood.

"No, John, I am truly glad that you're here; and I am sorry for wising off. But, really, how can you possibly help me? There's a helluva lot of big brass out there that you'd have to climb over if you did want to help me."

"Why don't we just start from the beginning and we'll see."

"OK, what do you want to know?"

"Well, first of all, did you shoot the guy?"

"No. Hell no."

"They say you threw a rifle in the water just before they boarded you."

"Let em say that. They have no proof."

"I've heard otherwise. Regardless, why don't you start by telling me exactly how it went down. If you want, you're welcome to check me for a wire. Like I said, I'm here to help you, but I need you to help me, too. And, since I swear to you that I do want to help you because I honestly believe you're innocent, would you even care if I did tape this conversation?"

"No, I don't care and no use to check you. Even if you've got a wire, you can't do me much more harm than I already got."

"If what you tell me is gospel truth, then it would probably be of benefit to have it on record."

"Probably. What do you want to know?"

"Were you fishing in or near Glacier Bay?"

"No, I was east of Gustavus in Icy Pass."

"Where were you when you got stopped by the Coast Guard?"

"Just west of Swanson Harbor."

"Were you alone in your boat?"

"Yeah, but it wasn't my boat."

"Who does it belong to and how did you come to be fishing the vessel?"

"It belongs to my friend, David Royce. I sure hope he's my friend because they say I stole the boat."

"Did you?"

"No. We were drinking at his place. He has a trailer near where I used to live on Thane Road. We were drinking and talking. I guess we had a little too much to drink, and he passed out."

"Did you take his keys to the boat while he was passed out?"

"Well, yeah, but he said earlier before he passed out that it was o.k. to borrow the boat."

"You're sure?"

"Real sure. Regardless, that's my story and I'm gonna stick to it."

"Yes, you better stick to it because, as flimsy as it is, that's all you've got."

"Well, he's let me fish it alone in the past."

"Maybe so, but, if he should say he didn't give you permission this last time, then what do you say?"

"I'd have to stick to my story, I guess. What else do you want to know? I mean about the shooting of the Fed?"

"I want to hear how it went down. See, I'm inclined to think someone else shot him, but I need you to help me prove it."

"Who?"

"Just tell me what happened and this time be completely truthful. I've been had by experts, Pinky, so I can usually tell when I'm being conned. Where did you get the rifle?"

"Well, John, I sure hope you're on the square with me because that not yet dry-behind-the-ears lawyer the court assigned to me ain't gonna do me much good."

"If you trust me, then I'm going to trust you by telling you what I think. Then, if I hit it pretty close to right, I want you to fill me in with the rest, and truthfully."

"OK, shoot. I mean go ahead."

"First, I believe the brass when they say they saw you throw a rifle overboard. I also think that the rifle was attached to something."

"God, I hope you really do want to help me, John. I'm putting my life in your hands when I tell you this. Yeah, it was bolted on to a board."

"Where did you get it?"

"It was in a plastic bag. I must have hooked it while I was trolling on the bottom."

"What kind of bag?"

"One of those big black garbage bags."

"You were trolling on the bottom?"

"Yeah."

"You always troll on the bottom? You can get hung up there."

"Yeah, but in that spot its almost all sandy bottom. Anyhow the big fish are usually on the bottom so I decided to try it. And, as I'm pulling in one line and tossing a salmon in the hold here comes this plastic bag on one of the other lines."

"What did you do then?"

145

"Well, I baited up the line and winched it back down. I just threw the bag aside."

"Then what?"

"I kept fishing – really nailing some nice salmon. When the tide turned I did too. I started trolling toward Juneau."

"Did you see any other boats around when you were fishing and, later, when you were pulling in your lines?"

"No. Not a soul - just the fog and me. There could have been somebody else around but I didn't see or hear anybody. Oh, I saw a Coast Guard chopper later. He went right over the boat heading into Bartlett Cove. So, I got out of there fast."

"Why fast?"

"Well, I heard some talk on the radio about some Feds being brought in there, and I figured it might have something to do with the rifle?"

"The rifle?"

"Yeah, when I first pulled the bag off the hooks I could see the barrel of a gun sticking out. If that's what they were there for, and I had it, then I was gonna head for Juneau and fast."

"If you were worried about the gun, why didn't you throw it back in the water right away?"

"I don't know. I just thought I might have found myself a nice new rifle with scope and I sure didn't want to let go of it if I didn't have to. Somebody stole my rifle four or five years ago. So, I thought I might be getting even. I didn't even have a chance to see everything that was in the bag. Hell, for a while there, I thought maybe some other stuff like cash might even be inside."

"How did you know it had a scope on it if it was all wrapped up in the plastic bag?"

"I could feel the outline of the rifle and the scope through the plastic. I didn't have time then to unwrap it. I was busy catching salmon."

"Just when did you unwrap the plastic bag and how was it wrapped?"

"It was wrapped around this board and it was taped closed with duct tape. Everything was inside the bag. Maybe six inches or so of the barrel and a few inches of the board was stickin' out of the bag."

"When did you unwrap it?"

"I did it a little bit at a time as I was heading east in Icy Strait. I didn't want to stop to do it. So, in between steering the boat and looking where I was going, I started to unwrap it. Whoever threw the bag in the water never wanted it to be found or to come apart in the water."

"Why do you say that?"

"Well, whoever threw it overboard used two bags. There was a rock in the inner bag to help make it sink. The rock had a bunch of string wrapped around it, and the bag was taped real good – way more than was needed."

"What else was in the bag?"

"Nuthin much else of interest."

"I'm interested. What else was in the bag?"

"I really didn't see everything that was in it. There was the board that the rifle was attached to, and an extra U-bolt."

"It was loose? By itself? The U-bolt?"

"Yeah."

"You said the rifle was attached to a board?"

"Yeah, with two U-bolts - a bigger U-bolt was around the stock and a smaller one held the barrel."

"When you finally threw the rifle in the water, was it still attached to the board?"

"No. I took off the big U-bolt and then slipped the barrel back out of the little one. I wanted to get a close look to all sides of the weapon, and I wanted to look through the scope. It kind of looked like my rifle that was stolen years ago in Spokane."

"What did you do with the board?"

"I just laid it down on the deck. The Coasties took all that stuff with them – the board, the bag, the U-bolts, everything. Oh, and I remember there was a hammer and some nails in the bag, too. That's all I remember."

"Was the board rectangular?"

"No, a triangular piece was cut off the end near the stock."

Those were the magic words that John wanted to hear. It was now almost a certainty that the board Pinky had pulled out of the deep would match the piece he had photographed in the locker at Upper Salmon. So, he said, "Well, Pinky, the Feds or Fish and Game or somebody might get you for stealing the boat but, hopefully, I can now help get you off the hook on the shooting."

"Well, if you can help me with the shooting part, I hope you can help about the boat, too."

"Pinky, I promise you, I'll do my best. First, however, you shouldn't do a lot of talking to your fellow prisoners here at Lemon Creek. Talk only to your attorney. He might be young, but he is on your side and he will do all he can to help you."

Their conversation ended there and Pinky was returned to his cell. John, instead, almost floated out of the jail. He was really on a high. It was all coming around, but would it be enough? He still had to somehow connect Rex to the Glacier Bay shooting.

If the FBI could prove that the subject rifle was used to shoot the wildlife officer, then they might also be able to prove that it first shot Mary. Since JPD had in their hands the bullet that killed Mary it might be that the FBI would be willing to share their evidence.

He knew for sure that it would be necessary for JPD to now work with the FBI to coordinate their efforts, but would they be willing to work with JPD? History showed that they were not noted for doing that.

TWENTY-SEVEN

THE CONSULTATION

Once back at JPD, Santori telephoned Fred Wolters and told him he had something important to talk to him about. He was pleasantly surprised when Fred said, "Come on over now." Needless to say, he didn't waste any time getting there.

As he was being ushered inside Fred's office, he asked his host if he would close his door so they could have a private chat. After shaking hands and exchanging pleasantries, John got down to business, saying, "Fred, I'm here to talk to you about the shooting out in Glacier Bay."

"Oh?"

"I assume you sent the rifle and all the other evidence to your people back East?"

"Yes. I got a phone call this morning before you phoned. They matched the two slugs to the rifle. So, we have the shooter. The evidence package is on its way back, and I already have a call into the U.S. Attorney in Anchorage. We'll want him in on this to start the necessary proceedings."

"That's why I'm here, Fred. I don't think you do have the shooter."

"Oh?"

"If you'd be willing to work with us and share your evidence with us same as we are willing to share ours with you folks, I believe you will conclude that someone else was the shooter."

"What makes you think that, John? Where are you getting your information?"

"Let's just say that I've been working on this for longer than you have."

"Perhaps, but what we have is pretty conclusive."

"Well, I think what I have is pretty conclusive, too. In fact, I feel confident that I can prove that the rifle you have was used to kill Mary Franz here in Juneau weeks before the Fish and Wildlife Officer was killed."

"How can you prove that, John?"

"Before I answer that, Fred, will you agree to tell me what you have in the way of evidence, and will you work with us on this?"

"Well, I won't say yea or nay right now but I can tell you that the serial number on the rifle has been traced back to the original owner."

"And, who is that?"

"Aloysius P. McInerney."

"You've got be kidding?"

"I'm not kidding, John. So, now, what do you have?"

"Right now I have a terrible headache and a real hurt in my gut."

"Yeah, I thought that might startle you a bit."

"Well, what I do have is the slug that killed Mary Franz. However, I might have to change course because you now make it look like McInerney killed both people."

"I'm not too knowledgeable about the Mary Franz shooting or any of the events leading up to it. However, if that slug did come from the same rifle then I do agree that Pinky appears to be the shooter of both people. He was working in the area near where she was killed wasn't he? I am told that there was bad blood between McInerney and Rex Franz. He might have been trying to shoot Rex, and instead got his wife."

"I don't know, Fred."

"Well, you must admit it hangs together pretty darn good."

"Yes, I'll grant you that."

"He was also found in the area where the Fish and Wildlife Officer was killed. So, if you suspect another person is the shooter of these two people, can you also place him at both places?"

"No, not right now, but believe me I'm going to be working on it a lot harder. First, however, will you send this slug off to Washington to see if it matches the other two? Secondly, when the evidence package gets back here, will you let me have the board for a few days? I feel confident that I can show you how it was involved in Mary's killing."

"So, you have some additional evidence?"

"Yes, Fred, I do. However, there is no use talking about it now. By the time you get the slug matched to the other two I hope to have some more to talk to you about. So, how about we meet again as soon as you hear back from Washington?"

"Ok, John, let's leave it at that. I'll call you when I get the board back and when I hear about the slug."

They parted company, and John walked out of the FBI office with considerably less bounce than he had when he walked in. Earlier, he thought he was on a path that would show that Rex had killed his wife. Now, he not only had to prove him guilty, but he had to prove Pinky was innocent. To suggest that one person killed Mary and another killed the Fish and Wildlife Officer all with the same weapon would be very difficult to prove. Absolving Pinky of any blame in either murder would be an almost impossible task, especially since it was Pinky's own rifle that probably killed both people. Either scenario seemed untenable.

He commiserated about his bad fortune the rest of the afternoon, and his bad mood carried on all the way to the dinner table. Just before sitting down, he saw what was being served. His comment was, "Leftovers again?"

Liz didn't even reply. She simply shook her head and muttered to herself, "I can't believe this man."

TWENTY-EIGHT

MUSHROOM HUNTING

On August 18, just after completing his day shift, Rex Franz received a phone call from Pete Tyler offering to take him mushroom hunting. "Sounds great," replied Rex. He really had very little alternative. To refuse might create suspicion. "Where are we heading, and when?"

"Over to Young Bay on Admiralty. There's a big stand of Hemlock in a spot where I've always had good luck finding Boletus. I realize it might be a little early for the King Boletus, but we should find plenty of the Rough-Stemmed Boletus this time of year."

"Good," replied Rex, "We can look for the Chicken of the Woods as well. They probably grow well in that area, too."

Pete then asked, "How about Monday? We can go in my boat. It's got radar in case we get into any fog. You know where it is, stall 7, the 'Tyler Two.' It's a Uniflite with blue trim."

Rex answered, "Yes, sounds real good, I'll be at your boat there at about 9:00 a.m., Monday." Then, as an afterthought, Rex asked if he should bring a lunch.

"No, no need. I'll have a cooler with lunch, and some beer," Pete replied.

Once he was off the phone, Rex unloosened his belt and removed the checklist. He added "METAL RAKE FOR TYLER," and he smiled as he replaced the list back in its hiding place in his belt.

On Monday morning he gathered together two plastic pails, two paper bags, and two pocketknives. From the bunch of old gardening tools he found the small hand rake that had nothing to do with mushroom hunting but would suit his purpose if the situation called for it. As he got ready to depart for Auke Bay he thought about how that situation might arise and how he would deal with it. By the time he rode his bike out to the penstock, parked it inside, and walked down the steps to his car, he was ready for any eventuality.

He met Pete Tyler by the side of his 36-foot Uniflite and commented about the size of the boat and all its accessories, "Well, we're sure going to travel in style today. All I got is that little 22 foot Bayliner."

As they started loading their gear aboard, Pete answered, "Hell, if I had your money I'd get rid of that slab of yours and I'd buy me a new 50 foot Grand Banks or even a bigger Princess."

"How do you know if I have any money?" asked Rex.

"I've got my spies," laughed Pete.

The sleeping tiger started to stir.

As Rex was loading the cooler full of beer and a lunch on to Tyler's boat he noticed that the man had a side arm holstered to his side. "So," he said, "I see you brought a weapon. Good thinking. That's real bear country over there and I forgot to bring my 16 gauge with the buckshot, but it's just as well. It's a nuisance to carry. Your weapon – it looks like a '45 - will only be good up close, though. So, if we meet a big fella, you fight him off while I run for help." They both laughed loudly.

Once underway, Tyler started his questioning again. Rex now knew the fat was in the fire. Pete started it with, "I see you got rid of the orange paint off the side of your boat."

"Yeah," answered Rex. "I commissioned some kid to clean it and patch it, but I don't know if he got it done. I haven't heard from him wanting to get paid so I assume he isn't finished yet."

Rex was able to divert the conversation away from this sore subject when, luckily, a whale surfaced in front of them. Seeing one of those huge mammals up close will interrupt just about any conversation. So, for the next few minutes the talk shifted to whales. Later, they noticed five or six porpoise racing alongside the bow of the boat and this further distracted Tyler and his questions. It was only as they were approaching shore within Young Bay that the subject came up again. Then, Pete Tyler came across with a real eye opener, "A friend of mine at Fish and Wildlife told me that the zodiac the Fed was piloting when he got shot appears to have been in a collision. You know, Rex, those zodiac bows are usually orange."

"So, what are you getting at, Pete? Damn, if you aren't starting to sound like a detective. Hey, aren't you getting too close to shore here?"

"No, I've been here before. But go ahead - drop the anchor off the bow. We can take the skiff in from here."

As Pete got into the skiff, Rex handed down the buckets each with a paper bag and a small knife in it. He had the hand rake handle tucked into the front of his Levis and his loose fitting jacket hid the claws of the tool sticking out above his belt. He now intended to use it. There was no longer any question in his mind.

No other boats were in the area and as the skiff touched the shore Rex felt certain they were the only humans around. Pete pulled the skiff onto shore and helped steady Rex as he too scrambled onto dry land. They both dragged it above high tide line, and then walked into the trees to start their search.

As they walked, Pete in front didn't notice that Rex picked up a large rock and placed it in his bucket. As they walked and searched, Pete started in on another just as troubling piece of conversation: "You know, I've been thinking of expanding the marina out into deeper water. My property extends out far enough so I could add at least one hundred more stalls, but I just don't have the cash to do it right now. Up on shore I'd like to build a condominium complex as well. I've got the room for that, too. How about coming in with me?"

Rex paused, and then answered, "So, you're looking for a partner with money?" As he asked this last question, Rex was already concluding that what Tyler really wanted was an influx of money from somebody that he would never have to repay.

"Yeah, I'd still want to run the marina but ..."

He never finished his proposition because just then Rex saw a beautiful yellow and orange spread of Chicken of the Woods straight ahead of them and he yelled out, "Look at that."

As they were prone to do, these colorful fungi almost surrounded an old stump and they really were a sight to behold.

Even the bright red-capped poisonous Amanita Muscaria with its white dots on top pales in comparison. There is little in the woods so bright and beautiful. Rex warned Pete, "Don't pull them up. Cut them at the base with your knife so their spores will still be in the ground and in the stump. That way they'll reproduce again next year."

So, with bucket in one hand and knife in the other Pete bent down to harvest the feast. He never saw the rock in Rex's hand and when he did sense something coming at him it was too late. Rex made sure to aim for the man's temple and he did it with tremendous force and pinpoint accuracy.

The blow knocked Pete Tyler to the ground and as he lay there unconscious Rex applied the tines of the hand rake across the man's face, from behind his ear, deep along his cheek, and all the way to his chin. The intent was to make it appear that Tyler had been attacked by a bear. He did it well. The wound was very convincing. Later, during the coroner's inquest, it would bolster the initial ruling that the cause of death was a bear mauling.

Rex had read much of his Mayo Clinic book, especially the chapter on intracranial hematoma. So, he was well prepared. A hard blow to the temple area of the skull can cause internal bleeding between the skull and the brain if a vein or artery is ruptured. Blood then seeps into that space which will cause compression of the brain tissue with resulting progressive lethargy, and then a lapse into unconsciousness. Death would soon follow if Tyler weren't treated immediately.

Rex made sure that treatment would not be forthcoming any time soon. The rock to Tyler's temple crushed his skull causing severe damage to the brain. The bone shards in his brain coupled with the blood seepage made for a short unconscious state and a more rapid death. Rex waited until he was sure Tyler was dead. Then he took off the baseball cap he was wearing and used it as a glove to remove the '45 from Tyler's holster. He dropped the weapon on the ground near the victim, feeling that the authorities would conclude that he tried to use it before being mauled by the bear.

Rex again donned his cap, picked up the rock and the hand rake, and proceeded to row the skiff back toward Tyler's boat. He rowed past the boat, however, into deeper water and threw the rock and the rake overboard. He then returned to the bigger boat, climbed aboard, and made a frantic sounding mayday call. Upon receiving the call, the Coast Guard dispatched their helicopter to Young Bay. They first arranged for a doctor from the Bartlett Hospital Emergency Room to accompany them. An Alaska State Trooper was also on board when the chopper landed on the beach near where Rex stood next to the beached skiff.

There was no need for medical assistance for Pete Tyler. The doctor quickly determined that the man was dead and the cause was obvious. The side of his head showed clearly that he had been struck a mortal blow and the claw marks solidified everyone's conclusion that this was in fact a bear attack.

The Trooper took pictures of the scene. He and Rex then gathered the remaining gear and placed it in the skiff. The crew of the helicopter carried the body to their chopper and departed along with the doctor to deliver Pete Tyler to Bartlett. Rex and the Trooper checked the area again and then rowed out to the Uniflite to head back to Auke Bay.

While Rex piloted the boat the trooper questioned him about the incident and made notes of the entire conversation. There was not much to write about because Rex explained that he and Pete had separated during their mushroom hunting. He said that he heard him yell and that he went running toward the sound of distress. He added that he came upon the bear hovering over the prone man. "I yelled out as loud as I could a bunch of swear words and threw my bucket at him. Fortunately, all of that scared him away. I kept yelling louder and louder hoping it would discourage him from coming back. I guess it worked because he didn't return. I laid Pete on his back and tried to help him, but I'm no doctor. So, I took the skiff out to his boat and called in the mayday."

When Rex and the Trooper pulled into Auke Bay and headed for Pete Tyler's stall they saw that Percy Weisenburger was waiting for them. He said that he had heard about the mauling on the radio in the marina office.

They handed the boat keys to Percy, answered a few of his questions, and then walked toward their respective automobiles. The Trooper asked Rex to follow him to the Alaska Department of Public Safety headquarters in town. He explained that he wanted to get Rex's account down on paper together with both of their signatures.

A few hours after Pete Tyler met his death the phone rang in Fred Wolters' office. It was Fish and Wildlife Juneau Field Office Chief Robert Gerdes:

"Fred, this is Bob Gerdes."

"Yes, Bob, what's up?"

"Well, quite a bit. First, the other day one of my guys gets a phone call from Pete Tyler who owns the marina out at Auke Bay."

"Yes, I know who he is."

"Well, it seems Tyler was nosing around for info on the shooting of our fella at Glacier Bay. He asked a few questions."

"What kind of questions?"

"First question was whether the officer's craft had been damaged. Second question was whether any part of it was painted orange."

"Well, that could well make you suspect that he knew something."

"Of course. Unfortunately, it seems Tyler didn't give any information back. He just asked those two questions and that was it. What's disturbing is that I just got off the phone with Mel Lonard and he told me they got a mayday call a few minutes ago from a guy out at Young Bay who was mushroom hunting with Tyler. He says Tyler is dead - killed by a grizzly."

"My God, that's terrible. Naturally, it's a shame he's dead but it's also too bad we'll never be able to find out what caused him to ask those questions of your guy. He probably had some evidence that might have incriminated someone other than McInerney."

157

"I agree Fred. So, I asked Lonard to have his people double-check the hull of that fishing vessel they confiscated to see if it has any damage or orange paint on it. If it doesn't, then that would strengthen the suspicion that some other boat was involved and that Tyler might have known whose boat it was. Lonard is going to call me back."

"Let me know what he finds, if anything, Bob."

"I will."

This news was a real shock to the FBI Agent. He now concluded that John Santori might be on to something, and this latest happening could somehow be connected.

When John heard the news of the mauling he was sitting in Chief Parker's office. They were both shocked and surprised. It wasn't so much that a prominent local marina owner had been killed by a bear, but rather that Rex Franz was there during the attack. As they sat there puzzling over the latest event, the Chief commented, "Everywhere that guy goes, death seems to follow."

TWENTY-NINE

THE PUZZLING QUESTIONS

That night, as John tried to sleep, he kept going over and over in his mind the last two killings and how Rex could have accomplished each one. It was evident to him that Rex killed Mary and then later tried to get rid of the evidence. These last two people must have gotten in his way and suffered the ultimate consequence. Perhaps he had attempted to get rid of the evidence in Glacier Bay and was intercepted by the Fish and Wildlife Officer. But, why go all the way to Glacier Bay? Perhaps Pete Tyler found out something. What could Tyler have known about Mary's killing? Very little. What could he have known about the shooting near Glacier Bay? Well, if Rex dumped the plastic bag and the rifle near Glacier Bay, he had to have done it with his boat. So, did Tyler know something about either the boat or its voyage? All of this kept John awake for too many hours.

He was in a bad mood when the alarm went off the next morning. Liz took the brunt of it and hit back, "Don't be grouchy with me, Mister. If you will remember, I'm on your side."

He apologized, hugged her, told her she was right, and further that she was the most important thing in his life. He offered to take her out to dinner to the Summit Hotel (one of the few places in town with fine dining and linen table cloths) to make up for his outburst. She accepted with a small, but satisfied, smile. That evening they enjoyed the intimate dinner at the Summit, and as they were savoring the meal, the mood, and their after dinner drinks he suggested that they should perhaps get out of town for a few days:

"How about we fly out to Gustavus and stay at the Inn?"

"I don't want to look a gift horse in the mouth, John, but why Gustavus?"

"Well, first, so that we can at least spend a little bit of quality time together. Second, maybe I can think out my work problems in that quieter setting. If the weather is nice while we're there maybe we can even rent some clubs and play some golf on that little nine-hole course. We haven't done that in a long time. Finally, speaking of a long time, if you bring along one of your sexy nighties, maybe we can start on a little brother for Andrew."

"Get that out of your head right now, Mister," was her smiling reply. Except for his last suggestion, Liz agreed to the short sojourn. So, when they returned home John phoned the Gustavus Inn and made reservations for the two of them. He then called Chief Parker. First, he told the Chief that he had yet to enjoy any vacation time since starting at JPD, and he asked if he would authorize a little time off for him. He said that he and Liz were going to spend a few days in Gustavus, returning late Sunday the 27th.

"Hopefully, the evidence will be back from Washington by the time I get back," he told Chief Parker. "Then, when I get my hands on that board I'll go back up the hill to find where it was nailed. This time it should be easier because we now know where to look. We have the line of flight from where the bullet hit Rex to where it finally came to rest in the tree. I'll just line it up in the opposite direction with the surveyor's scope, and that should show me where the rifle was mounted. I'm pretty sure it will be where two trees are close together. Secondly, Chief, can you assign somebody to determine from the Coroner the exact cause of Pete Tyler's death beyond any doubt. The officer has to do it quietly and with absolutely no fanfare. If it was anything other than a bear mauling and Rex was involved I wouldn't want any comments to that effect to somehow get back to him."

"I'll do it myself, John," replied the Chief. "We'll both feel better about it that way. And, John, I hadn't realized you've been so dedicated to your work. Of course, it's all right for you to take some time. You and Liz have a good couple of quality days. Relax and enjoy your off time with her."

"Oh, Chief, one more thing. I sure would like to put a 24-hour tail on Franz. I have a funny feeling that he might up and get out of town before we get to nail him. He's easy to watch during his ten days at Upper Salmon, but he could slip away during these next few days. He should be walking up the steps toward Upper Salmon some time Wednesday in the early afternoon. But, before then he might fly out of here in a small plane into Canada without our knowing it. Then, we'd play hell getting him back."

"Ok, I'll take care of that too, John. You and Liz have a good time in Gustavus. Appears it'll be nice weather at least the rest of today and tomorrow."

He thanked the Chief and then telephoned Chad at Upper Salmon and asked him to phone him when Rex was back at work. He told Chad, "If we're not here just leave a message. And, again, don't say anything to Rex. Avoid him like the plague. What time does he go back to work?"

"He starts back on the swing shift tomorrow. He relieves me. So, I'll phone you from the house when I get there. Better yet, I'll have the door to the plant open so I can keep an eye on the flume. As soon as I see him coming in on his bike, I'll call you."

"Good, Chad, the quicker I know he's up there the better for me. I think I'm gonna take Liz over to Gustavus for a few days. We should be back sometime Sunday afternoon. Call me, though, if anything wild should happen. We'll be at the Inn unless you hear from me to the contrary."

John and Liz were on their way the next morning and they did have a nice few days together. When they returned home from their little adventure there were three calls on their answering machine. The first was from Chad saying that Rex was back at Upper Salmon. The second was from Fred Wolters telling John that the board was back from Washington together with the plastic bag and all its contents. The third was from Chief Parker telling him that he had found something quite interesting at the Coroner's office. When John called him at home the Chief told him that some bits of rust were found in the claw marks on Tyler's face. John's first reaction to that development was that it again pointed directly to Rex: "Looks like our boy might have had his hand in this one too, huh, Chief?"

"We'll talk about it when you get to work in the morning," replied the Chief.

John, upon putting down the phone, thought that this new angle would be an interesting one to explore further. Almost for sure it seemed to him that a thorough search, especially during a real low tide, of the waters near where the two men had anchored in Young Bay would probably turn up still another murder weapon - probably a metal hand rake or something similar. For now, however, he had two chores to take care of yet this Sunday afternoon. He was going to Tyler's Marina to talk to the people there and then he would look at Rex's boat.

Pete Tyler had been widowed for almost ten years and had not remarried. He lived alone in his apartment above Tony's Deli. His office was on the same floor but separate from his apartment, and each had their own entrance. His assistant, Percy Weisenburger, had been working at the marina even before Tyler purchased the facility. When John entered the office, Percy was sitting at Tyler's desk.

John first expressed his condolences. Since he was not in his police uniform he took out his badge and identification and introduced himself, "I'm John Santori with the Juneau Police Department. Chief Parker asked me to see what I could find out about Pete's recent conversations. I'm especially interested in his recent telephone call that he had with a man at Fish and Wildlife."

"I'm sorry, but I didn't hear him having any such conversation. I'm usually down on the marina or at the gasoline dock."

"Have you heard him having any conversations with anyone lately that had anything to do with anything other than the business of the marina?"

"No."

"Did you know he was going to go mushroom hunting Monday?"

"Yes, he told me he would be gone most of the morning. He said he was going in his boat and he was taking Rex Franz with him. He has a Bayliner moored here."

"What stall number?"

"Let me get the book and I'll check. Here it is. Stall 32. Yes, I remember this guy. He hadn't paid his stall rental in a couple of months and Pete had me prepare a notice of eviction."

"Did you serve it?"

"No, Pete took care of it. He went down to post it on the man's boat and the guy was down there asleep in his boat."

"What day was that?"

"It was a couple of weeks ago."

"Do you remember the exact day?"

"No, I don't. Just that the guy had come up to the office and paid his bill up to date."

"Would your records show when he paid it?"

"Yes, but the accountant has the books at home, and I think she's out of town."

John handed Percy his business card and said, "Can you check with her when she gets back, and call me at the station?"

"Sure, I'll do that."

"Did Pete say anything else?"

"No, except Pete asked me if I knew what color the buoy out in front of Tee Harbor was painted. I don't know what the hell that had to do with anything."

"Did you ask him?"

"No, a customer came in then, and I went back down to the marina."

"Anything else you can tell me that you thought was strange in the last week or two?"

"No."

As John left the marina office, He also asked Percy to not mention their conversation to anyone. The man promised to keep quiet as requested.

John walked down to the docks where he found stall 32 and Rex's Bayliner. It was tied snug to the dock and he right away saw a dent in the starboard side. He leaned down to more closely inspect the damage and noticed that a small area within the dent had been scraped or sanded down below the original yellow paint of the hull.

If Pete Tyler telephoned someone at Fish and Wildlife to determine if the slain officer's zodiac appeared to have been in a collision, then maybe the dent in Rex's boat might have something to do with it. If Pete also asked about the zodiac's color, then maybe the scraping inside the dent had something to do with that, too. Maybe Pete Tyler noticed a bit of orange paint inside that dent and asked Rex about it when he woke him that day. It was wild speculation, but it could have gone down just that way.

To carry that theory a bit further, one might then conclude that Rex would have been concerned enough to want to clean that orange paint from his boat. Hopefully, a small speck of that paint or at least some of the scraping might still be on the side of the hull or possibly on the dock alongside the boat. "You should be so lucky," he thought, "that just a little bit of dust might still be around." With that hope in mind he walked up to the pay phones outside the Deli and called the JPD dispatcher telling her what he needed and where to deliver it.

Thirty minutes later, as he sat on a bench outside the Deli, a patrol car drove up and the officer inside handed him a paper bag that could have passed as John's lunch. Instead, he now had a box of glass slides, a roll of clear scotch tape, and a camera.

With the goodies in hand, he went back to the side of Rex's boat. He first went aboard the boat and took a couple of pictures. Then, he took several photos of the boat's dented starboard gunwale. He also collected every bit of debris that he could find on the dock adjacent to and on either side of the damaged area and he did the same to the entire dented area itself. He did that by using the scotch tape as the collector and affixing that piece of tape to a glass slide. He was hopeful that one or more of those slides would help him to finally nail Rex Franz. He collected more than twenty slides of something or nothing. He would see later what good it did.

From what he was able to see it appeared that the area had been washed down, both on the boat and on the dock to which it was moored. "I guess Rex was really working at covering his tracks," he commented to himself. He was hoping to see specks of dust or even bits of fiberglass from where the damaged gunwale had been sanded. To the naked eye there was none. Hopefully, the FBI's microscopes would find something. The fact that there had been some heavy rains the past two weeks did not help the situation either. If Rex's housecleaning hadn't done the job, perhaps the rains had completed it. Fortunately, John came up with one last important thought. Tiny particles containing some evidence might have found their way into the cracks and crevices of the wooden dock alongside Rex's boat. He took out his pocket knife and dug out a small amount of debris that could well have some of the sanded material. He added that additional small amount of hopeful treasure to one more slide.

After finishing with the slides John gathered up his gear and headed for the ramp leading to the parking lot and his car. As he was about to start walking up the ramp, Percy Weisenburger hollered to him. He caught up with John and gave him some additional information. He said, "I checked our records at the gas dock. That fella Rex Franz used his credit card to fill up the morning of July 26, and then again the next morning. So, Pete must have talked to him on either the 26th or the 27th."

He thanked Percy for the additional news and headed home thinking that it had been a good day. As he drove along Glacier Highway his thoughts were on his friend, Rex Franz, who seemed to be getting a little careless. Hopefully, no one would report to Rex what they saw the man doing by his boat. John's thoughts were also on Pinky. In spite of what he was finding out about Rex, the evidence that Fred Wolters had collected really did not bode well for the Irishman. John felt somewhat reassured, however, in that it was now evident that Rex had used his boat on the day the Fish and Wildlife officer was shot. It was an overnight trip to somewhere – a full tank of gasoline to go to Glacier Bay and back, perhaps. Unfortunately, he still had no proof as to where Rex was that day. He could have gone anywhere besides Glacier Bay. The slides and what could be on them now seemed more critical than ever.

THIRTY

WHAT EVIDENCE?

The next morning John was again in Fred Wolters' office. He handed him the slides and asked him to send them off to his people. At the same time Fred handed him the board that he had been waiting for. He assured Fred that he would return it in a few days. He also told him who his suspect was and what he thought the slides would reveal.

Fred's reply was, "Well, husbands have been known to kill their wives. So, the odds might be in your favor in that regard. However, if that slug you handed me should prove to have come from the same rifle that killed the officer, how can you put the weapon in the hands of the husband out near Glacier Bay? I have proof that my suspect was there. Do you have anything that will prove that your suspect was anywhere near Glacier Bay that night, other than these slides?"

"No, but that doesn't mean that he couldn't have been out there and back to Auke Bay before Pinky was apprehended."

"Another thing, John, and the most damning, is that the officer was shot with a Winchester that was registered to Pinky McInerney, which you already know. In addition, he was seen throwing a similar looking rifle into the waters near where the shooting took place. You probably already know that, too. Finally, and not that it will help either of us or that it has any relevance, we have copy of a Trooper's report of a stolen weapon filed by your suspect."

"Is that right? Well, let me take a wild guess and say that the report was filed just before his wife was shot."

"It was filed July 2nd."

"How about that. She was shot July 9th."

"Let me take another wild guess. It wasn't a Winchester!"

"You're right again, John, but right now it's my suspect that will go to trial, not yours."

166

"In that case, Fred, you would be part of a miscarriage of justice, and I think down deep you agree with me. If the slides show any evidence to connect Rex Franz's boat to the zodiac, then I believe my suspect moves to the front of the line."

"Perhaps so, John"

"There's no perhaps to it, Fred. You know darn well if there is or was any sign of orange paint on Rex's boat, that and the fact that he tried to remove it proves something. Then, if your people can match the slide evidence to the zodiac's bow, we've got him."

"The people at Bartlett Cove are flying over a small piece of the damaged bow, so I'll be sending that to Washington for comparison with anything that might be on the slides. Their report should be back before the end of the week. I'll telephone you as soon as I hear anything. If those slides show evidence that the zodiac did collide with the Bayliner, then I'll reconsider my position."

John thanked Fred, even though he felt the man really didn't want to be on his side, and headed back to the friendly confines of JPD. There he sat down with the Chief and talked about what they had and what they didn't have:

"The thing that still bothers me, Chief, is that they say the rifle is registered in Pinky's name. How do I put the rifle in Rex's hands, if that's true?"

"I think you should go have another talk with Pinky. We need to know exactly what he told the Feds. It might be that he can shed some light on how the rifle found its way here."

John did what the Chief recommended. He visited Pinky again and then he started delving further into the rifle's history. Based on what Pinky told him he was able to contact the man's former insurance carrier in Coeur d'Alene and the authorities in Spokane. Both told him exactly what he wanted to hear. Pinky did, in fact, file a stolen property report with both entities. He later obtained a copy of Rex Franz's stolen property report from the Troopers office in Juneau. That report was almost completely devoid of information. Of course, Rex would want it that way.

Days later John sat in the Chief's office again and went over with him what he had learned. He then laid before the Chief his theory about which stolen property report was the most credible, and why:

"It doesn't seem logical that Pinky would lie to authorities in Spokane and to his insurance agent in order to get a few dollars more for his rifle than if he just tried to sell it in the local newspaper. Secondly, if a person were moving to Alaska he would most likely want to purchase a rifle rather than to sell one. If he, instead, wanted to get some traveling money and keep the rifle at the same time by filing a false stolen property report, that too doesn't seem logical because he would need to wait such a long time to get his money and he would always have to keep the rifle hidden for fear of being found out."

"That sounds plausible," said Chief Parker.

John continued outlining his theory, "He was actively working as a powerhouse operator in Coeur d'Alene during that time. It just doesn't follow that he would lie about the rifle being stolen in order to gain a few extra dollars. He already had a good paying job. Also, until he came to Alaska he had no criminal record of any kind. It was when he got here and started some serious drinking that he got into all kinds of trouble. Even then, it was mostly for being drunk and disorderly. He had a couple arrests for assault but even those weren't major. They were the result of drunken brawls in barrooms. One thing you can say about Pinky, he wasn't selective. He'd fight with anyone. He even bloodied up some Coast Guard SP's down on Franklin Street one time when they tried to take him in."

"Yes, I remember that incident," laughed the Chief.

"I think Rex was lying through his teeth the day he reported his rifle had been stolen. His work application at Juneau Hydroelectric shows he listed his previous residence as Cheney, Washington. That isn't too far from Spokane. His last employment before coming to Alaska was as a sales and repair rep for a photocopy outfit headquartered in Seattle. His territory included Eastern Washington and all of Idaho and Montana. It isn't completely out of the realm of possibility that he either stole that rifle at the rest stop in Spokane or he bought it from someone who did. If he had purchased it legally, there would be a record of it someplace. Most people who buy weapons legally usually register them and some people (like Aloysius) have them covered by insurance with their other personal belongings. Why would Rex report the rifle stolen out at Herbert River Trail? The answer, from my point of view, is that if he intended to kill his wife with it he would want to show well in advance that he no longer had the rifle. Why would Rex lie and say he bought it in Seattle? I think he would want to show its origin as anywhere other than Eastern Washington if he stole it or got it from someone who did steal it."

"Well, John, we agree on that, too."

"Yes, Chief, I realize it's more than a million to one shot that the same rifle could have traded hands just like I've described. Even more unbelievable is that it would float its way into the hands and back out of the hands of Pinky into the deep of Icy Strait via the path that I am proposing. But, it is possible and it better have gone just that way or the D.A. will hang Pinky. That's just what he intends to do, by the way. I told Wolters that they should wait at least until all the avenues are explored. Pinky is in jail, and he isn't going anywhere soon. So, why rush it? Wolters told me they're going o go to the Grand Jury in a few days. It's already in the hands of the District Attorney's office."

At the Chief's suggestion he next wrote on the blackboard what each agency had in the way of evidence, real or suspected:

	(Slug that killed Mary Franz
	(JPD Report on Mary's shooting
	(Flume pictures taken at Mary's shooting
	(John's experimental mount
	(Vise impression from Upper Salmon workshop
JPD	(Picture of contents of gym locker
	(Stolen Property Report from Spokane
	(Insurance Claim filed by Pinky
	(Tape of John's questioning of Pinky on 8-11-72
	(Picture of damage to side of Rex's boat
	(Slides of debris from dock and side of boat

169

(Rifle registration showing Pinky as owner
(Board on which rifle was mounted
(Slugs that killed Fish and Wildlife Officer
FBI (Plastic bags with all their contents: hammer, ammo,
    screw eyes, netting, nails, U-bolt, rock, and string
(Tape of Pinky's questioning on 7-27-72
(Rex Franz's report of his stolen rifle
(David Royce's statement

The Chief agreed with John that almost every item on the FBI side of the board was pretty solid, with the exception of Rex Franz's report concerning his stolen rifle. That is, as far as they were concerned, it was suspect. The average juror would think it was a perfectly honest declaration. On JPD's side of the board they saw that almost everything listed there could pertain to either Pinky or Rex. There was no way to prove that only Rex was in the workshop because both Pinky and Rex had worked at Upper Salmon. How could anyone prove that only Rex was able to build the contraption there? The slug that John recently handed to Fred Wolters would almost certainly be proven to have been fired from the same rifle that killed the Fish and Wildlife Officer, but either man could have used that rifle to kill Mary.

If the slides did not support John's theory (if they had no paint residue on them) he'd have little or nothing with which to connect Rex to the Glacier Bay shooting. It was now looking rather bleak. While his hypothesis of the first killing and the possible need by Rex for the last two sat well with the Chief, still, he had just as many misgivings as John did. Both men sat silently pondering their predicament until the Chief asked, "What about the picture of the inside of the gym locker? Did anything ever come of that?"

"No, Chief, I haven't seen any of those items again. I sure would like to have that scrap piece of wood shown in the picture. I'd bet it would match the bigger piece that Wolters gave me the other day. By the way, I'm going to go back up the hill with that board tomorrow afternoon when Franz is at work. I'll take some pictures once I have it mounted on the trees."

As they talked on they concluded that the only good piece of evidence they really had was the bullet that killed Mary and even that item was suspect because they really couldn't prove for sure who used the subject rifle to fire it. In actuality, even the board that John was sure he could match to nail holes in two trees was suspect because they had to admit, "Pinky could have built the damn contraption."

John's whole theory seemed to be coming apart. When he first walked into Fred Wolters' office back in early August, he felt that Pinky had little to worry about other than a fishing violation and, possibly, cirrhosis of the liver. Now, it didn't look so good. All his evidence was pretty much circumstantial and/or suspect. Some might not even survive the test of admissibility. Fred's report from Washington showed that there was evidence of gunpowder residue on the large board but that, too, would not convict anyone. It still seemed difficult, if not impossible, to put the rifle in Rex's hands at either Glacier Bay or Upper Salmon.

So, John concluded that he had more work to do. First, however, he would go back up to the scene of Mary's shooting with the large piece of sugar pine. He would match the nail holes on the board to those on the two trees and they would go from there.

Later that evening, as he sat in deep thought and moped about his predicament, Liz commented, "I sure will be glad when this case is over. About the only fun times I've had with you these past couple of months were those few short days in Gustavus."

His reply to her was, "If only they had tested Pinky for powder residue when they pulled him over in Icy Strait. They'd have found that he didn't fire a weapon." As she walked into the kitchen, she replied to no one in particular, "If only I had a bedmate instead of a poor man's Sherlock Holmes."

That comment woke him from his ill-directed fixation and sent him hurrying after her into the kitchen. It started with a lot of kissy-face and it got better from there. It was his way of apologizing. He felt it was the least he could do.

THIRTY-ONE

THE INCRIMINATING EVIDENCE

A few weeks after Pete Tyler's mauling death, Rex telephoned a boat repair shop near Auke Bay and made an appointment to meet the shop owner that afternoon at stall 32 of the marina. As they stood by the side of his boat, Rex told the man that he wanted him to repair the damaged gunwale. They haggled and then settled on a price to be paid for the repairs. The keys to the boat were handed over and it was agreed that once the repaired vessel was back in its stall Rex would be called to come by to pick up the keys and to make payment.

As the two men talked, Rex leaned on the boat. His fingers happened to touch the inside of the boat pole holder that was built into the top of the gunwale, and he felt something foreign. He looked down inside and was surprised to see the shell casing that he had frantically searched for that night near Glacier Bay. Instead of being ejected into the water he had instead made a ringer into that small opening.

Without the other man noticing, Rex palmed the empty cartridge and then slipped it into his jacket pocket. Later, as he drove back toward Salmon Creek he commented to himself, "I know just where to deposit this little item and when I do I'll have taken care of still another thing on my checklist."

As always seems to happen, and in spite of the FBI's attempts at complete secrecy about any ongoing investigation, information will occasionally leak to the press. So it happened that Rex, while reading his evening newspaper from the night before, noticed the article about the recent incarceration of Aloysius McInerney and his upcoming trial. It talked about his being charged with theft of a fishing vessel and for not having a current salmon-trolling permit.

Rex smiled as he read the account. He was especially pleased when he saw in the same article mention of the slaying of the Fish and Wildlife officer near Glacier Bay. The reporter did not attempt to tie the two incidents together but did make mention that both occurred in the same area.

"Aha, this might be my chance to help the authorities find the killer of the officer," Rex laughed to himself. "You just sit there in that jail cell, Aloysius. I'll be out here helping you as much as I can."

The next morning, just after 9:00 a.m., the telephone startled Rex. This was one telephone call he never expected to receive. It almost threw him for a loop but he handled it quite well by feigning sleep.

"Mr. Franz, this is Trooper Ingersoll. I hope I didn't wake you."

"As a matter of fact you did, but what can I do for you."

"I'm sorry, Sir."

"No problem. What do you need?"

"Well, you reported your rifle stolen?"

"Yes, I did."

"Well, Sir, we have a rifle down here that we'd like you to look at."

"Where did you find it?"

"It was confiscated from a stolen fishing vessel. Could you come down to our office to see if you can identify it?"

"Sure. You say you have it there?"

"Yes, Sir."

"You're there on Whittier?"

"Yes, Sir. When you come in, please ask for me, George Ingersoll."

"Aren't you the fella that wrote up the report back in June or July?"

"Yes, Sir. It was July 2nd."

"Ok. I'll be there sometime this morning. It sure would be great if you found my rifle."

"Thank you, Sir. See you then."

Upon breaking the connection with the Trooper, Rex grinned to himself, "So, is it possible that my dear friend,

Aloysius, found my rifle in the deep and now he's stuck with it? Just to be sure, Mister, I'm gonna nail you even better."

When Rex arrived at Trooper Headquarters that afternoon, as promised, he told the receptionist that he was there to see George Ingersoll. When she telephoned his office to announce Mr. Franz, the Trooper told her he would be out in a few minutes. She asked Rex to have a seat.

While Rex waited, Ingersoll went to the property room and checked out the rifle that had been recovered from the deep by Denny Gustafson. He came out with the rifle and handed it to Rex.

"Is this your stolen weapon, Sir?"

Rex looked it over carefully. He quickly recognized that it was his, but he handed it back to the Trooper, saying, "No, it's not mine. This one is in nice shape. The stock on my weapon was much darker and it was scratched up pretty good. I wish it was mine. Anyhow, mine was a Remington and this is a Winchester. When I filed the report with you I thought I told you mine was a Remington. Isn't that what you wrote down?"

"I have the report here and I see that I did write down 'Remington.' I guess I had 'Winchester' on the brain when I telephoned you this morning. Well, regardless, if you say it isn't yours, then I'm really sorry to have brought you down here for nothing."

"No problem, Officer, I needed the exercise. Wait, let me see the rifle again."

As the Trooper handed it back, Rex looked at it more intently and then said, "This weapon sure looks in good shape. Do you people ever offer these confiscated items for sale? I'd sure be interested in buying it."

Ingersoll replied that items like this are usually part of an auction of unclaimed or confiscated items that is held once a year at the local National Guard Armory. He then added, "This rifle, however, is still part of an ongoing investigation. It probably will not be included in this year's sale, if at all."

This prompted Rex to ask, "Did somebody get shot with it?"

"All I can say again is that it's part of an ongoing investigation, so I can't talk about it, Mr. Franz. I'm sorry."

That now gave Rex the opportunity to end the conversation. He looked at his watch and commented, "Well, it's time for me to go to work, but thanks for trying."

With that they parted company and, as Rex walked to his car, he commented to himself, "I wonder if there was some ulterior motive in having me come to view the weapon? Well, if there was, I don't think I helped them in any way." He felt very comfortable with his situation."

When Rex was back at Upper Salmon later that afternoon, John Santori and a fellow officer walked up the steps and on to the flume to post #32. John carried the suspected board, a borrowed Winchester .30-06 rifle with scope. His partner carried four thin long nails, a hammer, and a pocket camera. He also carried a surveyor's scope. It didn't take them long to find the shooting perch.

After taking a few photographs of the subject trees with the four nail holes still showing, John secured the board in place on the two trees. It was, of course, as he suspected. The nail holes fit exactly to those on the board.

He then attached the rifle to the board with the U-bolts, and took more photos of the mount from in front and from behind as well as from the side pointing down to post #32. All that was missing was a picture looking through the scope at the target. That photo could always come later using more sophisticated equipment.

For now, John felt that even without being able to put the rifle in Rex's hand, he was closer to placing both pieces of the board in the man's possession. If only they could find the smaller piece that was cut from this one.

Fortunately, or unfortunately, (depending on whose side you were on), Rex Franz found it about a week later after his shift. He was on his way out of his house having planned another dastardly deed. This time he was going to frame Pinky for the shooting of the Fish and Wildlife Officer.

He had the empty shell casing in one hand and his flashlight in the other. In his jacket he also had a pocketbook with two old sales slips as bookmarkers. These slips covering hardware purchases from months before had, luckily for Rex, never been thrown away. They, too, would be used to hurt Pinky.

It was just past midnight and there shouldn't be any people awake at either Upper or Lower Salmon. His plan was to carefully sneak down to Pinky's apartment and deposit the shell casing and the book in a convenient place inside the residence. Then, he would drive to town and make an anonymous phone call to the Troopers telling them where they might find some very interesting and incriminating evidence.

As he walked out onto the porch of his house and reached back to shut the door, he accidentally dropped the shell casing. He directed his flashlight beam to the floor and found the casing near the back of his woodpile. He also spied the scrap of pine that he had forgotten weeks ago. It had fallen behind the woodpile. He smiled and said, "What a lucky break for me that I didn't burn it. Now, Aloysius, you'll soon own it and it'll be just another nail in your coffin. They'll get you for both murders."

He stepped on to the flume to start walking toward the penstock, and then he hesitated. "Why walk when I can ride," he told himself. So, he went back onto his porch and rolled out his trail bike. Now, he would have a slow leisurely ride to settle Aloysius's destiny. He was even humming a jolly tune as he rode along. His bike's headlight showed him the way in the dark with no problem along the first straightaway. It was a little more difficult on the turns. So, he slowed in those areas.

When he reached the post #32 area a little bit of nostalgia took over his senses. He didn't stop but he did slow down. He looked at the post and thought about the days before that morning in early July.

He commented silently, "If only things had been different. Mary was such a good woman, and she was beautiful both in face and in spirit. Why did I take my anger out on her? She didn't want to lose those babies. She longed for a child just as much as I did, if not more. It wasn't her fault."

As he slowly moved past this so familiar spot he moped. Then, finally, he came back to reality and sped on again toward the penstock. When he reached the little cabin he parked his bike inside and started down the stairs. With the aid of his flashlight he carefully negotiated the steps almost down to the parking lot. A few yards above the flat paved lot he found the worn trail from the steps to the company houses. None of this area was too familiar to him. He knew only that Pinky's apartment was atop the house closest to the Lower Salmon powerhouse.

When Rex first went to work for Juneau Hydroelectric at Lower Salmon he was still living at home. When he moved to Upper Salmon and was living up there, he never had need to take this path to the company houses at Lower Salmon. As he now started to step off the stairs and on to the trail he directed his flashlight beam ahead only to reveal two bright animal eyes staring back at him followed by loud barking. He unknowingly had aroused the pet dog of one of the tenants. Fortunately for Rex, the dog was within a chain link enclosure. But, its persistent barking caused Rex to decide this was not the night to visit Pinky's apartment. The dog's enclosure was attached to the middle house of the three, and Rex saw immediately that he had to walk alongside the enclosure in order to reach the stairs to Pinky's apartment. He stopped, doused his light, and carefully traced his way back to the steps. As he began his long walk back up the steps to the penstock he thought about this new dilemma with which he was now confronted. This appeared to be a real problem – in the daytime, someone might see him if he attempted to enter Pinky's apartment. At night, this seemingly large dog could alert one or more of the tenants that a stranger might be nearby. So far, all his planning had gone forward without a hitch. Now, as he walked, he contemplated his next move. He was almost to the top of the steps when it came to him – 'frankfurters.'

The next morning he began his four days off with a little less villainous intent than he had the night before. This time he was going to give some treats to a nice 'doggie' at Lower Salmon. It took him almost the entire four days, but by the time he started his graveyard shift the following Friday morning just after midnight he had a new friend who no longer barked but instead now wagged his tail every time Rex drew anywhere near. In that short period, with the aid of his store bought packages of franks, he had weaned a once unfriendly German shepherd away from threatening and loud barking and instead into a wimpy, slobbering canine puppy. It took quite a few trips up and down the almost 876 steps from and to the path leading to Pinky's apartment. He did this mostly during the day when, fortunately, all the tenants of the three company houses were at work. The night before he was to make the actual delivery to Pinky's apartment he gave it the very important acid test. Near midnight he approached the dog, gave him half of a frank through the chain link fence, and walked on past to the end of the path near the last of the three houses. He waited there a few minutes while he again surveyed the area. During the first daytime training of the problem German shepherd, he saw that the steps leading to Pinky's apartment were on the side of the house closest to the second house. That middle house had windows on the side facing Pinky's stairway. So, it was imperative that the dog not bark as Rex scaled those stairs of the first house where Pinky's apartment was located. As he started back toward the steps leading to Upper Salmon, he gave the remaining half of the frank to the dog as he passed by him. He reached the steps without so much as a yip from his new found friend.

Rex was rewarded for his efforts by a soundless greeting the next night when he did finally deposit the incriminating evidence into Pinky's apartment. Unseen and unheard, he conveniently placed the spent cartridge shell, the pocketbook with the sales slips bookmarkers, and the piece of scrap pine in areas of the apartment that would later be searched by authorities. As he was exiting the attached porch he noticed an empty can of Copenhagen on the floor. He stooped to retrieve it and smiled, saying, "I have a better place to throw this bit of trash, Pinky."   A short while later he was back on the path where he rewarded the dog with the final contents of the package of franks. From there he walked down the remaining steps to his car where he would finish his efforts for his other 'friend' - Pinky. He drove the roughly two miles into town to Franklin Street, parked his car, and walked almost unnoticed into the still busy Lucky Lady Bar. He used their payphone and with the background noise of the jukebox and the arguing pool players almost drowning him out he dialed Public Safety and asked to speak to a trooper. Had none been available his voice and his subsequent story would have been recorded on the dispatcher's machine. Instead, he was connected to a sergeant who had just come on duty. In a slurred and drunken sounding voice he explained how his drinking buddy, Pinky McInerney, had bragged to him weeks before that he had committed the perfect crime. He went on to say that Pinky did it with some kind of contraption that he built at a company workshop up in the mountains where he worked. He quickly hung up the phone before the startled Trooper had a chance to question him or even determine the caller's name.

When Rex returned to Upper Salmon that same night he walked over to the workshop where he deposited the empty can of Copenhagen into the bottom shelf of the locker. The next day Pinky was deeper into the soup. In fact, he was now up to his armpits in it. While Pinky was still enjoying the hospitality of the folks at the Lemon Creek Jail, two Alaska State Troopers with search warrant in hand walked into Pinky's upstairs apartment near Lower Salmon and confiscated a few very interesting items. One was a spent cartridge shell that was later microscopically compared favorably with the spent shell that was found in the rifle recovered near Swanson Harbor. They also took from his residence a scrap piece of sugar pine and a murder mystery that they found on his nightstand that, coincidentally, had on its cover mention of the execution of a perfect crime. The same two men then took a long walk into Upper Salmon and into the workshop where they found, lo and behold, an empty can of Copenhagen.

Pinky was unaware of all the happenings, but it now seemed that just about every government agency (federal, state, and local) had in their possession some kind of incriminating evidence against him. It was not long before his court appointed attorney learned about it, and he conveyed the bad news to his very unhappy client.

As he told Pinky what the Troopers had found in his apartment and in the workshop, Cameron Switzer voiced a somewhat oversimplified conclusion when he said, "I really think we've got a few additional problems." In his usual soft-spoken voice that this time was heard almost throughout the entire Lemon Creek facility Pinky yelled, "**WE** GOT PROBLEMS? I'm the one with the problems, Sonny, and you're one of them unless you can get me out of here. People are planting things in my apartment and you tell me **WE** got problems?"

In a most humble, and yet offended, tone the young man replied, "There's no need to be hostile, Mr. McInerney."

The now very red-faced Irishman answered, "**HOSTILE**? Sonny, you haven't even begun to see what hostile is if something doesn't start going my way soon."

"So, Mr. McInerney, that mystery novel they found on your nightstand wasn't yours?"

"Hell no. I don't read that stuff. They could have found a Playboy magazine, but I don't even read that. I just look at the pictures."

John Santori, too, was a rather unhappy man just a few days later when he heard more bad news. Fred Wolters phoned him to say that the FBI lab in Washington had found nothing of value in the slides to match to the zodiac. They did agree that the slug was fired from the same rifle as the other two, but that was already a foregone conclusion.

When Fred explained what the Troopers had found in Pinky's apartment and at the workshop this, too, was not good news in that the uninformed would quickly conclude that Pinky had indeed shot both the Fish and Wildlife Officer and Mary Franz. However, since the scrap board had now found its way from the gym locker into Pinky's apartment it was obvious to Santori that it got there courtesy of Rex Franz. As far as Fred Wolters was concerned, though, it was simply more solid proof that they had the right man in their sights. Probably, the only question remaining would be what branch of government would prosecute Pinky – state or federal?

For the next few weeks there was very little activity at JPD aimed at helping Pinky or incriminating Rex Franz. John felt that the department had gone about as far as it could unless some kind of miracle happened. On the other side, the Feds and the Troopers were at work with District Attorney Aaron Stoneman putting together a case for presentation to the Grand Jury. That body was convened on Monday morning, October 8, and, after hearing a number of witnesses that included Coast Guard and Department of Public Safety personnel as well as FBI Agent Fred Wolters, an indictment was handed down charging Aloysius P. McInerney with the murder of Fish and Wildlife Officer Aubrey Hutchison.

To his credit, Defense Attorney Cameron Switzer was not idle during those same two weeks. He obtained from Pinky the list of fishermen and/or their boats and he contacted and obtained signed statements from a number of those individuals. Each swore that they had seen or even had radio contact with Pinky when he was fishing David Royce's boat. Those that had seen him said that he was often alone in the boat.

With these statements in hand, Switzer visited the District Attorney and suggested that the stolen boat accusation might not be worth prosecuting. "After all," he said, "these signed statements now show that the owner of the boat did, on occasion, allow Mr. McInerney to fish the boat alone."

Since he already had the Grand Jury indictment in his hand, Stoneman gave no resistance. He instructed one of his assistants to proceed to court to request that the theft charges against Aloysius McInerney be dismissed. So, the next morning, Pinky stood beside his attorney, Cameron Switzer, and heard the judge dismiss the theft charges against him. He smiled down at his shorter companion as the judge said, "You are free to go, Mr. McInerney."

It now appeared to Pinky that his problems were down to a probable fine by Fish and Game for commercial fishing without a proper permit. When his attorney reached over to shake his hand, Pinky put his arm around him and said, "You did good, Sonny."

"I'm glad for you Mr. McInerney," said Switzer.

With his widest Irish smile, Aloysius said, "Oh, you can call me 'Pinky' anytime ."

The smile disappeared a few seconds later, however, when the Assistant District Attorney spoke up and said, "Your Honor, the people herewith request the immediate arraignment of Mr. McInerney for the murder of Fish and Wildlife Officer Aubrey Hutchison pursuant to indictment handed down by the recently convened Grand Jury."

Pinky's vacation from the Lemon Creek Jail lasted just over an hour, but his actual freedom from the law was for less than three minutes. After pleading not guilty to the charge before him, he was again on his way back to jail. He was again remanded without bail. Cameron Switzer would not have it as easy this time around. A few other people also would not have it very easy.

THIRTY-TWO

THE WIDOW JORDAN

A few evenings after his ten day shift on graveyard, Rex was on his way downtown to the Horseshoe Saloon where he intended to start recouping his losses. He hadn't played poker there in many months, and the regulars missed him and his money. Upon entering the backroom of the saloon, he was greeted warmly and offered condolences on the loss of his wife by everyone at the table. Later, at the end of the evening and whether it was by good fortune or perhaps a setup, he walked away from the table with quite a few dollars. In fact, it was many hundreds of dollars. He marveled at the thought that his success this night was due mostly to his bluffs. On one hand, with only a pair of threes, he had raised and re-raised and won the biggest pot of the night. It seemed that when he would bluff by raising and even re-raising (especially on the larger pots) most if not all the other players would drop out and he would end up the winner of that hand. When he had a good hand and played it cautiously – not raising – he seemed to win then, too. No matter which way he played the hands, he did win big this night and thus left the table in a much happier mood than usual.

Except for the recent one night splurge of beer drinking outside Glacier Bay, Rex wasn't a serious drinker. He might have an occasional glass of wine when having dinner out, but that was about it. He especially did not drink when he played poker in spite of the fact that the only poker he played was at a table that was located in a saloon. He always thought - wisely so - that he needed all his senses to be alert while he played. However, tonight after the game was over, he felt that he could safely have one drink before heading home. It being a Saturday night, the Horseshoe was crowded at the bar and as usual it was a friendly gathering. As he sat on his stool after ordering a 'seven and seven' he chatted with customers on either side of him. When one of those two stools lost its sitter, a young woman took it over. Normally, Rex would not be one to initiate contact with anyone, let alone a young woman. This time, however, his mood was warm and friendly. He turned his head toward her, smiled, and said, "Welcome." It took him another split second before he realized, "I know this lady."

Bev Jordan lost her husband in the spring of 1971. He had previously been working as a lineman with Juneau Hydroelectric when he was offered a much higher paying job installing transmission lines at the construction site of the Snettisham Hydroelectric Project, located 28 air miles southeast of Juneau. Up until his death the entire project had suffered only one minor lost time accident and was without a single contractor claim in spite of the fact that hundreds of men and much heavy equipment was being used in an almost impossible mountainous area. In addition to building of the main powerhouse itself, the task involved construction of over 8000 feet of unlined power tunnel, a 900 foot deep surge shaft, an underground machine shop and an underwater lake tap into a high mountain lake under more than 200 feet of water. There were also under construction several large underground chambers that required removal of some 30,000 cubic feet of rock from the smaller chambers to as much as 150,000 cubic feet of material from the larger ones. At the time, the project was the highest head lake tap put into operation in North America. Many years before a similar lake tap facility had been constructed at Annex Creek in the Taku River drainage, but on a much smaller scale.

Drexell Jordan was only one of many who were responsible for the aforementioned installation of high voltage transmission lines within and outside the facility. Much of his work was done on high transmission towers, but he actually met his Maker deep in the waters outside of Gilbert Bay east of the Snettisham construction area. On their day off he and a fellow worker were trolling for salmon in a twelve foot skiff when Drexel fell overboard. He made three mistakes earlier that afternoon. He forgot his lifejacket in his car. He didn't share enough of his twelve pack with his fishing partner. And, he wore fishermen's boots instead of slipons. His most fatal mistake, however, was made years before when he always seemed to be occupied elsewhere when free swimming and water safety lessons were offered after classes at the local high school. Just before his final demise, he made his last mistake of standing up in the boat in order to reel in his big salmon. When he lost his balance and fell overboard he sank like a stone.

When Bev Jordan became a widow, after only six months into her marriage, her dead husband's former employers never considered asking her to vacate her residence in the company house near Lower Salmon. Whether they really needed more help in their billing department or because they felt sorry for her loss, she was offered a position at their headquarters in downtown Juneau which she later accepted. So, she remained there in her house which, like the similar unit at Upper Salmon, had a separate upstairs apartment accessible only by climbing a long outside stairway. The apartment atop the house to the west of hers, coincidentally, was now rented by the presently incarcerated Aloysius McInerney.

Rex Franz first met Bev in 1970, shortly after she and her husband moved into one of those company houses at Lower Salmon. They had taken a hike along the trail to the Salmon Creek Dam and on their return had stopped in at the Upper Salmon powerhouse while Rex was on shift. After her husband accepted the job at Snettisham, he lived in company barracks erected there for the construction crews. So, he would only return to Juneau one week out of each month. While she was alone at the house near Lower Salmon she would occasionally visit the plant in order to use their phone to reach her husband at the Snettisham construction site. It was there at Lower Salmon that she also met another operator, Pinky McInerney, after he was transferred there from Upper Salmon.

There being no telephone lines between Snettisham and the outside world, communication could only be accomplished by the powerhouse operator who would then connect with Snettisham by telephone to the company's headquarters in town and marine radio beyond. There were also times, during weekends and especially on those rare occasions when the sun was shining, when she in the company of a friend or two (or even alone) would hike along the flume to the Upper Salmon plant and on to the dam. In those early days, Rex still had a happy home life. So, if she stopped in at the plant while he was on shift and asked him to place a call to Snettisham for her, he only looked at her as an interruption to his solitude and nothing more. She was just a skinny but cute little thing that could turn a few heads if she was all made up and nicely dressed. Instead, during her visits to either of the powerhouses she was usually dressed in a baggy sweater and jeans and she thus made no lasting impression. After talking with her husband she might tarry a while trying to delay going back to her empty house by talking with the operator on duty there in the powerhouse. In those instances when Rex was on duty, he was courteous to her but not very verbose.   This night as he was finishing off the last of his drink, he was startled when the young woman on the stool next to him greeted him, "Well, hello Rex Franz, how nice to see you again. It's been a long time."

His reply, while guarded, was considerably warmer than it had ever been in the past. He noticed that she had filled out where she needed to and that she had done her hair and her makeup to now more fully compliment her pretty face. They made friendly small talk and each expressed condolences to the other for the loss of their spouse. He offered to buy her a drink which she accepted even though he soon concluded that she might have already downed on or two before sitting down next to him.

As they sipped their drinks their conversation got friendlier, a little more intimate, and to the complete exclusion of all the other people on either side of them at the bar. They were soon comparing notes on life as widowed and now single people and it turned out that both had much in common. Neither had done much of anything except work and stay at home since the death of their spouse. Soon, both glasses were empty whereupon Rex opined that perhaps he should be heading for home. Bev interrupted his departure by suggesting that she should now return the favor by buying him a drink.   Again, out of character, he smiled and accepted, "Ok, one for the road."   As their conversation continued he thought to himself that while this might be a relationship begun here by chance it should probably be continued to a greater degree in the future. So, when they finished their second drinks, Rex made the first approach by saying, Well, Bev, I'm sure glad that I thought to come down here tonight. I used to spend a lot of time here playing poker during my four days off, but this is my first time back since Mary's death. I hope I'll run into you again soon."

Her answer was considerably more direct, "I've really enjoyed seeing you again, too, Rex. And, I hope that you consider doing something besides playing poker when you do come back." They shook hands, and Rex headed for his parked car.

Rex started the engine and slowly moved the car back and forth trying to squeeze out of the small space there on Franklin Street where the other two cars – the one behind and the other in front - had him pretty much hemmed in. He was interrupted in his effort to escape by a tap on his driver side window.   To his surprise it was Bev Jordan who offered, "I'll guide you out of there if you give a girl a ride home."

"This is turning out to be a pretty good night," he thought to himself just before rolling down his window. He answered, "Get in. I'll get us out of here even if I have to push each of them a little." Bev got in on the passenger side as directed, and Rex did just what he had promised. He pushed the front car forward with his own front bumper and the car behind with his back bumper, and they were soon on their way. As he turned on to Glacier Avenue to head out of town, he asked Bev, "Well, where would you like to go, young lady?"

Her reply really startled him, "Well, Miami Beach if you have enough gas. Or, my place if you'd like to come in for a cup of coffee."

Without thinking he replied, "You make an offer that's difficult to refuse. So, where are you living these days?

"I'm still in the same place."

"You're still at Lower Salmon – all alone in one of those big company houses?"

"That's right – just me and my dog."

At that moment he did not pick up on the significance of her comment. He had other things in mind. He continued, "You shouldn't be alone – a nice looking lady like you should have a man around to keep you warm at night." He was surprised at his own forwardness. He hadn't talked to a woman like this since before he started going out with Mary. Maybe it was the two drinks at the Horseshoe that emboldened him. The truth was that he had to talk and keep talking to hide the stark realization and alarm that befell him upon hearing and now fearing that her dog might be the one that had thwarted his initial visit to Pinky's apartment. Could it be that the dog woke her that night; and did she possibly see him when he did finally go up the stairs to deposit the incriminating items in his much despised fellow operator's apartment? He was searching for some additional thing to say when Bev answered his just offered and slightly suggestive comment.

"Thank you for saying that, but since Drex died I haven't gone out much. That's only the second time that I've been to the Horseshoe since Drex died, not that we went there very often when he was still alive. I was only there because the girls at work talked me into joining their billiards team. We had our first tournament tonight. I was going to be an alternate, but one of our girls didn't show so I got to play."

"So, how did you do?"

"I lost my match – I scratched on the eight ball."

"When they reached Lower Salmon, Rex parked in front of the middle house. He asked, "Are you're still in this middle unit?"

"Bev answered simply, "Yes." Then she added, "Would you like to come in for a while?"

Rex was out of practice when it came to the opposite sex and their needs and demands. But, he didn't have to be a Rhodes Scholar to realize that there was much more potential here than just a cup of coffee. He didn't get a chance to answer her because

188

she was already opening her passenger side door when he looked over at her. So, he simply turned off the engine, got out of the driver's seat, and went around to help her out of the car. He took her hand and they walked up the few steps to her front door. Once inside Bev pointed to the fireplace and said, "Start a fire and warm us up while I brew up some coffee."

It turned out that a fire was not really needed that night. It got very warm real soon – so much so that neither of them ventured out into the cold for the next two days. The warmth was only interrupted during the preparation and enjoyment of meals. In fact, the heated affair carried over into Monday when Bev phoned in to work to say that she had a fever. When she returned to work on Tuesday morning, one of her co-workers asked how she was feeling. Her reply was, "I am feeling much, much better!"

Rex Franz, too, should have been feeling good. Instead, he was feeling anything but better. He was still very much concerned. He was back at Upper Salmon beginning his ten days on the day shift. The busy part of the morning increasing power output was over and he was sitting in his cubicle quietly contemplating what he now considered a situation possibly much more serious than not. There were many pleasant events in the recent past and some even better ones coming up in the future that warmed him. The upcoming murder trial of Aloysius McInerney was one of those. So was the anticipation of one day enjoying the millions he was due to acquire upon the settling of his late wife's estate. The recent revival of his sex life was at the top of the list, but it was worrisome in that the source of this new pleasure might now be a very dangerous one. So, he was 'betwixt and between.' If Bev Jordan saw him the night of September 12, when he got into Pinky's apartment or on one of the days when he was attempting to befriend her watchdog, the consequences of her telling someone of that sighting would be disastrous. What should he do? One thing he decided to do immediately was not to panic. It was too early for a checklist since he didn't even have a plan. Most importantly, he had to talk to Bev to see if he could tactfully

189

determine what she had seen, if anything, and what she knew, if anything.

Prior to departing Bev's house that Monday night, Rex was asked point blank, "Was this a one-night stand for you?"

He answered truthfully, "No, and I hope it wasn't for you either."

She smiled and replied, "It was not. So, when will I see you again? Then, with an impish smile, she added, "I realize that you have a long way to travel, but I would like to cook you a real dinner one night soon."

With his own bit of sly humor, and appearing to have hurt feelings, he asked, "You didn't like the bacon and eggs I fixed for us?" Then in a more serious vein he added, "I have to do some double shifts during the next ten days because of vacations. So, can I come to visit for a while after that?"

"Yes you may," she replied, "and that will give me time to stock up on enough food to see us through your upcoming visit. Certainly, we should have a little more variety than twelve straight meals of bacon and eggs."

They both laughed heartily before and after he asked, "You didn't care for the variety that we shared in between the bacon and eggs?"

His last smart comment left her speechless. So, she simply put her arms around his neck, gave him a most passionate goodbye kiss, and sent him on his way back to Upper Salmon.

As he drove the few hundred feet from her house to his parking area at Lower Salmon, and again as he walked the steps up to the penstock, he asked himself some questions and he even took a stab at answering them. Unfortunately, he was not sure that his answers to his own questions were right on.

"Could she have seen me that night? If she had, wouldn't she have asked me about it by now? Do I dare ask her? Suppose I ask about her dog and then ask if she or any of her neighbors have ever had any prowlers that got scared off by the dog? How well does she know McInerney? Surely she should know him quite well since he was a next door neighbor. She also must have talked to him when she went into the plant at Lower Salmon to phone her husband."

Rex concluded that if her answers were all positive, he should then ask her what she thinks about Pinky's upcoming trial. "Was she aware of Pinky's drinking problem?" Perhaps, during his next visit, he might get to the answers by casually mentioning the upcoming trial and acting as if he was hoping the best for his co-worker. If she indicated any bias in Pinky's favor, he might then be able to steer her to giving him answers that might relieve his apprehension about his own well being. Since Pinky could only reach his apartment by walking up the stairway that faced her house, Rex thought of asking her if her dog ever barked and woke her when the man was stumbling up that stairway in a drunken stupor. "Yes," he thought, "that's the way to start. Make Pinky the center of the conversation, and keep mum about my unpleasant association with the man unless she brings it up."

Rex did work several double shifts, both day and swing. During the hours when he was not busy increasing or reducing the power output of the plant, he continually thought about what he was going to do about the Bev Jordan situation. He was far from being madly in love, but he did feel warmly for the woman. In fact, he actually hoped that nothing would upset the relationship that had started out so beautifully. He truly wanted it to continue and to flower. If, on the other hand, she might know or reveal something untoward about his own past actions, then he was already making plans that were not so beautiful. She had been alone for many months now - since the death of her husband. So, Rex was already making plans for her suicide – just in case.

THIRTY-THREE

PLANNING THE FUTURE

After ten long days and almost as many nights of work, Rex Franz started his four days off with a long sleep, a shower and shave, and the donning of clean and long unused sporty clothes. Earlier in the day he had telephoned Bev at her work to confirm that he was still invited to dinner and, once his assumption was validated, he went shopping. When he arrived at her door that evening he presented her with a bouquet of roses, a box of chocolates, and a bottle of Korbel Chardonnay wine.

During one of their earlier phone conversations, Bev asked him about some of his favorite dishes. So, their first sit-down dinner that could truly be called such (not just bacon and eggs) consisted of shrimp cocktails, oysters Rockefeller, chocolate cake with a side of vanilla ice cream covered with whipped cream – all washed down with a glass of the aforementioned wine.

During their first course, Rex started on his planned bit of questioning, "I guess you've heard that Pinky McInerney is being tried for murder of a Fish and Wildlife Officer?"

"Yes, it's a shame. He's such a nice man, and I know he's not guilty.

"How do you know he's not guilty? Do you know something that the authorities don't?"

"No, I don't. It's just that I can't believe that he would kill a man for no good reason."

"Have you talked to him lately?"

"No. I haven't talked to him in months. The last time I did talk to him he was in pretty bad shape."

"Drunk?"

"Yes, poor man. He was drinking a lot after he got let go by the electric company. In fact, the last time I talked to him he was sprawled out at the bottom of his stairway that leads up to his apartment. If my dog hadn't started barking and woken me, Pinky probably would have spent the night there."

"So, you have a watchdog. That's good."

"Well, she's not really a watchdog. She's almost a lap dog. She's usually in the house unless I'm gone. Then, a friend of mine comes by to feed her and give her a little bit of exercise."

"How come she's not inside now?"

"She's a pest when you're trying to eat dinner. She wants to be included, and she drives you crazy."

"What breed?"

"She's a German shepherd on paper, but she could pass for a teddy bear."

"I'd like to see her. Are you going to let her in after dinner?"

"I hadn't planned on it – certainly not tonight."

"Why? She doesn't like strangers?"

"On the contrary. If you come toward her from inside the house she considers you a friend, and she'll lick you to death if you get close to her. If you approach her from the outside, you're a stranger and she will bark until you leave or I call her back."

"You know, I think I heard her barking quite a bit some weeks ago when I walked up and down the steps. It was during my four days off. Can she see or smell people as they walk by on the steps?"

"It could have been her. I was in Seattle the first two weeks of September. So, she was in her enclosure that whole time, and she gets pretty unhappy when she's left outside that many days. If my friend, Bonnie, doesn't feed her or let her out until real late every day, she probably gets even more sensitive when someone is nearby."

"What's her name?"

"Josie!"

"Josie? You could have named her 'Josephine' just as well. That's a little more feminine."

"I was going to name her 'Josephine' which is also my mother's name."

"Oops. I'm sorry. I meant no disrespect."

"None taken. It's just that when I first got her as a puppy she seemed so sweet tempered, just like my Mom, and I thought it would be a compliment to name her 'Josephine.' I'll admit, even my Mom was taken aback at first. Then, when I explained my reasoning, she was no longer offended. However, she suggested that it might be a little less embarrassing to her if I used the shorter name. So, 'Josie' she is."

Rex was breathing a silent and unnoticed sigh of relief as Bev explained the origin of her dog's name. Now, he felt secure that Bev did not see him before, during, or after he deposited those critical items in Pinky's apartment on the twelfth of September – she was out of town. So, he moved on to the only other part of the worrisome past – could any of her neighbors have seen him during that same period?

"Do any of your neighbors ever complain about her barking? She must be a pretty big dog. She has a rather deep voice."

"No, the lady above me and the guy in the upstairs apartment in the last house both work for AEL&P, but they spend a good part of each month down at Snettisham just like Drex did. Ed Sloan lives in the unit under Pinky and he's such a nice guy – he wouldn't complain if you shot him with a new gun. The guy in the other downstairs unit also works for AEL&P – he's on shift at the Gold Creek facility. I've never met him. He's fairly new with the company."

This last bit of information that Bev imparted just about relieved all of Rex's previous anxieties. So, as their dinner ended and they were clearing the dishes, he felt it was time to change the subject on to a more intimate path. He asked, "After we finish the dishes, do you want to play some scrabble or gin rummy?"

"No, you damn fool. I don't want to do either of those, but I do want to play!" She moved against him, placed her left arm around his neck, grabbed a handful of his crotch with her right hand, and kissed him. The rest of the evening ended in her bedroom – the dishes remaining in the sink unwashed.

It was not all lovemaking those next three days that they were together. There were times when they stopped to eat and even to talk. Some of the latter had to do with what their future might be like. She started it one morning when she voiced the opinion: "It's really not fair that I have to wait another ten days before you get back here to fix breakfast for me."

Rex's reply didn't solve anything: "Well, you could come to live with me at Upper Salmon. You'd save money on rent."

"Don't be silly," she replied, curtly.

"Or, we could both quit our jobs and take a world cruise," he suggested with a broad smile.

"Now, you're really trying to be funny."

"No, not at all. That would give us a chance to really get to know each other."

"Well, that sounds considerably less funny when you put it that way."

"In fact, Bev, before my next ten days are over, I could start to really get all my affairs in order. I could put everything that has to be done in the hands of my attorney. I could let him finish the settling of Mary's estate and the selling of my house in town. In just a few more weeks, we could be on the high seas heading toward the Greek Isles and beyond."

Their blissful exchange of ideas ended suddenly when Rex noticed that Bev was crying. "What's wrong?" he asked.

"Oh, Rex, I'm so sorry. I shouldn't have started this. I can't do anything like what you propose – at least not right now."

"You can't or you don't want to?"

"I want to. I really do, but I can't. I should have told you this early on. I'm leaving in a few days for Seattle. My mother has Pancreatic Cancer, and she has only a few months to live. I'm going down to be with her, and I don't know how long I'll be gone. She really needs my help and comforting."

"How about your father? Can he help?"

"He's there, but he's never been much help."

"Do you want me to come with you?"

"That's nice of you to offer, but I don't think this would be an appropriate time to meet my folks."

"Well, there's one thing I can do for sure. I can take care of Josie for you while you're gone. If you let me meet her and let us get acquainted, I can then take her to Upper Salmon when I leave here."

"That's sweet of you. Yes, let me go get her."

The greeting between 'two old friends' went just as Rex had expected. Josie couldn't get enough of him. Given the chance, she would have licked him to death.

Bev laughed and commented, "See what I mean?"

Some days later, Bev was on her way to Seattle, and Rex was back at work. He and his new roommate got along well from the outset. In fact, Josie became his companion both at home and even sometimes when he was on shift. He was in telephone contact with Bev in Seattle at least once or twice a week. She was keeping him abreast of her vigil at her mother's side, and he did his best to tell her about his own doings which, at Upper Salmon, were not too exciting. Much of his report had to do with Josie and how well the two of them were getting along. During the months while Bev was away, Rex was able to satisfy himself that all his worries were unfounded. He made it a point to stop in at Lower Salmon whenever he knew Ed Sloan was on shift. He would spend time with him talking about everything except his visit to Pinky's apartment. He felt certain that Ed would say something about having seen or heard him during those critical days and that special night. Ed never came near to touching on that subject.

At a union meeting, Rex made it a point to get acquainted with the new man that Bev had described as living there at Lower Salmon. He, too, acted according to script. He shook Rex's hand, made a little bit of small talk, and quickly removed himself from harmful consideration.

In the weeks and months that followed, in late 1972 and early 1973, Rex slowly but surely got all of his affairs in order. The settling of Mary Franz's estate, which had begun shortly after her death, was now complete. The house in town had now been sold, and all previous checking and savings accounts were closed and new ones established in Rex's name only. The gift shops had now been placed in his name and a contract executed with Jane Whitney that would someday bring about her outright purchase of the two units. So, now he waited for Bev's return.

THIRTY-FOUR

THE TRIAL – FOR THE PROSECUTION

Almost eight months after the shooting of Fish and Wildlife Officer Aubrey Hutchison, the trial of Aloysius P. McInerney began. He was charged with second-degree murder and was again defended by the lightly skilled Cameron Switzer. To his credit, however, the young lawyer worked hard at putting together a defense worthy of more astute trial attorneys.

The feeling at Police Headquarters was that he was spending more time at JPD conferring with the Chief and John Santori than he did in his own office. Actually, they were all he had. In order to free Pinky he had to prove that Rex Franz was the real killer or, he had to place enough doubt in the minds of the jury that they really would not be able to decide which man did it. Lastly, he had to convince himself and the jury that million-to-one occurrences do happen.

The jury was impaneled in just one day. A trial in Juneau, like in so many small cities and towns throughout America, would not be a TV or movie circus event. It would not drag on for weeks and weeks. Juneau Superior Court would serve as the stage and District Attorney Aaron Stoneman would be the main actor. Nevertheless, there would be little grandstanding.

Earlier in the year, the much-traveled Stoneman announced his intention to seek the Governorship of the State of Alaska. It was his intention to use the successful prosecution of this trial as a stepping-stone to that high office. His opening statement was short and professional. He told the jury that the rifle used in the shooting was registered to the defendant and that he had been apprehended only a few miles from the scene as he was fleeing in a fishing vessel not his own. The D.A. further stated that witnesses would testify that the defendant was seen throwing the rifle overboard just before being apprehended. He then concluded his opening remarks telling the jury:

"We will enter into evidence two slugs, one taken from the life jacket of the slain Officer after it had passed through his shoulder and the other that was found still imbedded in the skin of his back. This second bullet, as the Coroner's report will show, mortally wounded the Officer when it entered his chest, severed his ascending aorta and part of his spinal column. An expert will testify that microscopic evidence shows that the bullets were fired from the rifle owned by the defendant – the same rifle that Aloysius P. McInerney threw into the waters of Icy Strait."

Stoneman did not go into much detail at the last of his opening, but he also told the jury that there would be placed into evidence material actually found in the residence of the accused. As Santori sat there in the courtroom he felt that some of the jurors were already wondering why they were even there. A few of them were actually yawning. It was very depressing. Stoneman was making it sound so cut and dried.

In contrast, Cameron Switzer's opening statement was anything but short, and it seemed more theatrical than professional. John Santori liked it. But, of course, he was on Switzer's side. Unfortunately, he noticed yet another juror starting to yawn in addition to the ones he had seen earlier. It was not looking good. The only parts of Switzer's opening remarks that had any meat on them were his closing words:

"Throughout criminal history more than one fatal shooting has taken place using someone else's weapon. Simply because this rifle was registered in Mr. McInerney's name does not prove that it was he who fired it. Ladies and gentlemen of the jury, the District Attorney has in just a few short words attempted to convince you that this is an open and shut case. What he hasn't told you is that this same rifle was used to kill Mary Franz in early July of last year. Ballistics will show that the slug that killed Mary was microscopically proven to be a match to the two that entered the body of the Fish and Wildlife Officer. So, why hasn't the District Attorney also charged my client with the killing of Mary Franz? I'll tell you why. It's because he can't prove it. There is doubt in his mind, and there should be doubt in your minds. We will show you and we will help you decide that this is not an open and shut case. There are a lot of wrinkles that the District Attorney will be unable to iron out to your satisfaction. If he cannot prove that my client killed Mary Franz then it follows that he must think someone else killed her. There, ladies and gentlemen, is where he and I agree. I, too, believe that someone else killed her. If that is the case, then is Mr. Stoneman going to suggest that whoever killed Mary Franz with this rifle then lent it, gave it, or had it stolen by Mr. McInerney so that he could travel out to Glacier Bay to murder a Fish and Wildlife Officer with it?"

It was a good strong statement that might not prove anything, but it did wake up the yawners. Santori almost stood up and clapped. He was glad he didn't. It probably would have done more harm than good; and he sure would have looked stupid.

The first day of the trial was now over. It consisted only of the impaneling of the jury and the opening statements. The next day, Tuesday, the prosecution would begin with its presentation of the evidence and the witnesses. Before dismissing the jury for the day, the presiding judge, Glenn R. Stuart, admonished them not to discuss the trial, the evidence, or the testimony with anyone. He told them that court would convene again at 9:00 a.m., the next morning, and that they should all be in their seats at that time.

As the jury filed out, Santori had a chance to talk to Switzer for a few minutes. He complimented the attorney on his opening statement, and asked him a little more about his defense strategy. While he already knew that Switzer was going to introduce the Mary Franz killing into the mix, he was curious as to how the young man was going to choreograph it.

"Well, John, you and I will be discussing it at greater lengths in the near future. But, be assured that you will have a big part in the action to come."

On Tuesday morning, Stoneman called his first witness. He was a forensics expert who testified that the slug found in the life jacket and the slug found in the body of the slain officer were both fired from the same weapon - the one displayed to the jury. He showed photographs of the slugs placed next to one that had been test-fired from the same rifle at the FBI lab in Washington, D.C. The match was perfect. There could be no doubt that all three slugs were fired from the same weapon. The D.A. then presented into evidence those photographs together with the involved rifle, as well as its registration showing Pinky as its owner.

Personnel from the Coast Guard Cutter Intrepid testified as to where they saw the rifle being thrown into the water. The young sailor who had the best view of Pinky throwing something into the water was cross-examined by Cameron Switzer at some length. He admitted that it was quite a distance from the fishing boat to where he stood on the stern of the cutter, that there was considerable fog in the area, and that both vessels were underway at the moment he saw the weapon being thrown into the water. The young attorney asked the sailor if he thought it might have been a shotgun or even a .22 rifle. When his reply was that it could be, the attorney asked if it could be a piece of kelp.

"That would really be a stretch, Mr. Switzer," replied the sailor.

A few of the jurors smiled, so he quickly asked a follow up question. "You cannot say with any degree of certainty that it was a Winchester .30-06, can you?"

"That's right, Sir, I cannot."

Switzer headed back toward the defense table and just before sitting down he asked the young sailor one more question – the same one he would later ask of every witness who testified to being in that area the day of the shooting, "One thing that you probably can say with certainty is that anyone could have thrown that rifle into the water. Isn't that right?"

Before the young man could answer the District Attorney objected saying that it called for speculation. The judge agreed and sustained the objection. Cameron Switzer had done quite a job considering his lack of experience. At least, that's how it looked to John Santori.

The pilot of the Coast Guard helicopter, Lieutenant Sean Gallway, testified that he saw no other vessels in the area on his trip into Bartlett Cove and that on his outbound trip he saw only the vessel "Royce's Girl" that appeared to be fleeing the scene. When he was cross-examined he admitted that he flew over the suspected area of the shooting probably ten or more hours after the occurrence. It was immediately obvious that Switzer was going to try to make some real hay with this pilot when he started his questioning:

"Lieutenant Gallway, what was your point of origin that morning?"

"JIA."

"For the jury, Lieutenant, do you mean Juneau International Airport?"

"Yes, Sir."

"Did you fly over land the entire way from the airport to Bartlett Cove?"

"No, Sir."

"Then, you flew over some water, too, including Chatham Strait and Icy Strait?"

"Yes, Sir."

"Then, depending on the wind direction at takeoff from JIA, you also might have flown over Fritz Cove and from there over Saginaw Channel and even over Barlow Cove. And, yet, over all that water you say you saw only one boat? You saw only my client's vessel?"

"Sir, we saw more than one boat."

"That being the case, Lieutenant, wouldn't you agree you saw a lot of boats on the way to Bartlett Cove?"

"Yes, but that was the closest vessel to Glacier Bay that we saw."

"Oh, so then you also flew past Bartlett Cove to see if there were any vessels anchored in a cove or harbor west of the opening to Glacier Bay? You flew west of Glacier Bay to see if any vessels were fleeing toward Sitka?"

"No, Sir, we did not. We were instructed to look within Glacier Bay itself, and …..."

Cameron Switzer interrupted the man, saying: "Lieutenant, on your direct testimony just a few minutes ago you told this jury that there was only one boat fleeing the scene. I am sure you didn't mean to mislead them in any way."

"No Sir, I was not."

"Then, Lieutenant, would it be safe to say that the vessel with the real shooter aboard could easily have been anchored in Mud Bay, Idaho Inlet, Elfin Cove or someplace to the west of Glacier Bay by the time you began your search? Would it also be possible that the real shooter might have already been docked at his stall in Auke Bay or even in Sitka by the time you began your search?"

"Yes, Sir, it is possible."

"Would it be safe to say it is VERY possible because you only searched in one direction?"

"Yes Sir."

"Now, Lieutenant, referring again to your earlier testimony where you said my client was fleeing. Roughly how many miles was it from JIA to Bartlett Cove?"

"Approximately 45 air miles."

"So, if your chopper flew at roughly 90 miles per hour, you got there in about 30 minutes?"

"From takeoff to touchdown approximately 30 minutes, yes Sir."

"Whereas from the opening near Glacier Bay via water to Auke Bay, which is a distance of approximately 65 nautical miles, it might take a fishing vessel with a top speed of possibly 12 miles per hour to make the same journey in a little more than five hours. So, if someone were fleeing from the area of the shooting he would probably try to go as fast as his boat could go. He would try to make the trip in even less than five hours. Agreed?"

"That sounds about right. Yes."

"Well, Lieutenant, if the Fish and Wildlife Officer was shot sometime before the end of his shift which would have been at midnight, why was my client supposed to have been fleeing at such a slow pace? He was apprehended at 10:00 a.m., the next morning, and he was barely moving. Do you think he might have stopped to do some fishing as he was fleeing?"

There was some laughter from the gallery that interrupted the defense attorney. And, there was a reprimand of the gallery by the judge. But, Switzer continued because he now had the jury's full attention and he was on a roll: "After ten hours of supposed fleeing shouldn't he have been all the way to Harris

Harbor in Juneau where Royce's Girl is usually berthed and even at home in his warm bed? You would have to conclude that he really wasn't fleeing and that he probably had no reason to flee. Wouldn't you, in all honesty, have to conclude that?"

District Attorney Stoneman again objected and it, too, was sustained.

Before sitting down, Switzer asked one more question that was followed by a few more questions that were followed by a keen observation, "Lieutenant, for the benefit of the jury, so that they will have a clear picture of what you really saw, please tell us about some of the other boats that you now admit you also observed. Tell us, were any of them moving through the water at a faster speed than was the vessel Royce's Girl?"

"Yes, I guess some were."

"Were they also fleeing? My heavens, Lieutenant, just about every pleasure craft on the water travels faster than does a troller like Royce's Girl. Didn't any of them arouse your interest as possibly fleeing?"

"I can't say."

"Well, Lieutenant, let me see if there is one thing that you CAN say. You CAN say that Royce's Girl really wasn't fleeing. Isn't that right?"

Before the Coast Guard Officer had a chance to answer, District Attorney Stoneman rose to object. When the judge again sustained the objection, Switzer asked to approach the bench. He was adamant and stressed the fact that even the mere suggestion that Aloysius might be fleeing could imply guilt in the minds of the jury. Judge Stuart replied, "Young fella, you're beating a dead horse. You've got a bigger hill to climb in order to acquit your client than getting this witness to take back that one word."

The young attorney gave it still another try when he pleaded with the judge, saying, "If I have a big hill to climb, Your Honor, please don't let the District Attorney place boulders in my way in the form of slanted testimony by his witnesses. That Coast Guard Lieutenant didn't know if my client was fleeing, and he shouldn't have been allowed to say that he was."

"Ok, Mr. Switzer, you've made your point. Let's move on."

"Your Honor, you're not going to correct the witness's misrepresentation that my client was fleeing? He wasn't fleeing and the jury shouldn't be lied to by this witness."

"No, I will not. You have already made it clear with your cross that Mr. McInerney was not fleeing. Just go sit down!"

Cameron Switzer turned and started back toward the defense table, but after only a few steps he turned again intending to go back and challenge the judge further. He stood there for only a second and then turned and continued on to his chair. He wisely concluded that it was probably best not to belabor the point. He was unaware of it at the time, but he had scored some points with the judge. The latter thought to himself, "This youngster isn't as dumb as he looks!"

After that bit of fanfare the District Attorney called his next witness - the Coast Guard diver who accompanied Denny Gustafson when he recovered the rifle. A few minutes later, Denny followed with his own testimony. Each man described the area where the search was conducted, the depth of the water, their grid system method of search, and the problems that they encountered.

On cross examination Denny was asked if he searched for any other weapon in the nearby waters after he found the subject rifle and whether he saw any kelp on the bottom. He answered no to both questions.

"However, Mr. Gustafson, you cannot say with all certainty that there was not another weapon in that sandy bottom, can you?"

"No, I cannot."

"You said you saw no kelp in the area, but will you not agree that the strong tidal action could have swept away any jettisoned kelp."

"Yes, that's possible."

After the noontime lunch break the prosecution called as its next witness, Trooper Sergeant William B. Harrison. District Attorney Stoneman led him through the events of September 12, and the subsequent search of Pinky's apartment:

"Sergeant, what did you find when you conducted the search of the defendant's residence?"

"We found a spent shell casing."

"Is this the one that I hold in my hand which I herewith ask the court to record as Prosecution Exhibit 7?"

"Yes, Sir, it is."

"What is significant about this shell casing, Sergeant?"

"Sir, it was found in a nightstand drawer near the defendant's bed. It was sent to the FBI lab in Washington D.C., along with the spent casing that was found in the rifle."

"The rifle earlier submitted as Prosecution Exhibit 3?"

"Yes, Sir. The FBI was asked to determine if they were both fired from the same weapon."

"And what did the FBI comparison reveal?"

"They were a match."

"What else did you find?"

"We recovered a mystery novel that dealt with committing the perfect crime."

"Anything else?"

"Yes, Sir. The book had a couple of sales slips in it."

"What is significant about the sales slips, Sergeant Harrison?"

"One covers a purchase of some U-bolts and some screw eyes."

"When were these items purchased?"

"The sales slip is dated in January of last year."

"What did the other sales slip cover?"

"It was for a Yale combination lock."

"And, when was that item purchased?"

"Two weeks earlier and at the same store."

"Your Honor, we ask that these sales slips be marked as Prosecution items 8 and 9. And, we ask that this pocketbook be shown as Prosecution 10. Where was it found, Sergeant?"

"It was on the nightstand next to the bed."

"Did you find anything else in the defendant's apartment?"

"Yes, we found a scrap piece of 1x8 sugar pine on his porch."

"Your Honor, we ask that the court show this item as Prosecution Exhibit 11. What is significant about this piece of wood, Sergeant?"

"It matches a larger piece of 1x8 sugar pine found on the deck of the fishing vessel."

"The fishing vessel that the defendant was piloting when he was apprehended?"

"Yes, Sir."

"How does it match?"

"Well, when laid side by side with the larger piece it shows that the smaller piece was obviously cut with a hand saw from the larger piece. It was not a smooth perfect cut as would result if it had been done with a table saw."

"We will ask that the larger piece of pine be shown as Prosecution Exhibit 12."

"Did you conduct any other searches?"

"Yes, Sir, we also searched the workshop at Upper Salmon."

"What did you find there?"

"In the metal locker we found an empty tin of Copenhagen chewing tobacco."

"What is significant about this empty can of Copenhagen chewing tobacco, Sergeant?"

"It is the same brand as the chewing tobacco the defendant has been using while he has been incarcerated at the Lemon Creek Jail."

"Your Honor, we ask that this last item be shown as Prosecution Exhibit 13. I have no more questions of this witness."

As Cameron Switzer stood up to begin his cross-examination, one could almost see the gleam in his eye. He was facing only the judge and the witness at that moment, but he was already standing in front of the witness box almost before the D.A. had returned to his own chair. His first question surprised everyone in the courtroom:

"Sergeant Harrison, did you plant any of those items in the defendant's residence or in the gym locker at Upper Salmon?"

District Attorney Stoneman bolted out of his chair.

"Your Honor!"

The judge in his calm way settled Stoneman back down and then motioned to Cameron Switzer to approach the bench. The District Attorney came up, stood alongside the young attorney, and scowled in his direction. Judge Stuart quietly admonished Switzer, saying:

"Son, you have a tough case to defend here. So, do not make it tougher on yourself or your client with these kinds of antics. I will not have a circus going on in my court."

When the room quieted down, Switzer continued with his cross:

"What prompted this search, Sergeant?"

"We had a search warrant issued by Judge Fielding."

"I didn't ask that, Sergeant. I didn't ask whether you had a search warrant or where you obtained it. It goes without saying that you would have a search warrant. You would not want to do anything stupid or illegal, would you?"

"That's right, Sir."

"So, I ask again, what prompted the search?"

"We received a tip."

"Oh, you received a tip. That was convenient."

When District Attorney Stoneman again stood and objected, the judge simply told Switzer to move on:

"Get to the point, Mr. Switzer."

"Yes, Your Honor. Well, Sergeant, will you please explain about this tip?"

"Yes, Sir, I had just come on shift at midnight. The dispatcher on duty got the call and transferred it in to me."

"Who was the caller?"

"He didn't give his name."

"That was convenient."

One more time, the District Attorney stood and complained:

"Your Honor, how long can he continue doing this? This is not fair."

This time the judge spoke with considerable more authority:

"This is the last warning, Mr. Switzer. Wrap it up or sit down."

So, Switzer asked, "What did the tipster tell you?"

"He said that Pinky McInerney had bragged to him about committing the perfect crime. He also said something about Pinky having constructed some kind of contraption in the workshop at Upper Salmon."

"And you believed him?"

"I didn't get a chance to determine whether to believe him or not. He hung up on me."

"So, you didn't get his name?"

"No, Sir."

"Do you know where the call came from?"

"Yes, from a drinking establishment on Franklin Street."

"He probably sounded drunk?"

"Yes, Sir, he did."

"Sergeant Harrison, based on just that short drunken statement from a questionable source you were able to obtain a search warrant? Did you possibly suspect that this was a setup? Did you or any of your people check with the bartender to ask if he noticed a "drunken" stranger using their phone that night?"

"We did, Sir, but it's a pay phone in an alcove just outside the rest rooms, so anyone of the patrons could have used the phone without being seen by the bartender or anyone else."

"Regardless, Sergeant, with that flimsy bit of justification you were able to obtain a search warrant of my client's apartment. What other 'overwhelming' evidence did you have that even supported issuance of a search warrant?"

"Sir, because of the tip we had received, we felt evidence had to be there because nothing else had been found on the defendant's person or on the stolen vessel other than the items confiscated when he was apprehended near Swanson Harbor. The tip caused us to conclude that evidence would be found either in the residence of the defendant or in the workshop at Upper Salmon."

"When you conducted the search of Mr. McInerney's apartment, did you have anything specific in mind that you were looking for?"

"No, Sir. However, the tip sounded so genuine, we felt it imperative to search his apartment and the workshop before he might have the chance to destroy any incriminating evidence."

"Did you look for any weapons in his apartment?"

"We did, and we found a Model 1897 Winchester 16 gauge shotgun."

"Was it hidden?"

"No, it was on a gun rack hanging on a wall."

"Did you find any ammunition?"

"Only some 16 gauge buckshot."

"Was it hidden?"

"No. It was in a box on the shelf of the gun rack."

"You found no other weapons, hidden or otherwise, and you found no other ammunition, hidden or otherwise?"

"That's right, Sir."

"Was the apartment in disarray?"

"No, Sir, it was quite neat. Everything seemed to be in its proper place."

"Tell us again, Sergeant, where did you find the shell casing?"

"In the nightstand near the bed."

"I bet it was hidden in there, wasn't it?"

"Yes, it was kind of hidden."

"What do you mean by kind of hidden?"

"Well, it was under some papers in the drawer of the nightstand."

"Now, Sergeant, you have been in this business for a few years, haven't you?"

"Yes, Sir, almost 20 years."

"Do you then mean to tell this jury that you go into what seems like a rather neat and orderly apartment where everything appears to be in its proper place ... and, it was in an orderly condition, wasn't it?"

"Yes, Sir, it was."

"And, you find what you consider an incriminating item and it is hidden. Yet, everything else appears to be where it normally should be? Wouldn't a live round of ammunition or even a spent shell casing be more likely to be found in or on the gun rack rather than hidden under some papers in a nightstand drawer? Did you check for fingerprints on the drawer to see if someone other than Pinky had touched it?"

"No, Sir."

"How many troopers were involved in this so-called search of Mr. McInerney's apartment?"

"There were two of us."

"How long did it take to do the search?"

"About half an hour."

"You found all of this so-called evidence ......"

Switzer was interrupted by the District Attorney's shout, "Objection, Your Honor. Defense continues to use the term 'so-called' when, instead, you have already accepted it into evidence. It is real evidence. It is not 'so-called' and shouldn't be categorized as such."

"If, as I suspect, and as I am attempting to show the jury, Your Honor, this so-called evidence was placed there by someone other than Mr. McInerney, then it is not real evidence. It is a real conspiracy," pleaded Cameron Switzer.

Before he could continue, Judge Stuart chided him, "As you well know, Mr. Switzer, a conspiracy involves at least two people. Do you have evidence that at least two people were involved in placing things in Mr. McInerney's apartment?"

"Not at this time, Your Honor. However, I am attempting to get this witness to admit to me and the jury that what I suspect happened in that apartment is not really what he portrays it to be."

"What you suspect is not evidence for this court, Mr. Switzer. Move on with your questions and cut out the extra adjectives. We will consider it as evidence until the jury says otherwise."

The defense attorney was not going to let go, however. He asked the witness, "When you first arrived at Mr. McInerney's apartment, how did you gain access?"

"The door was not locked. We just walked in."

"You didn't knock first?"

"There was no need to – the defendant was in jail."

"He is the 'accused' – the wrongly accused, Trooper Harrison."

"I'm warning you, Mr. Switzer, stop pleading your case. Just ask the questions. And, make them short and to the point," Judge Stuart shouted – his face reddening.

Switzer continued: "So, you went directly to the night stand – you didn't look elsewhere?"

"We did look elsewhere. We searched the entire apartment – went through every drawer, every closet, and every cabinet. The items we found were hard to miss – almost right out in the open."

"You did all of that in thirty minutes? Didn't you even have the slightest suspicion that these items were planted?"

Before the Trooper had a chance to answer, the District Attorney again objected. Again, the objection was sustained.

Cameron Switzer persisted with another question, "Sergeant Harrison, did you perhaps look for any exculpatory evidence in the apartment of the defendant?"

"Exculpatory?"

"Yes, Sergeant, something that might help the defendant. For instance, did you look for any dust on the gun rack to see if it might show any indication that it held a rifle at one time in addition to the 16 gauge shotgun?"

"No."

"Sergeant, if the gun rack was dusty on all its surfaces, that might indicate to you that no other weapon had been stored thereon for quite some time. That could very well help the defendant in corroborating his statement that his rifle had indeed been stolen four or five years previously. Conversely, if there were some bare spots (some clean spots), it might indicate to you that a rifle might also have been on that rack, and that would dispute his contention. You have been in this business for almost 20 years. Did you possibly look for that kind of evidence?"

"No, Sir."

"Shouldn't you have?"

"Objection, Your Honor." hollered the Prosecution. "Calls for speculation."

Before the judge could rule on the objection, Switzer spoke up, "Well, Sergeant, the defense did what you should have done. We will later enter into evidence a photo of that gun rack showing it is still all covered with dust. There never was a rifle on it."

The judge, now a little more than angry, gaveled the court to order and again called Cameron Switzer to a side bar.

"Young man, I will hold you in contempt if you try any more shenanigans like that. You let me run this courtroom; you let me do the reprimanding. Just ask your question, and stop doing what you have accused the District Attorney of doing - editorializing. You ignore my instructions one more time and you will spend a few days in the same jail with your client. Do I make myself clear?"

So, Switzer sat down saying, "I have no further questions of this witness, Your Honor."

District Attorney Stoneman had originally planned to use Rex Franz as his final witness. He was going to walk him through an accounting of the stormy relationship between Rex and Pinky. He had intended to bring out the story that Rex had been constantly harassed and humiliated by the big man. He wanted to show that Pinky's transfer out of Upper Salmon had finally come as a result of that harassment and that he bore a grudge. However, after seeing the tactics of the Defense Attorney, it was decided that putting Rex on the witness stand would be right down Switzer's alley. The prosecution team saw the handwriting on the wall – the young attorney was going to base his entire defense on convicting Rex Franz, at least in the minds or suspicions of the jury. So, wisely, the prosecution rested.

Even though it was still early afternoon, Judge Stuart adjourned the proceedings until the next morning. It was a warm sunny day, and he wanted to still get in a little fishing. He told the jury that he would give them the rest of the day off and he told Cameron Switzer that he was giving him a chance to collect his thoughts and to ready his presentation for tomorrow.

"This time, Mr. Switzer, it will be in an orderly manner."

THIRTY-FIVE

THE TRIAL – FOR THE DEFENSE

Cameron Switzer began his presentation for the defense the next morning by first asking that there be placed into evidence a copy of the police report that Pinky filed with the police in Spokane, Washington, in 1968, which showed that his Winchester .30-06 rifle was stolen from his parked and unlocked truck at a rest stop near Sprague, Washington. He also was able to place into evidence the claim that Pinky filed with his insurance agent covering the same theft.

A third item was also allowed into evidence at that time. It was a sworn statement from the Chief of Police of Coeur d'Alene, Idaho, who indicated that Pinky had never been in any trouble with the law in that area and that he had been steadily employed at Idaho Power & Light for more than 15 years before he decided to move to Alaska. Finally, and with a little less fanfare than he displayed the previous day, Switzer asked that there be placed into evidence a photograph showing the results of a finger being drawn across the dusty gun rack. He then called his first witness:

"For the record, please state your full name."

"Chadbourne Allen Winkler, but everyone calls me Chad."

"What is your residence address, Chad?"

"314 Alpine Way, Juneau."

"What is your place of employment?"

"I work as a powerhouse operator for AEL&P."

"That is our electrical utility here in Juneau?"

"Yes."

"Where specifically do you work for AEL&P?"

"I work at the powerhouse at Upper Salmon."

"How do you know Aloysius McInerney?"

"He worked with me at Upper Salmon."

"How long did he work at Upper Salmon?"

"I believe he started in September of 1970. He replaced John Santori when John left to join JPD."

"You mean the Juneau Police Department?"

"Yes."

"Was Mr. McInerney always at Upper Salmon?"

"No, later he transferred to Lower Salmon."

"What was the reason for the transfer?"

"I believe it was arranged by the union rep."

"How so?"

"I believe it had something to do with Pinky not getting along with another operator at Upper Salmon."

"Who was that?"

"Rex Franz."

"In what way did they not get along? Was there some kind of altercation?"

"No, nothing physical. They just didn't like each other, and it showed."

"How did that dislike manifest itself?"

"Well, Aloysius likes to be called by his nickname 'Pinky' and, instead, Rex constantly called him by his given name. Pinky didn't like that. He asked Rex to address him by his nickname like everyone else did, but Rex paid no attention to his request. So, Pinky did his best to antagonize Rex in return. There was never a blow exchanged, but it was apparent that there was bad blood between them. Somehow the union rep got involved and Pinky was transferred to Lower Salmon. Everybody was happy with the move, especially Pinky."

"Did their animosity ever lessen?"

"No, but they never saw each other or talked to each other. So, it only lessened because they were apart. Otherwise, neither spoke well of the other."

"How did you get along with Rex Franz?"

Upon hearing that question the District Attorney objected and asked the judge what relevance this had to the guilt or innocence of Aloysius McInerney. When the judge agreed and put the same question to Defense Attorney Switzer, he responded that he would tie it all together if he were permitted to continue. So, he was allowed to go on.

"So, again Chad, how did you get along with Rex Franz?"

"I got along fine with him. We rarely talked. So, there was no friction between us."

"Did he talk much to Sam Phillips, the man who transferred up from Lower Salmon to replace Mr. McInerney?"

"No, he talked to no one. He was always a very quiet man and the last few years he became even more withdrawn. If the conversation got around to Pinky then he might display some emotion."

"How?"

"It was obvious he disliked the man."

"Might it be safe to say he wished the man harm?" Might he even try to implicate Pinky in the murder of Mary Franz or of the Fish and Wildlife Officer?"

District Attorney Stoneman objected before Chad could answer and the objection was sustained by Judge Stuart. Switzer said he had no further questions, and quietly returned to the defense table. On cross-examination, Stoneman asked Chad if he ever talked with Mr. McInerney. He answered that during the time that Pinky worked at Upper Salmon they talked quite a bit. Chad went on to say that after Pinky transferred to Lower Salmon they rarely spoke unless they met in the parking lot outside Pinky's work. Sometimes they might talk during a chance encounter at the Elks Club or at the grocery store. He said that in the period of more than a year since Pinky had moved to Lower Salmon he had spoken to him no more than a half dozen times. The District Attorney then asked:

"When you did talk to him, did he ever indicate he would like to harm Rex Franz?"

This time there was no objection from the other side. Cameron Switzer wisely allowed Chad to answer. His reply was simple and truthful:

"No, he did not."

Switzer called John Santori as his next defense witness:

"Please state your full name."

"John Aldo Santori."

"What is your residence address?"

"809 Fifth Street, Juneau."

"What is your place of employment?"

"I am an officer with the Juneau Police Department."

"Where did you work before joining JPD?"

"I was a powerhouse operator at Upper Salmon when the facility was still owned by Juneau Hydroelectric."

"Why did you leave the electric company?"

"I was offered a position with JPD. I was a police officer in California before we decided to come to Alaska, so I welcomed the opportunity to get back into that line of work."

"How long have you been with JPD?"

"I joined the force in September of 1970."

"How do you know Aloysius McInerney?"

"He was my replacement at Upper Salmon. I worked with him for my last two weeks there. It was my task to break him in on the job."

"How did you get along with him?"

"We got along well."

"How did you get along with Rex Franz? He was the other full time operator up there at that time, wasn't he?"

"Yes, he was. We got along well."

"Were you aware during your last two weeks at Upper Salmon that McInerney and Franz did not like each other?"

"Yes, it was obvious."

"Might it be safe to say that Rex Franz wished the man harm? Might he even try to implicate Pinky in the murder of Mary Franz or of the Fish and Wildlife Officer?"

Again, this question, or the answer to it, never got any further than it had when it was posed to the previous witness, Chad Winkler. There was an immediate and loud objection from the District Attorney who said quite firmly that this called for speculation. The judge agreed and sustained the objection. He then instructed Switzer to continue with his questioning, "Or sit down." So, the questioning continued:

"Have you kept in contact with these two men since leaving Upper Salmon?"

"No, I have not kept in contact with either one, but I did interview Mr. McInerney at the Lemon Creek Jail on August 11, of last year. I interviewed him a second time at the same facility four days later."

"What was the reason for those interviews?"

"Well, I was working on the case involving the shooting of Mary Franz, and I thought that Mr. McInerney might have some information that might help me."

"That shooting was ruled a hunting accident by an unknown shooter. Did you think otherwise?"

"Well, I was involved in that case from the very first day and I did file a report saying what you describe. However, some things kept coming up that always caused me some concerns as to whether it was really an accident."

"You suspected there might have been foul play?"

"Yes."

"What caused your first suspicion?"

"Well, both the other operators indicated that they saw Rex Franz spending a lot of time putting together something in the company workshop. It's a separate building just outside the powerhouse at Upper Salmon."

"Both operators volunteered this information to you?"

"No, only Chad Winkler did. He told me about it one night when we were together. He indicated that Sam Phillips, one of the relief operators, had commented to him that he, too, saw Rex spending a lot of time in the workshop."

Before Switzer could ask his next question, District Attorney Stoneman objected, saying, "Relevance, Your Honor?"

Cameron Switzer spoke up, "If I am allowed to continue, Your Honor, I will show a very clear connection."

Judge Stuart allowed him to proceed.

So, Switzer asked Santori, "Did you ask Mr. Winkler if he ever saw the defendant in the workshop?"

"I did, and he said that he might have seen him there once or twice."

"Was Mr. McInerney in there for any extended period of time?"

"It appeared not."

"Did any of the other operators ever see what Rex was working on?"

"No. Whatever it was, he apparently kept it locked up in the workshop."

"How was it locked up?"

"There is an old gym type upright metal locker in there and he had a combination lock on it. I assumed what he was working on was in the gym locker."

"Did you ever find out for sure?"

"Yes, I did. I got the combination from a local locksmith using the serial number on the back of the lock."

"What did you find?"

"I found a U-bolt, two metal screw eyes, and a piece of scrap sugar pine. I took a photo of the inside of the locker with its contents and then replaced the lock."

"Your Honor, we request that this photograph be entered as Defense Exhibit 5."

District Attorney Stoneman rose and objected to the photograph being placed into evidence, saying, "Your Honor, since this photograph was taken illegally it should not be admitted. It certainly has no relevance to the innocence of the defendant."

Judge Stuart answered simply that he would allow it for now, and he would rule on its admissibility later. Attorney Switzer then continued: "Now, Officer Santori, tell the jury what happened next to cause you to think Mr. McInerney was innocent and that someone else might be the shooter not only of Mary Franz but also of Fish and Wildlife Officer Hutchison?"

"When I was able to determine exactly what was found on the fishing vessel involved in this case I suspected that some of it might have been involved in the shooting of Mary Franz."

"How so?"

"There was a large piece of 1x8 sugar pine found on the vessel together with some screw eyes and some U-bolts. If that board that was now in the hands of the FBI could be matched to the piece I had seen in the gym locker then it probably could be tied to the Upper Salmon shooting."

"What did you do next?"

"I went to the Lemon Creek Jail with the intention of interviewing Mr. McInerney."

"For what purpose?"

"I wanted to hear his side of the story, and I wanted to know about the shape of the board. If the board he pulled out of the water was rectangular, then my earlier theory wasn't worth much."

"Were you satisfied with the results of the interview?"

"More than satisfied."

Switzer now looked over at the judge and asked, "Your Honor, the defense would like to place into evidence this audio tape of the interview. We would ask that it be marked as Defense Exhibit 6 and that it be played now for the jury."

The District Attorney again objected and he asked the judge to rule on its admissibility saying that if it was obtained illegally it should not be admitted into evidence, nor should it be played to the jury. The judge replied, "No, counsel, I will listen to it in chambers and I will decide there if it can be admitted. We will take a short recess while we listen to this tape."

When court reconvened the tape was admitted and it was played for the jury. Cameron Switzer then continued with his questions. He asked: "So, Officer Santori, you now believed that the board really was involved in the Mary Franz shooting?"

"Yes, I did, and I do now."

"Why are you so certain?"

"First, I believed that Pinky told me the whole truth throughout my entire interview with him. Secondly, he did not know in advance that I was coming to interview him. So, it was unlikely that he would have been practicing answering questions since he didn't know which ones anyone would pose. He answered everything I threw at him with no hesitation – no indication at all that he was making it up as he went along. I have studied investigation techniques in my years in police work. We are taught ways to determine whether a person is stretching the truth. Finally, there simply was no logical explanation for him to have taken all of that paraphernalia on the boat with him in order to kill someone. A rifle by itself – perhaps. But, why a contraption such as was found in those plastic bags?"

Santori then went into a long explanation, after specific questions from Cameron Switzer, in order to describe how he himself would have constructed and used a contraption like the one found in Pinky's possession when he was stopped near Swanson Harbor. He was asked, for benefit of the jury, how he lined up the shot from Rex's buttocks to the nicked 4x4 post to the imbedded slug and then back from that post to the shooting perch. He described how he was able to obtain the large board from the FBI and how he took the board to that perch and lined it up to the old nail holes in the two trees. As he was continuing his explanation Cameron Switzer interrupted him and asked, "What are you really trying to say, Mr. Santori?"

"Sir, I believe that I can show the jury exactly how Mary Franz was killed. I believe I can prove that it was not an accident but instead a premeditated murder and that it was not Aloysius McInerney who did it."

"How would you propose to do that, Officer Santori?"

"I would set up the contraption at the actual site of the shooting using all of the admitted evidence – the rifle, the board, the U- bolts, etc. - all the things that Aloysius McInerney found in the plastic bag that he pulled from the deep in Icy Pass. Then I'd fire the weapon to show that it would have killed the person sitting where Mary Franz had been purposely positioned that ill-fated morning in July of 1972."

"If you could prove to this jury that Aloysius McInerney did not kill Mary Franz, how could you then convince them that he also did not kill the Fish and Wildlife Officer?"

"The District Attorney would do that."

"How and why would he do that?"

"Well, he has already proven that the subject rifle was used in the killing of the Fish and Wildlife Officer, and I can prove that it was used to kill Mary Franz. So, if I can show the jury that it was impossible for Aloysius to have killed Mary Franz with that same rifle, then how is the D.A. going to explain how the killer of that lady was able to put that same rifle in Mr. McInerney's hands so that he could go out to Glacier Bay to shoot that Fish and Wildlife Officer."

It was no surprise that the courtroom erupted. First, the District Attorney leaped to his feet and objected that the defense was trying to turn the trial into a circus, "Something that you admonished defense counsel not to do, Your Honor."

Then, because of all the whispering and talking going on throughout the entire courtroom (in the gallery, at the prosecution table as well as at the defense table) Judge Stuart pounded his gavel and declared a recess. He called both counsels into his chambers where considerable back and forth occurred.

When they exited the judge's chamber there was a smile on the face of Cameron Switzer and a scowl on the face of the District Attorney. As soon as it was again quiet in the courtroom, Judge Stuart announced that the jury would be taking a little helicopter ride the next morning. There were a few oohs and aahs from the jury and from the gallery.

"So," Judge Stuart added, "those who have trouble flying are welcome to walk up the 876 steps and along the flume for another almost two miles. You should all plan to be at the site at 11:00 a.m." The courtroom erupted again.

The next morning, on the flume near post #32, Santori's demonstration began. At each step of his presentation Defense Attorney Switzer asked him what he was doing and why. His purpose was to make Santori's testimony seem more like a courtroom session rather than an exhibition.

He placed an inflated balloon where Mary's head had been that fateful day in July of 1972 while cautioning the jury and the other observers to stay well back on the flume as he set up the contraption. As he looked out at them he noticed a familiar face in amongst the gallery. It was Rex Franz. Santori then went back to work, nailing the board with its rifle in place on the trees. As he knelt to replace the screw eyes in their original holes he described each part of the setup. He made it a point to explain to the jury that he was placing the nails and the screw eyes back into the same holes that had been made when the real shooter had set up the contraption back in 1972.

He tied the string to the trigger, sighted in the target through the scope, and made a slight adjustment of the rifle within the U-bolts. He sighted in the target one more time and then placed a live round into the breech. He ran the string from the trigger up the hill through the screw eyes and back down to a large round rock. He wrapped the string around the rock, again describing his actions and those of the real shooter. He then went through the theoretical photographing scene saying, "Move over a little, and smile." With his back resting against the sheltering tree, he kicked the rock. The shot was deafening and it echoed throughout the small valley. Needless to say, when it popped the balloon many if not all the jurors were frozen in the stark reality of what they had just seen and heard. Most of them probably pictured in their minds how it could have looked that day more than a year ago when a real living person was there instead of that balloon.

As John looked down at the serious faces of the jury he explained that he, too, could have been nicked with that same bullet if he had positioned himself properly. He felt that he had clearly proven how easy it was for one man to shoot two people simultaneously. He looked out in the direction where he had just a few moments before seen Rex Franz, but he was gone.

Everyone was deathly silent for what seemed an interminable amount of time. Then Santori woke them from their stupor by calling attention to what the shot had done to the upright 4x4 post. This time the bullet hit just a little farther down in the middle of the upright post. The slug remained in the post because the cartridge had been specially loaded with considerably less powder just for this display. He concluded his presentation, saying: "If the defendant, Aloysius McInerney, planned a murder with this contraption, he sure wasted a lot of time and effort on a big gamble. If his target had elected to sit anywhere but in that exact spot he could never have fired at her. Only someone who knew where she was going to sit – someone who purposely positioned her there - used this contraption."

District Attorney Stoneman objected, saying that now the witness was making a closing argument – a highly speculative one. The judge sustained the objection telling the jury that they should disregard Officer Santori's last statement. John still felt that he had done some damage to the prosecution's case because Switzer was smiling and Stoneman was not.

The judge then told the jurors that they had the rest of the afternoon to relax and enjoy the sunny day by walking back down to the parking lot via the steps or up to the helicopter pad for a scenic flight and the return to the ground below. He again admonished them to not discuss the trial and to return to the courtroom the next morning at 9:00 a.m.

The next day Cameron Switzer continued questioning John Santori on the witness stand. As he prompted him with just the right questions, same as he had done throughout his earlier testimony, John proceeded to outline how he felt the murder of Mary Franz was planned and executed. He suggested that the Fish and Wildlife Officer had gotten in the shooter's way when the latter tried to dispose of the incriminating evidence. He opined that the officer paid with his life for interfering in the shooter's ultimate plan.

Aaron Stoneman was just as eager to get at Santori as had been the young Defense Attorney when he cross-examined Trooper Harrison the day before. His first question brought the first laugh, the first objection from the defense, and the first warning from the judge.

Stoneman asked, "Officer Santori, did you say you were from Hollywood?"

After the laughter, followed by the judge's reprimand, John was able to answer: "I was born and raised in San Francisco, Sir."

"Your testimony, especially your presentation, was quite hard to believe, wasn't it?"

"On the contrary, Sir, it was quite plausible and, as you saw and heard, quite accurate."

"No, Officer Santori, while it might have been good theatre it fell way short of proving Mr. McInerney innocent. In fact, you did not come anywhere near putting the rifle in anyone else's

223

hands other than those of the defendant. It is still his rifle. It was still thrown overboard by him and it was still recovered from where he had thrown it. He, too, worked at Upper Salmon, and he, too, had access to the workshop there. You did not in any way exclude him from that little building and you certainly did not disconnect the defendant from the Yale combination lock, the locker, or the items found therein."

Cameron Switzer stood and asked, "Your Honor, have you already called for closing arguments? That sure sounds like what the District Attorney seems to be doing. Does the District Attorney have any questions of this witness, Your Honor?"

The questions did finally come. There were many of them and they all cut deep. Most were so deep they hurt. Some were to the point and others were slanted. During the last part of the District Attorney's cross examination he attempted to paint Santori as a personal friend of the defendant. Stoneman's questions seemed to imply that Santori's investigations as well as his testimony leaned toward helping a friend rather than as a policeman doing his unbiased civic duty. At one juncture, Stoneman asked him, "Did you feel that your friend was being framed?"

John answered calmly and respectfully, "Sir, I have known the accused for only two weeks and I interviewed him for no more than two hours since his incarceration. I form my friendships over long spans of time – even years. My friends and I have either been in school together, worked together, played together, fished and hunted together, and even suffered together. Our families have almost always been involved in those same activities – again together. I have done none of those things with the accused, Aloysius P. McInerney, except to spend a few days showing him how to run the powerhouse at Upper Salmon – a task that he already had years of experience doing."

When Santori stopped for a second to catch his breath, the District Attorney jumped in, "Just a yes or no, Mr. Santori."

So, John went on, "The evidence found by the Troopers was just too conveniently placed in Mr. McInerney's apartment, Sir. So, yes, it smelled like a setup to me. I would have come to the

224

same conclusion and my testimony would have been exactly the same even if it was your apartment and you were the one on trial – and we've never been friends, have we?"

There was a brief moment of stunned silence in the courtroom. The District Attorney was taken slightly aback. He turned to the judge and said, No further questions, Your Honor."

Cameron Switzer took quick advantage, saying, "Redirect, Your Honor." While he felt that Santori had perhaps made the District Attorney look like he had some egg on his face, this was not the time to add to it, but rather to apply just a little more defense.

"Officer Santori, did the Juneau Police Department ever approach this case as a rescue mission in behalf of Aloysius McInerney?'

"No Sir. To the contrary. I think it is safe to say that policemen suspect everyone until strong evidence clears them – one by one. In this case, we were still eliminating when the District Attorney preempted our investigation by bringing this action against Mr. McInerney. In my testimony I have sought to show the evidence that we have collected and to present our theory that the real perpetrator is yet to be discovered."

The Defense Attorney continued, "Officer Santori, yesterday you were stopped by the District Attorney when he said you were speculating about the shooting of Mary Franz. So, I will ask you a direct question. Did Aloysius McInerney use that contraption you displayed to shoot Mary Franz?"

"No, Sir. He could not have killed her with it."

"Why do you say that?"

"It was set up to shoot only in one direction and to hit a specific target. It had to be a person sitting in that exact spot right in front of that 4x4 upright post. Anyone sitting there six inches to the left or six inches to the right of that post would not have been hit with that bullet."

"So, what does that prove?"

"Sir, it proves that someone had to position her there."

"Well, couldn't Mr. McInerney have positioned her there?"

"No, Sir. He could have, but he didn't."

"Why do you say that?"

"Sir, after she was shot I interviewed her husband. He recounted all the events leading up to the shooting and the events after the shooting. If the judge will allow you to play for the jury the tape of that interview you will hear that Rex Franz never mentioned Aloysius McInerney being anywhere near the flume on that day. Certainly, in view of his dislike of the man, he would have brought up his name throughout the interview as being responsible for positioning Mary by that post."

District Attorney Stoneman rose and said, "Your Honor, I object. We are here to prosecute the defendant for the murder of a Fish and Wildlife Officer near Glacier Bay. If the defense wishes us to prosecute Rex Franz for the murder of his wife, let them go through the proper channels at another time and in another place."

Cameron Switzer loudly protested the objection. Judge Stuart stopped him, saying, "Mr. Switzer, I am going to sustain the objection. You are trying to go around to the back door to bring in more speculation. That's all it is – speculation. As plausible as it might sound on the surface, it is not evidence. If you have some concrete evidence, enter it. If not, call your next witness."

John Santori was now sweating as had Pinky that day when he was questioned on the ninth floor of the Federal Building. John's sweat, however, was from around the collar. He was really irate that he had not been allowed to continue to prove his point. He wanted the jury to hear Rex's interview to prove his point that it was not Pinky who positioned Mary at Post #32.

Not being an attorney, he always questioned why some good old solid speculation should not be allowed. Regardless, this part of the fight was over and he was excused. As he walked out past Pinky he could feel a warm, unspoken thank you coming from the man - an appreciation for his effort even if it wasn't totally successful. Still, John did his best. While he may have created some doubt in the minds of some jurors, he feared that he was still a long way from convincing enough of them to acquit Pinky. At least that is how it appeared to him when he finally walked out of the courtroom.

The judge then asked Switzer if he had any more witnesses.

"Yes, Your Honor, I will have one more witness."

"That being the case," said the judge, "we will break for lunch and, hopefully, finish up this afternoon."

The last defense witness was the defendant himself. After the opening questions as to name, place of birth, and work history, Switzer asked his most important and expected question: "Did you shoot Fish and Wildlife Officer Hutchison?"

"No, Sir, I did not."

"Did you shoot Mary Franz?"

"No, Sir, I did not."

"You were out near where the Officer was shot?"

"Yes I was, but I was fishing. I wasn't shooting. I had no rifle to shoot with."

"However, Pinky, it is your rifle, isn't it?"

"Yes, Sir, it is. How it got all the way from near Spokane to here is beyond me. No matter. I haven't fired or even seen that rifle in more than five years."

"Now, Pinky, since the District Attorney will ask you this question if I don't, tell us which interview was and is more truthful, the one you had with the FBI and the other people in the Federal Building on July 27, of last year or the one you had with Officer Santori at the Lemon Creek Jail two weeks later?"

"The one with Officer Santori was completely truthful, even though I wasn't aware that he was taping our conversation. The one with the FBI was a little off, but I was between a rock and a hard place then. I didn't know why I had been stopped and since it seemed the rifle might be the reason I figured it was best to get rid of it and to deny I ever saw it. I just didn't think they would believe a fairy tale about me catching a garbage bag with a rifle in it on my trolling lines, which of course is what really did happen."

"You said you did not shoot Mary Franz?"

"Yes, I said that, and I will continue to say that all the way to my grave. I only met her one time when she stopped in at Lower Salmon when I was on shift. She seemed like a nice lady.

227

I had no reason to dislike her. I sure as hell would never want to shoot her."

"Where were you working when she was shot?"

"I was working at Lower Salmon, but I was not on shift at that time. I had been on swing, and I was still asleep in my place."

"Swing is from 4:00 p.m., to midnight?"

"Yes, and after my shift I sat around and talked to my relief, Ed Sloan, for almost an hour before turning in."

"During that early morning of July 9, did you go up those steps to the penstock and along the flume to post #32 to set up a contraption to kill Mary Franz?"

"No. First, I had no reason to kill her. Secondly, I hated every one of those 876 steps. I had walked up and down those steps for months and I was glad as hell to now be at Lower Salmon. Lastly, I definitely am not crafty enough to build a contraption like the one Officer Santori used in his display up there on the mountainside."

"Did you go up there, instead, to shoot her husband?"

"No, I didn't like that worm, but I sure as hell wouldn't shoot him or anyone else."

"No further questions, Your Honor."

It was now time for District Attorney Stoneman to have his day, and it would be quite a show. The man didn't get to his high position in State government by accident. He was good and he was thorough. He was also relentless. At one point he tried to bring out Pinky's violent history by calling attention to his numerous arrests for drunkenness and disorderly conduct. Cameron Switzer objected. The objection was sustained, but the jury still heard enough of Stoneman's portrayal of a recalcitrant and obstreperous Aloysius to get the message.

After the judge gaveled the courtroom to quiet, the questions continued and they got tougher. Pinky was composed early in the cross-examination, but by late afternoon he was reacting harshly to many of the questions. The District Attorney was asking relatively innocuous ones, but they were laced with innuendos and Pinky simply could not cope.

Finally, in desperation, Defense Attorney Switzer asked Judge Stuart to admonish the prosecution for editorializing instead of questioning. The judge asked Switzer if this was an objection, and Switzer replied, "Yes, Your Honor. The District Attorney is again using his cross to make his closing argument, rather than asking any substantive questions."

Judge Stuart overruled the objection and allowed Stoneman to continue until, finally, even the judge thought it was time to rest. He called a recess.

When court resumed so did the questioning and again Pinky did poorly. There were a number of heated exchanges between the two men. In all of them Pinky was his own worst enemy. During those exchanges Cameron Switzer did his best to save his client by objecting even when objections weren't warranted or accepted. He was trying his best to give Pinky some breathing room. But, by the end of the day it seemed like Stoneman had wiped away all the gains that Switzer had exacted from this difficult case. The District Attorney did his own bit of Hollywood with his final questions:

"The registration for that rifle hasn't changed, has it? It still shows the name of Aloysius P. McInerney, doesn't it? And, all the theatrics of Officer Santori and of your own attorney cannot remove that fact. Nothing has taken that rifle from your hands and put it in anyone else's hands, has it?"

Cameron Switzer objected but it was almost lost in the whisperings of the gallery. The closing arguments by both the prosecution and the defense were presented the next morning, and they were almost anticlimactic. In fact, they were obligingly short. All the real damage had been done earlier – most of it to Aloysius.

District Attorney Stoneman drove one more nail into Pinky, however, with his penultimate comment when he said, "If the defense wants to speculate, we can go them one better by suggesting that the defendant shot Mary Franz from an area close to the two trees without any props but built the contraption and mounted it there to plant suspicion on the lady's husband. No matter. He used no props to murder the Fish and Wildlife Officer.

He did it with his own rifle and then, unfortunately for him, was seen trying to dispose of it in the deep. Ladies and gentlemen of the jury, there should be no doubt as to who killed Officer Hutchison. It was Aloysius McInerney."

After the judge's instructions were read to them, the case went to the jury. It was now late in the day, so they had only enough time to pick a foreman and little else. The bailiff was then called in and a request was made that they be excused for the day. The jury had been told early on that they would not be sequestered, so they were all anxious for a change of scenery – back to the warm friendly confines of their own residences.

Before exiting the jury room one less than dedicated juror suggested, "How about a show of hands as to how many of us feel he is guilty? We might still be able to get this over before dinner." Amazingly, nine of them raised their hand including the foreman. They did not sit back down, however, because it was apparent that deliberations were going to be necessary - the three dissenters were not smiling.

It took many hours the next day, but the majority finally wore down the remaining innocence voters. The jury had one more free lunch - courtesy of the State of Alaska. Then, more than two hours later, eleven of them finally convinced the remaining holdout, a widow nee Margaret O'Callahan, that this particular Irishman, Aloysius P. McInerney, was indeed guilty of that terrible crime.

John Santori was not there in the courtroom to hear the jury's 'guilty' verdict. He was later told that Pinky created quite a scene and had to be restrained. Rex Franz was there, however, and he gloated before, during, and after Pinky's outburst. In fact, he was still gloating when he departed the courthouse. He was also smiling when in late afternoon he deposited into his checking account the proceeds from the sale of his Bayliner. He had advertised it in the want ad section of the local newspaper, and it sold in just two days. Everything had gone well for him, and the future looked bright. Now, he had only to wait for Bev's return. A week earlier, she had called to say that her mother had passed away.   Soon, she would be returning to Juneau where they, hopefully, could resume their plans for the future.

Now, as far as Rex was concerned, all obstacles had now been removed. All worrisome items or thoughts had been set aside, and only a few minor tasks remained to be finished. As for now, he was going to have a nice dinner at the Summit Hotel capped off with a glass or two of their most expensive wine.

THIRTY-SIX

HOME FREE

When Bev Jordan returned to Juneau on Alaska Airlines late afternoon flight, Rex and Josie were at the airport to greet her. As they were driving toward Lower Salmon he explained that he had one more night of graveyard before his four days off. After this last shift and a little bit of sleep he would come back down to her house because he had some things to go over with her. Not surprisingly, Bev wanted to know what it was that he wanted to talk to her about. He told her that the subject was too important to discuss while he was driving. She persisted, and he did the same. He told her, "When serious matters are to be discussed between two people, it should be done 'eyeball to eyeball' and not while one of them is otherwise occupied."

In order to keep her from pursuing the matter further, he changed the subject to her mother's last days, the funeral, and the situation as pertained to her surviving parent. Her reply took up the rest of the drive to Lower Salmon and the carrying of her luggage into her house. Once inside, she quickly got back to their earlier conversation. She stood up close to him and said, "Now, what do you want to talk about?"

His reply, he explained, was a quote from what Mark Antony once told Cleopatra: "I did not come here to talk!" They both laughed as he picked her up and carried her, squealing, into her bedroom. When their lovemaking subsided for a few moments, Bev smiled coyly and suggested, "Now that we're eyeball to eyeball, what do you want to talk to me about?" This time there was no laughing and not even the hint of a smile. He said, "I want you to marry me!"

She screamed, happily, "Yes! Yes! Yes, I will."

"Good. Now that we've settled that matter, can we get back to what I was talking about a minute ago?"

"Oh, you're terrible!   And, you weren't talking. Just like your friend, Mark Antony, you were only 'oohing and aahing.'

Rex then added, "And, our honeymoon will be spent aboard the Queen Elizabeth II on her next world cruise. How does that sound?"

Her uncomplicated reply was simply, "Ooh, aah."

Later that evening, Rex Franz started up the 876 steps to the penstock and his bike for the return trip to his little house by the flume. When he reached the top of the steps and made the short walk to the penstock he turned and looked back toward Gastineau Channel. At that moment, as far as he was concerned, all was right with the world. It could not be better.

He rolled his bike out from where it was parked in the penstock and started to motor in toward Upper Salmon. When he reached post #32 he stopped and parked the still idling trail bike. He dismounted and sat on the platform near the upright post where Mary had been killed. One last time he commiserated about what was and what could have been. He would miss this beautiful place, he thought, but he wouldn't miss the sad years that had just recently passed. The future beyond would be much more peaceful and even more beautiful. Right then and there he vowed to forget the past.

As the bike sat idling on the flume its exhaust fumes slowly wafted up the mountain toward the den of the sow and her cub. Whether it was the odor or possibly the movement of her cub, she awoke. If she actually smelled the exhaust or if she even remembered the other event years before when her two previous cubs had been threatened is moot. All that mattered now was that her newest youngster was already yards ahead of her heading down toward the flume.

She and her cub had been asleep in a small hollow up the mountain above the flume - just one of the many resting spots that they occupied together during the year. When she saw her little one heading toward the apparent danger she reacted with a fierce growl. In just a few quick leaps she was past her curious cub and onto the flume. Rex had by this time returned to his bike and was

233

about to continue on toward Upper Salmon. He didn't even get started. Almost before he could react, the sow was on top of Rex and his bike. Her momentum coupled with his attempt to avoid her catapulted the three of them (the sow, Rex, and his bike) over the edge of the flume and down to the rocks 20 feet below. Unfortunately for Rex, they landed in the wrong order. The first to hit the rocks was Rex followed by the bike, and on top of those two came the five hundred pound bear. Rex's body cushioned the blow for the sow, but her weight atop the bike did just the opposite for him. He landed head first on the rocks sustaining probably as much damage to his skull as had befallen Pete Tyler.

Rex lay unconscious, bleeding in that small space between his brain and his skull. He, too, suffered an intracranial hematoma. He also suffered a broken neck. This time there was no mayday call and no one was there to help. The sow limped off to recover her cub and she did that rather roughly. She probably in her own way pounded into him the need to be wary of people and their motorbikes.

Rex, instead, joined his three victims in the beyond and his body was not discovered until the next day. He and the bike had fallen into deep underbrush onto the jagged rocks below. Both were almost completely hidden from anyone looking down from atop the flume.

THIRTY-SEVEN

A DIFFERENT SEARCH

John was enjoying the last few mouthfuls of another of his favorite meals when the phone rang that next morning. This meal was one he had prepared himself – Eggs Benedict with a side of cold lox. It was Chad Winkler reporting and at first it appeared that one of John's worst fears was being realized. Chad said that Rex Franz had not shown up for his graveyard shift. He was now more than seven hours late and no one seemed to know where he was.

Rex's house was searched but there was no evidence of a planned departure. His suitcases, his clothes, and his toiletries – everything was still there. Chad said that he took a ride to the penstock and back but didn't see any sign that Rex might have gone off the flume. He added that Rex's bike was not at his house nor was it in the penstock. Since Rex's bike was missing John had to conclude that the man had gone off the flume somewhere.

John told Chad that he would meet him at the penstock in thirty minutes. After hanging up the phone he went back to his almost cold eggs and lox. Nothing would keep him from it. After breakfast he considered phoning Alaska Airlines, all the local small feeder airlines, and the Ferry System people to see if Rex had departed on any of them, but he decided to wait until he and Chad finished their search. All indications pointed to an accident off the flume.

Almost an hour later, John was just about at the top of those familiar 876 steps. It took him a little longer to reach the top – He was not in as good a shape anymore. Chad greeted him when he reached the penstock. He could see John was huffing and puffing, and he laughed, "Getting old, huh, buddy?"

They double-checked the little cabin and made sure that Rex's bike was indeed gone. This further bolstered John's suspicion that he might have fallen off the flume during the previous night. So, they started to walk in toward Powerhouse #2, with John on one side of the flume and Chad looking down from the other side. When they were between posts #32 and #33 they noticed a tire skid mark that went off the flume at an angle. They stopped and looked down to the bushes below. There appeared to be something that might warrant a closer look. Whatever it was, it wasn't green like the heavy foliage around it. They decided it was worth looking at from down below.

This particular spot was one of the areas where the flume was suspended fairly high above ground for some distance. So, they had to walk farther along the flume to reach an area where it was again closer to the ground. From there they carefully inched their way down through the bushes and the small trees back to where they found the bike atop the now dead Rex Franz. He, even in death, still had his arms wrapped around the handlebars. It was a lurid scene – in his last moments as he dropped to the rocks below it was the only thing left for him to embrace.

When John attempted to call JPD on his radio he couldn't make contact, so he asked Chad to hike up the trail to the powerhouse. "Call Chief Parker. Let him take care of sending either the Troopers or the Fire Department guys to get the body out of here. I think the best way to get him out is along the trail up to the helicopter pad. Might as well have the Lorenzen Helicopters people come in here again. They were the ones who took his dead wife out. Tell them to bring a stretcher and a body bag."

While Chad hiked up to the powerhouse, John stayed behind. He searched the area for any evidence of intended flight on the part of Rex, but he found nothing. He searched Rex's pockets and even the inside of his wallet. He found only the usual items that one normally finds in a man's pockets – his keys, his ID, and his money. There was nothing in his jacket pockets, even though there was the smell of tobacco. This was strange because John didn't remember ever seeing Rex smoke or chew. He hadn't talked to the man in quite a while, so maybe Rex had changed his habits since John's departure from Upper Salmon more than two years ago. Then he remembered that one of the troopers during his testimony told of finding the empty Copenhagen can in the gym locker. "Yes," he said to himself, "he probably carried that tin around for quite a while before he found the right opportunity to further implicate Pinky. Now, it's probably too late to be used by the defense to suggest how it could have been planted in the gym locker by the real shooter."

Later that morning, when John was back at JPD, he telephoned Fred Wolters to tell him what had happened to Rex. He told him about the tobacco odor and the lack of any other evidence he was able to find on or near the body. Fred tried to poke a little fun at him by asking if John thought Rex might have planted the empty Copenhagen tin purposely to incriminate Pinky. "You damn right he did, Fred. Even you know that Pinky, if he really was the shooter and the architect of that deadly contraption, would not have placed one of his signature cans of Copenhagen in that locker in order to incriminate himself." They both laughed, and Fred acknowledged that John really had a good point. John thought to himself, "A lot of good that will do me or Pinky now."

THIRTY-EIGHT

THE IRONY

The next morning, before leaving the station to head out on patrol, John received a strange telephone call:

"Officer Santori?"

"Yes, this is John Santori."

"This is Victor Rapp. I'm the Funeral Director here at Spruce Acres Memorial Park. We have the body of Rex Franz here for disposition."

"Yes, Mr. Rapp, how can I help you?"

"Well, I remember reading some time ago that you were involved in the investigation of the shooting death of this man's wife."

"Yes, I was."

"Well, I have something here that I think you might want to look at."

"Can you tell me about it on the phone?"

"Well, it's a checklist that we found on the body."

"On the body?"

"Yes."

"That's strange because I searched the man thoroughly from head to toe when we discovered his body, and I found nothing like you describe."

"Well, Officer, it was strange to me, too. That's why I would like for you to come out here and see it."

"Ok. I'll be out there this morning."

"Thank you, Officer Santori. I'll be here until at least 5:00 p.m., in case you don't make it this morning."

"No, I'll be there shortly."

After that conversation John decided to telephone Fred Wolters suggesting that they should both visit the mortuary. Upon their arrival they were greeted by the funeral director and, after introductions, they were taken to the work area of the mortuary.

Rex's body was on a metal table and it was still partially clothed. He was still in undershirt and trousers but his shoes and socks had been removed. Rex's western style leather belt had been loosened but was still around his waist. It was that item that the funeral director wanted them to see. On the back of the belt they found what Rex had hidden so successfully for all the past months.

Protruding from a cleverly sewn pocket on the back of the belt was a lined sheet of notepaper. John pulled it from its hiding place and both men started to read what Rex had so calculatingly planned over the past few years. Victor Rapp smiled at the two of them and said, "I found this in the back of his belt as I was starting to disrobe him and, after reading it, I put it back so you could see how it had been hidden."

Fred's comment was simply, "Talk about just desserts."

He then added, "Well, John, it seems you were right about this guy all along."

John smiled, "Yeah, how about that. He, too, had a checklist."

Victor Rapp said it best, however: "Seems he was hoisted on his own petard."

THE END

EPILOGUE

That same morning, after returning from the mortuary, Agent Wolters received a report from the FBI Lab in Washington advising that the slides had been tested again, this time with an electronic microscope and a chemical analysis. With this second and more sophisticated testing technique they were able to find traces of the orange paint on the slides that compared favorably to the orange paint on the zodiac of Officer Hutchison. Later that day, when District Attorney Stoneman in the company of FBI Agent Wolters and Funeral Director Victor Rapp visited the Juneau Courthouse with Rex Franz's checklist and the new slide evidence in hand, the result was that Judge Stuart overturned the jury's verdict and freed Aloysius McInerney.

One week later, Alaska Electric Light & Power Company asked Pinky to return to Upper Salmon to take the place of the recently deceased operator, Rex Franz. With a mile-wide grin on his no longer suntanned face Pinky accepted the offer saying, "Those 876 steps are a snap and they sure will keep me in good shape." It is said that soon after his rehire he also quit drinking. He wisely concluded that the steps and the flume could not be negotiated in a drunken condition.

John Santori saw his young son, Andrew, graduate from University of Alaska Southeast with a degree in Criminology. He did not see him graduate from the Police Academy in Sitka, however. John was killed in January of 1978 by a drunken driver who sideswiped his patrol car as he was exiting his vehicle to help a stranded motorist.

Almost nine months to the day after returning from Seattle Bev Jordan gave birth to a 7 lb.7 oz. perfectly healthy blue eyed baby boy.

At this writing, David Royce still hasn't gotten his boat back.